THE PLUNDERING OF MALAYSIA

Najib Razak And The 1MDB Debacle

Also by M. Bakri Musa

The Rot In Malaysian Education And Other Essays (2020)

Race, Religion, And Royalty: The Barnacles On Malay Society (2020)

The Son Has Not Returned. A Surgeon In His Native Malaysia (2018)

Cast From The Herd. Memories Of A Matriarchal Malaysia (2016)

Malaysia's Wasted Decade 2004-2014. The Toxic Triad of Abdullah, Najib, And UMNO Leadership (2016)

Liberating The Malay Mind (2013)

Moving Malaysia Forward (2008)

Towards A Competitive Malaysia: Development Challenges Of The 21st Century (2006)

From Malaysia, With Love (2004)
(With Karen E Musa)

Seeing Malaysia My Way (2003)

An Education System Worthy Of Malaysia (2003)

Malaysia In The Era Of Globalization (2002)

The Malay Dilemma Revisited: Race Dynamics In Modern Malaysia
(1999; Updated Edition 2017)

THE PLUNDERING OF MALAYSIA

Najib Razak And The 1MDB Debacle

M. Bakri Musa

Contents

World's Greatest Kleptocrat – Najib Razak

Failure Of Leadership And Institutions

UMNO Is The Problem

The 14th Malaysian General Elections

The 13th Malaysian General Elections (GE 13)

About The Author

Preface

This second of my three-volume collection of commentaries on Malaysian affairs written since 2008 focuses on the 1MDB debacle. The first, *Race Religion, And Royalty: The Barnacles On Malay Society*, contains my articles on those three elements that today form the ugly and dangerous troika of identity politics in Malaysia. My commentaries focus on another and more dangerous aspect. As per the title, those three are now the barnacles on Malay society, impeding its progress and threatening to sink it.

The third is *The Rot In Malaysian Education And Other Essays*.

This 1MDB scandal is now the world's most expensive heist of public assets by a national leader. Thus far the tab exceeds RM 42 billion (US $10 billion) and fast spiraling out of control. The central culprit is former Prime Minister Najib Razak, now facing multiple criminal charges.

Najib is not that smart to carry out a heist of this magnitude. He had many enablers, in government as well as in his party, United Malay National Organization (UMNO). These commentaries focus not only on him and his enablers but also the lapses of Malaysian institutions and those entrusted to run them.

This 1MDB robbery has been investigated by no fewer than six foreign jurisdictions, with individuals convicted, banks closed, and assets seized. In July 2016 the US Department of Justice (US DOJ) initiated its massive civil suits under the Kleptocracy Asset Recovery Initiative (KARI), its biggest thus far in terms of monetary value, seizing those assets bought through funds illicitly siphoned from 1MDB. DOJ's associated criminal investigations continue.

Those diligent and aggressive actions abroad notwithstanding, what broke the case wide open was the pivotal actions of those simple voters in the villages of Malaysia. They may not be worldly in their political sophistication or savvy in their financial understanding, but they could sniff a rat from afar. It was their collective decision on the May 9, 2018 14th General Elections (GE 14) that nailed Najib and his fellow crooks in UMNO.

Who could forget the surreal scene of Najib and Rosmah trying to make a late midnight getaway by way of a private jet provided by his Indonesian crony late on election night when it was obvious that he and the coalition he led had been defeated? The pathetic sight of the couple *sans* any police escort trying to sneak through the back gate at the subsidiary Sepang Airport said it all. Thanks to the social media a crowd had already gathered there to confront the couple. Ever the pariah, the couple cowered and turned tail.

A few days later there were the gaudy images of piles of boxes of cold cash in various foreign currencies being hauled away by the police from Najib's private residence. That flooded the media, local and foreign as well as mainstream and social.

There is still something that perplexes me. While the simple village folks understood intuitively that they had been had by Najib with his massive 1MDB heist—hence their pivotal collective decision on GE14—more than just a few any of the supposedly sophisticated and well-educated Malays still supported Najib. They refused to accept the evident reality. Many believed that the US DOJ suit was yet another sinister American attempt at regime change. They ignored the fact many of the defendants in that KARI civil suit have already copped a plea with DOJ, including the prime culprit, Jho Low. Meaning they admitted that the funds with which they had acquired those assets were illicitly obtained.

Some of Najib's cabinet ministers and UMNO Supreme Council members during the time Najib was siphoning billions from 1MDB were lawyers, accountants, MBAs, and former chief executives of major corporations. Najib's cousin and Minister of Defense Hishamuddin is a British-trained lawyer. Another, that Oxford graduate Khairy Jamaluddin, was with Najib right till the GE14 disaster. I have yet to hear any of them condemn Najib. On the contrary, many still praise their man. "*Malu apa bossku?*" (What is there to be ashamed about our boss!) is the slogan they—and Najib—proudly display today. Where is their shame, or to use the more appropriate Malay words, *amanah* (fidelity) and *maruah* (dignity)?

As GE14 was pivotal, I have included my commentaries on that, as well as on GE13 five years earlier. I expected Najib and his UMNO-led coalition to be booted out then. Had that happened, there would not have been an 1MDB, and Najib, Rosmah together with all the other crooks would not have been able to rob the nation. On the positive side, they would have been spared their current humiliations. Most of all, Malaysians would not have been burdened by this humungous debt that Najib and his fellow crooks had generated.

As with the other two volumes, I have arranged these essays thematically, and within a section they appear in reverse chronological order. Doing so would be less disorientating to readers and would make the earlier pieces appear as background or historical materials.

As these essays had originally appeared as independent pieces, some of the material would therefore be repeated. Where possible and when they do not disturb the flow or the theme of the piece, I have deleted or abbreviated those items.

Beyond that, as with the other two volumes, I have made only minor editorial and other changes.

Except for a few, these essays have previously appeared only in cyberspace. I thank the owners and publishers of the various Internet portals for their generosity in providing space for my thoughts and commentaries. Special note of gratitude to Lim Kit Siang, Datuk Din Merican, and editors of *Malaysiakini*, *Malaysian Insight*, *Malaysian Insider*, and *Malaysia-Today*.

Most of all I thank my readers who have gone further and shared their views directly with me and others through their postings.

The cover design is by husband-and-wife team of Jason and Su Pittam. I thank them for this as well the designs in the other two companion volumes.

Throughout all these, my partner in life as well as in my writing, Karen, had been unstinting in her support and encouragement in going over these essays both in the original as well as in this edition. Thank you again and much love!

M. Bakri Musa
Morgan Hill, California
May 2020
bakrimusa@gmail.com
www.bakrimusa.blogspot.com

World's Most Brazen And Costly Heist – 1 MDB

Malaysia Should Do A Lehman Brothers On Goldman Sachs

November 18, 2018

Malaysia should sue in American courts Goldman Sachs (GS), the investment bank associated with One Malaysia Development Berhad (1MDB), to recover not only the US$600 million it had charged the company (and thus Malaysia), but also the associated financial loss from the ensuing criminal activities through 1MDB.

Malaysia should go beyond seeking restitutive remedies and demand punitive damages to teach those bankers a lesson to never again collude or be complicit with Third World kleptocrats in robbing the world's poor. In short, inflict a Lehman Brothers on Goldman Sachs through a lawsuit.

Malaysia would be doing the world a great favor by exposing the weaknesses and inadequacies of the current regulations and oversight agencies, both international and domestic. Those agencies are impotent in curbing corrupt and illicit cross-border money flows because they are too beholden to the industry to effect meaningful reforms despite the many attempts.

A successful lawsuit would be a far more effective remedy than any legislation or international treaty. Former Wall Street executives are key players in current and previous American Administrations, Democrat as well as Republican. They are so used to calling the shots, quite apart from the hold their industry has on those regulatory agencies through their powerful and lucrative lobbying.

Malaysia would have no difficulty finding competent lawyers even on a contingency basis. This 1MDB mess could prove to be the most lucrative bonanza for American lawyers. GS is a deep-pocketed defendant. Already a few of the key players have in effect pleaded guilty.

By way of background, Lehman Brothers was an old white-shoe Wall Street firm forced into bankruptcy in 2008 for its overexposure in the subprime financial spiral. The company's leaders then considered themselves the new Masters of the Universe, the same hubris now afflicting GS top personnel in their dealings with corrupt Najib.

oing in Lehman was the most necessary and effective lesson on Wall Street for the 2008 economic crisis that nearly took down Western capitalism. A decade later that sting has been forgotten. Wall Street needs to be taught that lesson again, and very forcefully too. Malaysia through Mahathir is destined to be that strict teacher. He should not shy away from this unique and awesome responsibility.

I sniffed this 1MDB skunk long before it hit the headlines in Malaysia. When a senior Bank Negara official was in America on a private visit many years ago, I showed him articles in leading American financial publications of the unusually attractive returns on the 1MDB bonds managed by GS, with rates in excess of 300 basis points of what I was paying for my unsecured line of credit at my local California bank. This was during the post-2008 recession when money was dirt cheap. Surely sovereign Malaysia was a better credit risk than little me!

What stunned me was this official's non-reaction. He knew nothing about it. Surely such mega deals should have been the talk at Bank Negara's water coolers.

Meanwhile the American press was featuring how a Malaysian boy related to Najib was making a splash in Hollywood and the local ultra-luxury real estate market. Nobody questioned how Najib's stepson, whose father was but a retired junior army officer, acquired all that wealth. My suspicion deepened with firsthand knowledge of the super-lavish, gaudy shopping habits of Najib and his spouse on their frequent visits to California.

Then there was the extraordinary effort by the co-producers of the Oscar-winning film "The Wolf Of Wall Street" to excise Reza Aziz's name off the credit list at the Academy Awards ceremony even though he had provided the film's critical financing. Then in July 2016, America's Department of Justice (DOJ) came down with its massive civil asset forfeiture lawsuits under the Kleptocracy Asset Recovery Initiative.

Despite all that, the tipping point occurred not in the major financial Western capitals or courts in the West, rather in the simple Malay kampungs. At the May 9, 2018 Malaysia's 14th General Elections, those seemingly unsophisticated villagers booted Najib and his gang of plunderers out. With that, the rotten durian split, and the stink was no longer containable. Since then Najib, his wife, and no fewer than half a dozen of his ministers and top aides have been criminally indicted, with more coming!

America followed her civil suits with criminal indictments. Malaysia too should follow America's example and initiate civil suits against Najib and the others, attaching their assets. Najib would have little need for those palatial mansions and ultra-luxury condos, likewise his wife and stepson. Their room and board would be provided for gratis by the state, and for a long time.

Najib's elaborate corrupt schemes, obscene greed, and *dedak*-fed enablers must be exposed and put behind bars. Malaysia must make every effort to recover the loot.

Like those former high-flying Wall Street financiers, former Malaysian leaders too must be taught a very tough lesson. By teaching these former leaders, we would also be instructing current and future ones.

A Collective Malay Shame And Tragedy

November 4, 2018

Reading the US Department of Justice's (DOJ) criminal indictment of November 1, 2018 relating to 1MDB, as well as its earlier (July 2016) civil forfeiture lawsuit on assets allegedly linked to it, I am struck by three singular observations.

First is the appalling avarice of the alleged culprits; second, the utter impunity with which they conducted themselves; and third, the sheer stupidity of the man without whose authority those shenanigans would not have been possible–Malaysian Official 1, as referred to in both charges. The world now knows him as Najib Razak. While to date he has yet to face any DOJ charges, in Malaysia he is being prosecuted on multiple criminal trials, each of which could put him in jail for the rest of his life.

This 1MDB heist is by far DOJ's most complex as well as largest in terms of monetary value. Complex because its criminal activities span over at least six jurisdictions. At last estimate the loot was in excess of US$4.5

billion and counting. That does not include the added liabilities through the associated loans and leveraging.

The sheer hubris of the perpetrators to think that they could get away with it! As for Najib, he is not terribly bright, just wily enough to know that his fellow ministers and UMNO leaders could be bought cheaply with the loot from 1MDB.

As for his rise in UMNO, that too is more the consequence of Malay culture. Malays are suckers for *terhutang budi*, an excessive sense of personal gratitude. In the case with Najib, it was for his father, Malaysia's second Prime Minister who died unexpectedly while in office in 1976.

Had Najib not been a Bin Tun Razak, he would be but a middling civil servant, at best. At worst, he would have been flogged and jailed decades ago for "close proximity."

Think of it; had those religious police in Port Dickson been in their usual zealous mode back then in the 1980s and ignored Najib's Bin Razak status, or had the powerful not been *terhutang budi* to his father, Malaysia would have been spared much grief today, and a whole lot less debt.

The financial liabilities of 1MDB, though humongous and painful, is at least quantifiable. Not so the associated lost opportunities. Had the billions not been squandered on luxury real estate in London, Beverley Hills, and New York, or funding soft porno movies, but on improving national schools and FELDA settlements, we would be that much closer to the goals of *Ketuanan Melayu* (Malay Hegemony) and Vision 2020.

This being Malaysia, the dangerous race factor is never far from the surface. That is the most pernicious and consequential legacy of 1MDB. Already there are ugly rumors, and not just within UMNO but also other segments of the Malay community, blaming those smart, greedy Chinese once again taking advantage if not outright cheating sweet, innocent Malay leaders. Even Najib is now distancing himself from Jho Low. This potential explosive race angle is the most dangerous and incendiary. That risk too could not be quantified.

Even uglier and more painful to express publicly is this: Malays are downright ashamed by the outrageous behaviors of their corrupt leaders. Not stated but obvious is that all those charged in Malaysia are Malays, not ordinary ones but top UMNO leaders.

Malaysians must thank Prime Minister Mahathir for appointing Tommy Thomas as Attorney-General. It is amazing what you can achieve when you put a premium on diligence, integrity, and competence. Yes, there were many Malays who complained of Thomas not being a Malay or Muslim, as well as on his less-than-polished Malay. Regardless, he put to shame his predecessor, Apandi Ali. He, together with Najib, Zahid, Azeez and other UMNO leaders, is but an unmitigated disaster and gross embarrassment to Malays and Muslims, bar none.

By normal reckoning, Apandi should have been impeached. In a perversion of values, Najib made him a Tan Sri, Malaysia's high civil honorific, and the Agung agreed. Like it or not, to many non-Malays as well as Malays, the likes of Najib and Apandi represent the best that the Malay community could produce. That hurts!

As for those other champions of *Ketuanan Melayu*, their goals would be achieved that much faster and more efficaciously if they would first get rid from their midst these corrupt contemptuous characters.

With the DOJ's filings, a pivotal defendant in its criminal case has already pleaded guilty; with its civil, at least two have agreed to settle.

Much can be deduced from the local reactions, and even more so from the lack of same among some notable quarters. It is not surprising that some still believe Najib despite those charges and the boxes of gold as well as cash hauled from his residences right after the election. They still believe that the money was for them!

What stretches one's credulity is that UMNO leaders too bought Najib's snake oil, and they included many lawyers and accountants, as well as an Oxford graduate and even an Ivy League PhD in economics!

I can see a few who would be silenced by diverting some 1MDB crumbs their way as with funding their Hajjs. What about the stunning silence of the ulama class and sultans? Sly Najib had diverted chunks of 1MDB goodies to them too! Except for the sultans, mere crumbs would not do it for them.

That is the greatest Malay shame and tragedy.

Liquidate 1MDB And Appoint A Special Prosecutor

October 28, 2018

With former Prime Minister Najib, his wife, Deputy and other former top officials now facing dozens of serious criminal charges, the Mahathir Administration can no longer be accused of focusing only on the small fries in its fight against corruption. There is however a price to be paid for that diligence.

This 1MDB mess consumes an inordinate amount of attention and resources from the Administration to the detriment of its other responsibilities. Why not liquidate 1MDB and appoint a special prosecutor (or extend the terms of the present one) to investigate and prosecute all matters pertaining to 1MDB? That should free up the Administration and the Prosecutor's Office.

For all of Malaysia's frenetic activities and high-profile arrests, no financial institution has yet had its license yanked or anyone convicted. Singapore and Switzerland have shuttered a few banks and sanctioned the individuals involved. Singapore even jailed a few. America meanwhile has seized hundreds of millions of assets allegedly linked to 1MDB.

1MDB is a humongous mess, with labyrinthine international tentacles stretching from Panama and Cayman Islands to London and New York. Its transactions flout the borders of legality through its multiplicity and complexity. Regulatory agencies have proven themselves woefully impotent.

Malaysia must get to the bottom of this and punish those culprits and do so without mercy to deter others from even thinking about committing similar offences in the future. If Malaysia were to succeed in unraveling and exposing this grand robbery scheme, she would make a significant contribution towards making complex international financial dealings more transparent and thus less subject to corruption.

Mahathir was wise in enlisting a distinguished private attorney to be Attorney General (AG) and to lead the prosecution. I hope that the AG would seek lawyers, accountants, and forensic experts from the private sector to help him. Bypass the tainted, incompetent civil service with its "*Saya menunggu arahan*" (I await directives) mindset.

Najib's Attorney-General, the now disgraced Apandi Ali, had destroyed what little credibility and professionalism there was in the public prosecutors' office. Besides, many of those remaining were Najib's enablers. They could sabotage the investigations. Indeed, if not for their earlier collusion, or if they had been a wee bit professional or faithful to their oath of office, this boondoggle would not have happened in the first place. Najib is not that smart to have executed this massive heist on his own. He was smart only in recognizing and exploiting the fact that his ministers and top civil servants were *dedak*-dependent.

Beyond expanding the powers of the current special prosecutor to investigate all matters pertaining to 1MDB, Mahathir should also liquidate the company and its myriad subsidiaries, as well as associated entities.

A special prosecutor would be a far more efficient and effective route than a Royal Commission. With the former, charges could be brought in as soon as enough evidence has been adduced. With the latter, you would have to wait for the full report, which could be months or years. With a special prosecutor, the investigations and interviews would be private. The evidence would be made public only during a trial.

I would livestream the trials and give running commentaries in Malay so kampung folks and others would be apprised of the scheming of their leaders and institutions. These crooked leaders have betrayed citizens' trust in them. A public trial would expose them.

Liquidating 1MDB would contain and minimize the financial and other liabilities. The trial would also be a splendid teaching moment, educating citizens on the associated massive opportunity costs.

This colossal disaster did not arise out of the blue. The climate incubating it had long been nurtured. It began during Mahathir's first tenure as Prime Minister. He cannot escape the blame and responsibility. There had been many mini 1MDBs in his time, from the London Tin debacle to the Bank Bumiputra flop. Because those were tolerated and the responsible individuals not punished (neigh, they were amply rewarded!), we have this current massive scandal.

Were Mahathir to be successful in punishing those responsible for 1MDB, introduce laws that would prevent future recurrences, and repatriate some of the loot from abroad, then he would have expiated to some extent his earlier sins. He has started that process just by defeating

Najib's coalition in the 14th General Elections. He should go further and ensure that Najib is thrown into the slammer for good.

It is human to make mistakes. Refusing to learn from them would be the depth of stupidity. Liquidating 1MDB and appointing a special prosecutor would be the first step in this much-needed learning process.

1MDB Only A Symptom Of A Much Bigger Mess

May 27, 2018

Only a few weeks ago the CEO of 1MDB was telling everyone that the company's assets far exceeded its liabilities and it could service its debts.

Today Arul Kandasamy is exposed for what he is, Najib's campaign errand boy tagged with an impressive title and powered by a massive dose of *dedak*. Arul is but an inept executive and a bumbling campaigner. What can you say of a CEO who does not even know that his company is insolvent, and has been so for months, or a campaigner who could not draw a crowd? As for the title "Chief" Executive, he is 1MDB's only employee!

I could not care less about Arul or his erstwhile boss Najib Razak. Malaysians are rightfully concerned with 1MDB as they would end up with the liabilities, now fast ballooning to be in the multi-billions. What a sorry and very expensive end to what started out as a state-level, government-sponsored development agency, Trengganu Investment Authority (TIA), to manage the state's oil revenue. TIA was a combined Alberta Heritage Fund and Norwegian Sovereign Fund wannabe.

Najib morphed TIA into 1MDB and borrowed heavily. It is now near bankruptcy, needing frequent bailouts. Instead of the promised bounty, 1MDB burdens the *rakyat* and their descendants for generations to come.

Despite that, many still do not or refuse to see the connection between those boxes of cash hauled from Najib's residence and 1MDB's insolvency. That scene was more like a raid on a drug kingpin's house. I do not fault those simple villagers for still not believing that their Najib had perpetrated the largest fraud. Those figures and convoluted transactions are beyond their comprehension. Besides, they just could not believe that their leaders would ever betray their trust.

What surprised me instead are the reactions of the supposedly more educated urban Malays. Their denials border on the pathologic.

This 1MDB scandal is a symptom of a much deeper problem that afflicts all Government Linked Companies (GLCs). It is time to rethink the whole GLC concept.

GLCs and their antecedents, the crown corporations, have a long history. They are not unique to Malaysia. Both capitalistic America and Communist China have their GLCs, but they serve their different needs and objectives.

To Tun Razak, GLCs were to be the instrument to leverage and spearhead Malay participation in the corporate sector. His son, Najib, degenerated that into a not-so-sophisticated system for crooked politicians like himself to plunder. At least when the Sultan of Brunei wants some cash, he raids the public treasury. As there is no differentiation between his and the state's assets, raid is not quite the right term for his actions.

In Malaysia, Najib needed elaborate shell companies and trusts in such places as Panama and the Cayman Islands, as well as willing intermediaries like his stepson, that chubby moronic-looking fellow, and an Arab potentate among others to siphon off the state's assets through a GLC. 1MDB is Exhibit A.

The frequent exercise of one GLC selling assets to another, each with an ever-escalating price, is reminiscent of the tricks used by rogue Iceland bankers that led to that country's economic meltdown in 2008. All the associated paper-shuffling maneuvers with their expensive commissions and professional fees are schemes to plunder the assets of those GLCs.

Malaysian GLCs also have a negative influence on talented young Bumiputras, their idealism and brilliance squandered by the corrupt ways of these companies. Without those GLCs they could have started their own enterprises and be the local Bill Gates and Jeff Bezos or shine at the local branch of IBM or Morgan Stanley.

Yet another corrosive effect of GLCs is that they are a not-so-subtle but effective scheme to corrupt top civil servants. Be too critical of your political superiors and you jeopardize your chance of a lucrative post-retirement job as Chairman of Petronas. Note that of the four Tan Sri's connected to the earlier investigation of 1MDB who 'retired,' only former

IGP Khalid, the snitch, was given the chairmanship of a GLC. That is not lost on those bureaucrats.

The sultans too; a few millions thrown their way and they would *titah* (pronounce) what a wonderful leader Najib was.

As for the academics, a few thousand dollars for being on the National Professors Council would do it. For the ulama, a few crumbs thrown their way and they would quote *ad nauseam* hadith on the importance of obedience to leaders.

My solution to the Malaysian GLC mess is as simple as it is inexpensive, while being infinitely more productive and effective. It would also prevent future debacles like 1MDB or the many preceding ones like London Tin fiasco and the Bank Bumiputra bust.

Sell them all! Put the proceeds into a Trust Fund to benefit Bumiputras. Be a combination of the Norwegian and the Alberta variety. Like the Norwegian, be only a passive investor, as an individual would with a mutual fund. Half of the income would be reinvested in the fund and the other half be spent as with the Alberta Heritage Fund, to improve the quality of Bumiputras' human capital. This would include supplementing the education of Bumiputras in STEM studies, acting as a source of venture capital for budding Bumiputra entrepreneurs, and providing business infrastructures as with building marketplaces and manufacturing food trucks, as well as modernizing the rural sector through mechanizing farms and rural areas.

Malaysia should not be satisfied with only punishing those corrupt and incompetent individuals in 1MDB and other GLCs. They should demand more. Get rid of the sources of the problem. Sell all those GLCs!

Reactions To DOJ Lawsuits Reflect Ignorance And Corrupted Concept of Justice

June 26, 2017

America is a Rorschach Test to most foreigners. What they view as America reveals more of themselves than of America; likewise, how they react to events in America.

One visitor to Washington, DC, would see only the homeless under the bridges, potholes in the streets, and "adult" stores at every corner. Others see The Smithsonian, Georgetown University, and the National Institutes of Health. The contrasting observations reflect volumes on the respective observers.

Consider the Malaysian responses to the US Department of Justice (DOJ) lawsuits relating to alleged illicit siphoning of funds from 1MDB. I am not referring to the *kopi-o* babbling from the echo chambers of UMNO-paid "cyber-troopers" that pollutes the social media. They are but pet parrots echoing whatever is coached to them. With a different master offering more leftovers they could be made to change their tune with ease.

What interests me instead are the responses of ministers and mainstream commentators. Their utterances expose their appalling ignorance of the American justice system. They also reveal much of themselves, as per Rorschach's insight.

One minister, eager to be his master's favorite lapdog, asserted that DOJ is being influenced by the Malaysian opposition. On cue, the other hounds and bitches piled on. A hitherto severe critic of the establishment pontificated that Mahathir and Daim Zainuddin were involved in the intrigue to besmirch "Malaysia's good name."

Mahathir described it best those who believed such canards: *"Bodoh luar biasa!"* (Extraordinarily stupid!)

Those characters must believe that the American judicial system is like Malaysia's, where prosecutors could be influenced or paid off *a la* one Shafie Abdullah. *Sarawak Report* alleged that he was paid RM9.5 million from Najib's slush fund before being appointed special prosecutor in Anwar Ibrahim's second sodomy case. Shafie has not denied that.

Another minister declared DOJ's charges 'mere' allegations. A former journalist-turn-blogger echoed that, and proceeded, for emphasis, to reprint in bold the DOJ's caution.

Yes, DOJ's accusations, like all court complaints, are "alleged" until adjudicated. DOJ must have credible evidence to not waste taxpayers' money on frivolous lawsuits. The jury would not buy that.

Those who believe otherwise must think that DOJ and American courts are like Malaysia's where prosecutors could be bought to bring on cases with the flimsiest of evidences and still find judges to convict, as with Anwar's two sodomy cases.

That is not a far stretch. A few years ago, a defense lawyer known for his amazing 'skills' in getting his clients acquitted was caught on videotape assuring his listener on the phone that he had a particular judge in his pocket. The lawyer's utterance, "Correct! Correct! Correct!" would forever be embedded in the annals of shame in the Malaysian judiciary. He was speaking to no less than the country's Chief Justice.

Then there was the character who insinuated that the 'inactivity' of DOJ since its first filing a year earlier revealed its sinister political motive. Had that person followed the court's calendar she would have noted the flurry of activities since. Among them, the successful challenge by the new trustee of some of the seized properties to be represented.

This character went on to opine that since her initial filing in July 2016, US Attorney-General Loretta Lynch had been "fired," implying that the lawsuit was without merit. Such willful ignorance reveals a deliberate attempt to mislead. Lynch was a political appointee, and with President Trump's election, all such appointees were replaced. Further, the second 1MDB-associated filing was by her Trump-appointed successor.

Deputy Prime Minister Ahmad Zahid, a local PhD, implied that all the furor over 1MDB were fake news, the concoctions of hostile foreign media! It is instructive that this character did his dissertation on the local media. To him, the likes of *The Wall Street Journal* are like *Utusan Melayu*. His response reveals as much about him as the institution that awarded him his doctorate.

A junior minister accused the Americans to be in cahoots with the opposition in trying to topple Najib. That minister did not see fit to demonstrate at the embassy in defense of Malaysia. Some *jantan* (hero)! It is unfortunate that this non-too bright character's remarks resonated with simple villagers.

A senior minister, Hishamuddin Hussein, a little brighter being that he was a London-trained lawyer, dismissed the whole DOJ affair. Malaysia had other far more important issues to attend to, he sniffed. If the staggering sums of the loot did not impress him, what about the charges of corruption levelled at the highest government official, cryptically referred to as "Malaysian Official 1" in the DOJ filing? That should be his and all Malaysians' top priority.

Yet another minister advised everyone not to panic. The lady doth protest too much! Nobody was panicking except her and her crowd.

Attorney-General Apandi was miffed that DOJ did not consult him. DOJ's lawsuits were prompted to protect American financial institutions from the corrupting influences of dirty foreign funds. It does not need Malaysia's 'help,' more so considering that Apandi had earlier in his investigations declared no wrongdoing.

Apandi was also upset at the criminal insinuations against the Prime Minister. Apandi's comment unwittingly revealed what he thinks of his job, less chief prosecutor, more Najib's private attorney. No wonder his "investigations" exonerated Najib! Apandi also unwittingly confirmed that MO1 was in fact Najib and that the activities he was alleged to have been engaged in were criminal in nature.

If the responses were revealing, the non-response or silence was even more so. The lawsuits alleged that billions were illicitly siphoned from the company. That was mentioned umpteen times in the complaints. Yet 1MDB did not seek to be represented as a party of interest. This reflects its management's inability to separate the company's interests from those of its officers'. Najib is 1MDB's chairman. The management confuses Najib with the company. Management is not looking after the company's interest in not seeking legal representation, which was how the mess started in the first place.

Malaysian officials' responses to DOJ's lawsuits did not reflect well on them or Malaysia. I can hardly wait for their reactions or "spin" when this DOJ investigation goes on to its next inevitable phase, the filing of criminal charges and or when one of the defendants becomes a prosecution witness.

Meanwhile, fake news or not and collusion or not, MO1, his spouse, and stepson will not be stepping foot in America any time soon, if ever. *That's* revealing!

The Hyenas, Vultures, And Maggots Of 1MDB

August 22, 2016

1MDB is not yet a bloated carcass (it is bloated but only with debt) and already the hyenas, vultures, and maggots are feasting with glee. In the wild, hyenas and vultures wait till their prey is dead while maggots wait till it is rotting. Not these human varieties.

Scavengers are vital in the ecosystem; they help cleanse the environment of dead and decomposing bodies. In contrast, the human varieties now feasting on 1MDB are part of the rubbish. Perverse as it may seem, they have an exalted opinion of themselves. They view what they are doing–defending "Malaysian Official 1" and those associated like his stepson Reza Aziz–as honorable.

This 1MDB mess is humungous; it will burden Malaysians for generations. That is the grim and undeniable fact.

Other facts, also undeniable, include these. One, 1MDB's debt in excess of RM42 billion, and growing fast, exceeds the current budgetary allocation for education. No other entity, private or public, then or now could come even close. Those loans are the labilities imposed on taxpayers as well as those who do not pay tax. Those non-taxpayers, meaning the poor, are impacted because funds meant for them would have to be diverted to servicing those debts. A colossal loss in opportunity costs!

Two, 1MDB has gone through as many accounting firms as Britney Spears with her boyfriends. Its latest, Deloitte, has resigned, but not before making a most unusual declaration. It admitted that the US Department of Justice's July 20, 2016 asset forfeiture lawsuit contained information that, if known at the time of Deloitte's 2013 and 2014 audits "would have impacted the financial statements and affected [its] audit reports."

Along the same vein, the Auditor-General's Report on 1MDB which the government had promised to make public is now under the Official Secrets Act. Those reports have always been public.

Three, 1MDB has gone through as many chief executives in as many years, not the sign of a well-managed company.

Four, drive by the site of the proposed Tun Razak Exchange, 1MDB's signature development. It is empty.[1]

Last, 1MDB has yet to generate a cent of profit despite being in existence since 2009.

---

[1] Its signature The Exchange 106, Malaysia's tallest skyscraper, is now (Dec 2019) complete. Its launching occupancy rate is under 20 percent.

Meanwhile Switzerland has forced the sale of the bank involved with 1MDB and imposed an unusual and tough stipulation. Its new owner must not employ any of the existing senior managers of the sold bank. Singapore summarily closed the local branch of that bank and its head faced criminal charges. He was denied bail while awaiting trial, reflecting the gravity of the alleged crime. Singapore admitted to being lax in monitoring the bank's activities with respect to 1MDB. Singapore also froze the assets of Jho Low, Najib's financial confidant and key 1MDB player, an unprecedented severe action.

Then there are other 'facts,' Malaysian variety. The Attorney-General and Bank Negara have closed their investigations with no negative findings.

In America there is DOJ's asset forfeiture lawsuits and the related class-action suit filed by two Malaysians, Husam and Chang.

In America anyone can file a lawsuit. As such you may dismiss the American lawsuits but not the actions of the Swiss and Singaporean authorities. As for the Attorney-General and Bank Negara Governor exonerating 1MDB, I will let readers give that its proper weightage and relevance. Nonetheless that would still not explain 1MDB's huge debts, changes in management and auditing firms, empty TRX lot, and the Auditor-General's Report being kept secret.

For those who believe that Najib is God's gift to Malays, you cannot argue with them. It would be blasphemous to dispute Allah's choice. For the rest of us, we need a more rational explanation, one that does not assault our credibility or insult our intelligence.

Back to the hyenas, they are now uncharacteristically quiet, their former flamboyance gone. Perhaps they are enjoying their morsels while they can, in their penthouses of Manhattan, mansions of Beverly Hills, and luxury yachts cruising the South China Sea. One would expect that having benefited handsomely from 1MDB they would harbor some gratitude to defend their benefactor.

The vast majority of Najib's supporters are simple, unsophisticated Malay villagers still under the grip of feudalism. To them it is a simplistic "my leader, my race, my country, right or wrong!" Their loyalty to leaders is intense and unquestioning, up to a point. Betray that, and you pay the price. Datuk Onn was a hero for stopping Malayan Union, and for achieving merdeka. When they fell out of step with their followers, their drop from hero to villain was precipitous and merciless. Najib is nowhere near the caliber of those two giants.

What puzzles me are the many otherwise sophisticated and well-educated Malays (Najib's supporters are almost exclusively Malays except for the few well-compensated oddballs like 1MDB CEO Arul Kandaamy) who continue to believe in Najib despite the overwhelming evidence to the contrary.

Those aside, there are those vultures and maggots. They remain Najib's supporters. The hyenas should be vociferous, but for reasons best known to themselves have chosen to remain silent. That leaves the vultures to be Najib's noisiest and ugliest cheerleaders. Unlike the hyenas with their bounties in the millions, those vultures are satisfied with a promotion or two and a federal award (second or third class) thrown in. Satisfied because stripped of their new appointments, they would earn but a mere fraction back at their old law practices or whatever they did before prostituting themselves to Najib.

The maggots are there so long as there is a decaying carcass. A few *ringgit* tossed their way to fill the tanks of their used motorbikes, and they are happy parading in their red shirts or polluting the social media with their inane comments. Once the carrion is gone, so would they.

Some support Najib out of inertia, buttressed by the havoc of regime change in Iraq and Libya as well as the performance of the local opposition. Others reflect the forbearance of Malaysians. Najib, they rationalize, won the last election [GE 13] albeit without majority popular votes, and that victory was reaffirmed by the subsequent state elections in Sarawak as well as the two by-elections in Peninsula Malaysia.

That is a dicey defense. Winning elections is no license to steal or be corrupt. Nixon won a landslide in 1972, yet that did not stop the threat of impeachment and his subsequent resignation in disgrace for covering up the Watergate break-in.

A few would argue that Najib's shenanigans are no different from Mahathir's many opaque UMNO proxy companies' scandals, as with London Tin, Bank Bumiputra, and Forex debacles. To them 1MDB is merely a different crocodile, albeit much bigger and more menacing, but from the same fetid swamp.

Malaysia will never progress with that attitude of resigned acceptance.

Then there is the reflected glory argument. Reza Aziz, Malaysian Official 1's stepson, is one of the producers of the Academy Award-winning "The Wolf of Wall Street." Most would miss the irony as the film is banned in Malaysia. Nonetheless Malays, hungry for glory beyond their kampung stage, celebrate that achievement.

Malaysians too would have likewise celebrated the achievement had the film not been tainted. The Academy publicly demanded that Reza Aziz's name be officially deleted at the ceremony. It is like winning at the Olympics, and later disqualified for doping. Instead of glory, shame.

Another aspect to Najib's support is simply crude anti-American rage triggered by the DOJ's lawsuit. That was viewed as interference as well as double standards. America too is blighted with corruption, they sniff. True. As South Korean Tongsun Park and Indonesian James Riady, as well as former Attorney-General Mitchell and President's Counsel John Dean found out, the corrupt do get caught, convicted, and jailed. President Nixon was forced to resign under threat of impeachment. That's the lesson Malaysians should draw from America.

As for American interference, if Najib and other corrupt Third World leaders do not want that, then next time accept only Zimbabwean dollars and use a bank in Uzbekistan. Then buy properties in Bali or Cancun, not Manhattan or Beverly Hills, and bet at casinos in Macau not Las Vegas.

There are no shortages of hyenas, vultures and maggots in those countries to clean up your mess.

1MDB – Malaysia's Enron And Watergate Combined

August 14, 2016

The One Malaysia Development Berhad (1MDB) corruption is business as usual in Malaysia. That is a great tragedy as well as gross injustice. To Malaysia, 1MDB is "case closed." That reflects the nation's system of justice and quality of its institutions, as well as the caliber of those entrusted to run them.

Like ugliness, injustice is obvious to all and transcends boundaries. The US Department of Justice (DOJ) first shone the light at the hideous pox on 1MDB's face with the filing of the asset forfeiture lawsuit on July

20, 2016. That was only the beginning. Shortly thereafter, Singapore froze the assets of Jho Low, one of the culprits. Together with Switzerland, it also closed the bank involved.

There is now a racketeering suit filed by Hussam Musa and Matthias Chang, as private citizens, on August 11, 2016 in New York. That has yet to be certified as a class action suit. With the huge number of potential plaintiffs, it would have no difficulty meeting the numerosity criterion.

1MDB – Malaysia's Watergate and Enron combined

The US Senate Watergate Hearings of the 1970s, triggered by the "third-rate burglary" at the Democratic Party Election Headquarters in Washington, DC, saw many jailed. More than a few prominent lawyers were disbarred, including President Nixon's former Attorney General as well as the Counsel to the President. It forced Nixon to resign in disgrace.

The Enron debacle also saw many of its principals imprisoned. The main culprit had a fatal heart attack while being investigated. Enron's principal advisor, the giant accounting firm Arthur Andersen, collapsed. Quite a collateral damage!

Unlike the defendants in the earlier DOJ's suit, in the current criminal one they are individuals and firms, not assets. They include the usual culprits Jho Low and Reza Aziz, plus his principal accountant Debra Johnson, Goldman Sachs' bond salesman Timothy Leissner, and film producer Joey McFarland, together with their respective enterprises Metroplex Capital Advisors, Goldman Sachs, and Red Granite Pictures respectively.

Lawsuits in America are complex and expensive, both to initiate and defend. As for costs, we are looking at high six figures or even millions. That is US dollars and not devalued *ringgit.*

America however has the wonderful concept of contingency fees where plaintiffs' lawyers would get paid only from the awards. Meaning, they must prevail to get paid. That is laudable public policy as it would ensure that the poor get access to good legal representation.

It would be in the plaintiff lawyers' interest to ensure that there is a good or at least winnable case, as well as a pot of gold at the end of the trail, or trials. Meaning, their defendants must have deep pockets.

Reza Aziz's and Jho Low's major assets are now tied up in the DOJ's civil forfeiture lawsuit, while Low's are also frozen in Singapore. Reza

Aziz may have a super-rich stepfather or donor somewhere. As for the other defendants, Goldman Sachs has the deepest pocket, tantalizing enough target by itself.

While the other defendants and their enterprises may not have deep pockets on cursory examination, they may have generous liability and other insurances. It would be a hollow victory not to mention a an expensive one, if in the end you could not collect on your awards.

In their lawsuit, Husam and Chang seek awards of actual damages, restitution, or disgorgement of wrongful profits obtained by the defendants, triple damages as provided for by the racketeering Act and other statutes cited, punitive damages, as well as costs and expenses. Tallying all those would take a battalion of accountants. Insurances do not cover punitive damages or racketeering acts. The threat of both is motivation enough to make defendants settle early.

Husam and Chang have already won a victory of sorts in securing the services of top law firms. Those lawyers would not risk their reputation and resources to see their case thrown out of court at the first hearing. They must have done their research and found the case not without merit.

What's in it for Husam and Chang? Certainly not the money. For even if they were to prevail and the awards be in the mega millions, their share after their lawyers' cut would not be substantial. They must be doing it to ensure that justice prevails. They could not get that in Malaysia, so they came to America.

The irony should not escape Malaysians. The pair could not find justice in an Islamic country. Instead they flew ten thousand miles away to the land of the kafir to seek it. The paradox must have struck Husam hard, being a former PAS Vice-President. That should impress upon him the essential difference between label and content.

Lawyers have as much to do with justice as doctors to health. Lawsuits, at least the civil variety, have even less; they are but business decisions. Victory is settlement in their favor without having to go through an expensive and uncertain trial.

For others, justice would be served if Jho Low and Reza Aziz were forced to disgorge their illicit gains, and then be punished. For Malaysians, that would not be enough. For them justice would come only with full exposure, as with a trial, so all the ugly truth could be revealed. With that information they could make a better choice on whom to elect as their next leaders to ensure that such corruption and injustice would not recur.

As President Johnson once noted, the vote is the most powerful instrument ever devised by man to fight injustice. We must erase this perversity among Malaysians, leaders and followers alike, that corrupt and illicit gains are but rewards and gifts from generous donors or a benevolent Allah. An open trial would be a great effort in that direction.

The highest reach of injustice is to be deemed just when you are not, wrote Plato. Likewise, the most depraved act of corruption is to view it as otherwise. 1MDB is the most egregious corruption. That fact must be brought home to all Malaysians.

To Husam Musa and Matthias Chang, thank you for your initiative in taking that brave first step. Yours is the finest form of patriotism. The corrupt, the perverts, and the traitors would view your act as treason. That is the ultimate compliment!

1MDB Not An Overnight Monster; Likewise "Malaysian Official 1"

July 31, 2016

The colossal corruption scandal that is 1MDB is not an overnight monster, likewise its principal rogue "Malaysian Official 1" (MO1).

The loss from 1MDB, though in the billions and fast ballooning, is at least quantifiable. Not so the besmirching of Malaysia's good name by its leader, MO1, *aka* Najib Razak, being labelled the world's most corrupt kleptocrat by the US Department of Justice.

So hideous and unprecedented was Najib's conduct that I believe he was born and raised corrupt. Or to use Mahathir's words in his *The Malay Dilemma*, it is in Najib's genes to be corrupt. His upbringing further nurtured that hideous trait.

I go further. Even if you are inherently (that is, genetically predisposed to be) corrupt, you would not necessarily be so if you were to be brought up along the straight path. The only conclusion then with Najib is that he, in addition to being born corrupt, was also nurtured in and by a corrupt family.

That is a near-blasphemous statement to make in Malaysia. The memory of Naib's father is still held in high regards by most Malaysians. Most but not all. For those not lucky enough to be born of the right heritage to benefit from Razak's New Economic Policy, his image is less pristine.

In trying to defend his (and his spouse's) current wealth and profligate ways, Najib claimed that he was blessed with a bountiful inheritance. Offended by that statement, one of his siblings took the unusual step of publicly contradicting him, claiming that their father died while not quite in poverty was certainly not wealthy. At least that family has one honest member.

Najib has a long history, both personal as well as official. As for the personal, let us just say that he is a Malaysian Bill Clinton, minus the brilliance. There is little need to pursue that prurient path.

As for the official, as Minister of Education back in the 1990s Najib approved over 500 permits for private colleges during a two-year period. More than one application approved per business day! You would need a lot of grease to make the normally sluggish Malaysian bureaucracy go that fast and smooth. He must have received plenty of grease to let those applicants slide by.

A measure of his ministry's "thoroughness" was that many of those colleges closed shop soon, but only *after* their students had paid the exorbitant fees, stranding them, and dashing their hopes as well as that of their parents.

As Defense Minister, Najib gave his buddy Razak Baginda millions as "commission" to buy a billion-ringgit used French submarine that could not submerge. We may yet know more about that scandal as the French are reopening that corruption case. As for his buddy, he too shared Najib's personal morality. All that is now cleansed, in the eyes of the Malaysian brand of Islam, with their trip to Mecca.

Now with Najib as Finance Minister as well as Prime Minister, should Malaysians and the world be surprised then that 1MDB is the consequence?

One person however vile, corrupt, or greedy could not possibly execute a heist on the grand scale of 1MDB. Najib must have had many enablers. Not only that, the nation's institutions must also have been sufficiently weakened and their personnel emasculated not to have noticed the massive looting in front of their very eyes. The rotting of Malaysian institutions and the breeding of those enablers too did not happen overnight.

Consider that the heads of Bank Negara, Anti-Corruption Commission, and the Police, as well as the Auditor-General and Attorney-General during the looting of 1MDB were individuals appointed by other than Najib, specifically his predecessors. That would include Mahathir, Najib's now severest critic. The exception is the current Attorney General, that failed former UMNO operative, Apandi Ali. Najib appointed him after firing his predecessor.

The talk of the town was that Najib fired Apandi Ali's predecessor Gani Patail just as he was preparing the papers for Najib's arrest. If that were so, Malaysia at least had one upright officer, but not a brave one as he did not go public.

There may be some poetic justice if not perverse irony in that a few of those enablers now face the threat of being charged for treason, for *not* protecting Najib vigorously or enough.

I draw a difference between those enablers versus the UMNO ministers, divisional chiefs, and UMNO Youth "red-shirts" who mindlessly defend and sing praises of Najib. These latter characters are whores; they are *paid* to pleasure Najib. Destroy 1MDB and Najib, and with their lifeline cut off, watch them convert to be Najib's and UMNO's severest critics.

With the National Security Act (NSA) of 2016 now operative, criticisms of Najib would be that much more difficult and treacherous. Again, that NSA did not appear overnight. It took decades in preparation, going back to the constitutional amendment of 1994 which made possible for laws passed by Parliament to dispense with royal assent. Thank Mahathir for that.

That constitutional amendment, as well as the rotting institutions, is water underneath the bridge. No point wallowing in it. Yet many are still obsessed with the blame game and relish indulging their status as Mahathir's victims. They are more interested in settling old scores or getting even on earlier slights instead of helping solve the current problem. Some let their hatred and contempt for Mahathir get in their way of rational thinking. What's the point? *All* Malaysians are now victims of Najib's greed, except for the equally corrupt few who are the beneficiaries of Najib's "cash is king" mode.

Mahathir let possible all those things to happen during his watch. However, he has been off the stage now for well over a decade. Surely Malaysians could rise above and rectify his mistakes. Why still blame the man? He is over 90 now. No glory in beating up an old man. Besides, he is trying hard to undo his errors. Help him succeed, and once that is achieved you could then engage in a post-mortem and assign blame.

It would take more than a little bit of humility to admit to one's error. It would take an even greater courage to rectify it. Mahathir admitted that appointing that dud Abdullah Badawi to succeed him was a mistake. Being instrumental in Najib's ascend was also Mahathir's mistake. He was successful in correcting his first. Malaysians should now help him correct his second, that is, getting rid of Najib.

Malaysia would be the ultimate beneficiary, not Mahathir. He does not need the trophy. If 1MDB and Najib are not destroyed, both would destroy Malaysia. Then *all* Malaysians would be the victims.

The Malay Shame And Tragedy That Is 1MDB

July 25, 2016

Imagine had Prime Minister Najib Razak responded differently to the US Department of Justice Asset Forfeiture lawsuit [filed on July 20, 2016] and said instead, "I have instructed my Foreign Minister to seek clarification to determine who is this "Malaysian Official 1" so we could investigate him. I have also directed the Attorney-General to review the evidence in the DOJ complaint."

As for 1MDB, imagine if its spokesman had responded, "We view with deep concern allegations that assets meant for our company, a public trust, had been corruptly diverted. We seek clarification on who 1MDB Officials 1 and 2 are to make sure that they are no longer in our employ. We will review our policies to ensure that such pilferages as alleged by DOJ if they did occur will not recur. Additionally, we are engaging legal counsel to protect our interests in the American trial."

Instead, what Malaysians and the world heard last Wednesday were irrelevant and meaningless statements to the effect that neither Najib nor 1MDB are the defendants in the suit. True and obvious, needing no response or clarification. The defendants are the owners of those seized assets which are alleged to have been acquired with funds corruptly siphoned from 1MDB, a GLC of which Najib is the Chairman.

The responses from Najib, his ministers, and 1MDB only brought shame to themselves, to Malays, and to Malaysia.

As for the defendants, their options are either not to contest the suit and thus forfeit those assets or fight it. Negotiated settlement is unlikely. This is the biggest asset forfeiture in US history; Attorney-General Lynch is out to make a point to corrupt kleptocrats everywhere that the days of opaque, complex cross-border money laundering are over.

Before this, the biggest forfeiture suit involved the giant telecom company, Amsterdam-based Vimpel.com, and individuals close to the President of Uzbekistan. The Uzbeks ignored the suit while the company pleaded guilty to the criminal charges. Rest assured that those defendant Uzbeks would not be visiting Disneyland or Las Vegas any time soon, or ever! There is no statute of limitations for their hideous crimes.

This 1MDB corruption may be a legal case but politics is never far off the radar in both Putrajaya and Washington, DC, as well as in the potentially more volatile international arena.

No-Contest Option

Not contesting would save substantial legal fees and other costs, as well as the not insignificant personal hassle factor. Those aside, the biggest advantage would be in not further exposing the defendants and others, legally as well as in many other ways, during the pretrial discovery and actual trial. Spared a trial, the identity of "Malaysian Official 1" will never be known, at least not officially, a crucial consideration in Putrajaya.

The loss of those assets, even though in the hundreds of millions if not billions (in US dollars, not worthless *ringgit*), is at least quantifiable. However, even the Sultan of Brunei could not shrug off a loss of that magnitude.

Choose this option and Reza Aziz, one of the defendants who according to court documents is also related to Malaysian Official 1, would be well advised to pack up and find a country that does not have extradition or tax treaty with the US. He also had better get used to a much less luxurious lifestyle.

Were Reza to pursue this course, at least in his old age he could regale his grandchildren with stories that he once owned glittering condos in Manhattan and shared drinks with top Hollywood stars in Las Vegas.

That would also be a very Malay story. At Kampung Baru today there are many elders who look with nostalgic gaze at the skyscrapers in the Golden Triangle and lament, "*Ah, itu cerita dulu!*" (Those are old stories!)

The US Government would recoup its considerable costs from those assets. Rest assured that there would be itemized bills for every paper clip used, and DOJ lawyers would be charging senior partners' rates. Even after factoring that, there would still be substantial loot left. By statute, that belongs to the people of Malaysia.

If Najib were still to remain as Prime Minister, do you think those Americans would be dumb enough to return those millions to the same scoundrels? America could not disburse them to Malaysian NGOs either. As most are not sympathetic to UMNO, repatriating those funds to them could pose a delicate diplomatic problem. On the other hand, those precious funds could be leveraged into the most sophisticated and effective exercise of "soft power," more powerful than "boots on the ground" in effecting regime change in Malaysia.

In short, do not expect those Monet paintings to hang on the walls of kampung huts any time soon.

Contesting the Forfeiture

Contesting the DOJ suits would be no walk in the park. It would be expensive, protracted, and risk uncovering details that could trigger criminal charges. American lawyers are not cheap and potential defense attorneys would want their substantial fees paid upfront and from "clean" sources. With their assets tied, Reza Aziz and the other defendants better have other fat bank accounts. Even if he were to receive help from his "Malaysian Official 1" stepfather, Reza's defense attorneys would insist and need unchallenged documentation to prove that those funds are legitimate and that they are not siphoned public funds.

The earliest a trial could begin would be a year or two hence, in time for the UMNO Leadership Convention or worse, the next Malaysian election. A trial would also risk exposing the identity of "Malaysian Official 1, a consideration for Putrajaya.

Being a civil case, the burden of proof for the prosecution is lower, merely the preponderance of evidence, not the much higher "beyond a reasonable doubt" of a criminal trial. The burden also shifts to the defendants to prove that those assets were acquired with untainted funds.

In court documents Reza Aziz claimed that the millions he received were from some unknown Arab as a gift. An incredulous assertion that even his accountant did not believe him; hence the "attestation" from his "donor." If this be a trial by jury, it would be tricky to convince an American juror that receiving millions from a stranger is a "gift." Besides, the image of an Arab in America these days is far from pristine.

With a trial, the testimonies of those professionals who had advised the defendants would be scrutinized. The Watergate Hearings of the 1970s exposed the unsavory activities of the various advisors. Many prominent lawyers ended being disbarred as a result of revelations from those hearings, including the President's Counsel as well as a former Attorney-General.

A trial would also highlight an ugly truth that could prove explosive in race-sensitive Malaysia. That is, Reza Aziz excepted, those corrupt Malays got only the crumbs while the juiciest gravy flowed to that Wharton-trained Chinaman. That won't sit well with UMNO Youth's "Red Shirts" or PERKASA boys.

A trial would also showcase the professionalism and meticulousness of American prosecutors and investigators. That would not make the former failed UMNO operative and current Malaysia's Attorney-General Apandi Ali look good. The Malay image is already battered by the amateurs at 1MDB.

From the perspective of international politics, it may be shrewd not to identify "Malaysian Official 1." This forfeiture lawsuit is not the only game. After all, Obama did not tee off with Najib that Christmas of 2014 in Hawaii because he (Najib) was a Tiger Woods. It was part of Obama's "Pivot to Asia" show, with Najib the convenient prop.

There are other actors in this new shadow play. China is asserting itself, most visibly through military exercises in the South China Sea but more effectively elsewhere. Note the abrupt change of face at the recent ASEAN conference that had initially condemned China, and ASEAN's collective silence on the International Court's decision on the South China Sea dispute that favored fellow ASEAN state, the Philippines.

China could also play the Obama game, not on the greens of Hawaii's golf courses but FELDA's palm oil plantations. China could buy palm oil from Africa as well as not offer inflated prices for those rusty 1MDB assets.

Najib must now balance the interests of his stepson and former Beverly Hills real estate tycoon Reza Aziz versus that of FELDA settlers and their wooden huts. Not an easy choice for Najib; it should be for a genuine Malaysian leader.

The kampung boy in me longs to see a good fight by our modern-day Hang Tuah. Thus, I challenge Reza Aziz to be *jantan* (man) enough to fight this US forfeiture.

Back to reality, the winners in this 1MDB shadow play are many and obvious. Reza is one, though not as big as he was before the forfeiture; so too Malaysian Official 1 as well as IMDB Officials 1 and 2. As for that Wharton character Jho Low, he could still savor his shark's fin soup in Taiwan. The US DOJ too is a winner, and a big one.

As for the losers from this 1MDB debacle, that too is obvious. First, its current management. It should sue the previous board and management for incompetence as well as breach of fiduciary duties to recover some of the losses. Current management owes the company and Malaysians that much.

The other victims are less obvious. They include FELDA settlers now deprived of better schools, smart young Malays who excelled on their IB tests but now could not go abroad because of lack of scholarship funds, and those dedicated GLC Malay executives whose reputations are now tainted because of the shenanigans of those top monkeys at 1MDB.

Those who still strenuously defend Malaysian Official 1 have yet to recognize these victims of 1MDB. That is the terrible shame, and a great Malay tragedy.

The Noose Tightens On 1MDB

July 20, 2016

For those who missed the live streaming of the United States Department of Justice Press Conference on Wednesday, July 20, 2016 in Washington, DC, regarding the 1MDB scandal, here is a partial transcript. The full transcript is available at recapd.com.

A few preliminary observations. First, this civil filing of asset forfeiture is only the initial action following an intense and still ongoing investigation. There could be other charges later, including criminal ones against specific individuals. The presence of senior officials from the criminal divisions of the DOJ and IRS, as well as top FBI officials at that press conference would indicate this. Assets do not become corrupt by themselves; individuals through their corrupt acts created those assets.

Second, this is a *civil* complaint against the *assets* that were acquired from alleged corrupt acts perpetrated on 1MDB. Those assets are now legally tied up.

There could be two possible responses. At one extreme the owners of those assets would choose not to challenge the complaint at which point those assets become US Government property and would be auctioned off. The US Government would recoup its costs and the people of Malaysia would be entitled to claim the leftovers. The other would be for their owners to challenge the order. That would incur substantial legal fees as the filings are in many courts and your adversary is the US Government with its near unlimited resources. And American lawyers are expensive. With those assets frozen, their owners could not liquidate or mortgage them to finance their defense. Knowing that should be satisfaction enough for Malaysians.

A court challenge would be very enlightening. The ensuing trials would reveal much.

Third, this is by far the largest (in monetary terms) asset seizure in US history. As such those professional prosecutors would not settle for anything less than a total victory. Before this, the largest forfeiture under the Kleptocracy Asset Recovery Initiative involved the Amsterdam-based Vimpel.com, a telecommunication giant, and its subsidiary in Uzbekistan. That involved top Uzbek officials related to that country's President.

Fourth was the impressive performance by Attorney-General Loretta Lynch and her team at that press conference. It is not simply a matter that she is a seasoned professional prosecutor with a Harvard law degree while her Malaysian counterpart is a failed UMNO operative with a legal qualification from an obscure British Inn of Courts.

What follows is a truncated version of the press conference.

Attorney-General Lynch: Today the Department of Justice has filed a civil complaint seeking to forfeit and recover more than [US]$1 billion in assets associated with an international conspiracy to launder funds stolen from 1MDB. These are just a portion of the more than $3B that was stolen from 1MDB and laundered through American institutions in violation of US law.

. . . [Our] complaint alleges that from 2001 to 2015 [1MDB] officials and associates conspired to misappropriate and launder billions of dollars from 1MDB. They laundered their funds through opaque actions in bank accounts in countries around the world including Switzerland, Singapore, and the United States. The funds were then used to purchase a range of assets for the conspirators and their relatives and associates, including high-end real estate in New York and Los Angeles, and art works by Monet, and a Bombardier Jet aircraft.

Today's case is the largest single action ever brought under the Kleptocracy Asset Recovery Initiative. . . . .

Assistant US AG (Criminal Division) Leslie R Caldwell: . . . I'd like to focus on . . . allegations involving two bond offerings in 2012 through which 1MDB raised some of the money siphoned off by the corrupt officials and their associates. The stated purpose of the bond offerings was to allow 1MDB to raise money to invest in various energy assets of the Malaysian Government and people. Almost immediately . . . roughly 40 percent of the money that was raised, which was about $1.7B, was transferred out of 1MDB account and into a Swiss bank account that was in the name of a shell corporation incorporated in the British Virgin Islands. The . . . name of that shell company was chosen because it sounded like the name of a legitimate company that was involved in the bond offering but in fact the Swiss bank account was controlled by corrupt officials and associates.

From Switzerland the corrupt officials transferred money using a series of transactions involving more shell companies and bank accounts located all over the globe. Eventually more than $223M of that money found its way in the account of shell companies whose beneficial owner was a close relative of a senior 1MDB official, and that individual used the money to buy luxury real estate in the US and other assets, and . . . to fund a motion picture company called Red Granite who in turn used more than $100M of that money to finance the award-winning 2013 film "The Wolf of Wall Street." Neither 1MDB nor the Malaysian people saw a penny of profit from that film or the other assets purchased with funds siphoned from 1MDB. Instead that money went to relatives and associates of the corrupt officials of 1MDB and others.

US Attorney, Central California (Los Angeles) Eileen M Decker: Another phase of this money laundering scheme occurred in early 2013 in connection with a third bond offering arranged by Goldman Sachs International. In this offering 1MDB raised approximately $3 billion purportedly to form a joint venture with an entity from Abu Dhabi to promote growth. Instead, the officials misappropriated a significant amount of the funds raised. . . . [O]nly days after the initial bond sale, approximately $1.26 billion was diverted for the benefit of individuals associated with 1MDB. Approximately $137 million of the pilfered money was spent to purchase works of art, including a $34 million work by Claude Monet. . . . . [and] . . . to enhance the luxury and lavish lifestyles of those stealing money from 1MDB. Funds diverted from the third bond offering were also traced to the purchase of an interest in the Park Lane Hotel in New York. . . . The laundering of the proceeds continued throughout 2013 with an additional $106 million used to purchase an interest in EMI Music Publishing.

FBI Deputy Director Andrew McCabe: . . . Not long after 1MDB was established in 2009, corrupt officials at 1MDB and their associates began a sophisticated scheme to enrich themselves. In the first two years of their existence, almost $1 billion was transferred out of 1MDB to bank accounts in shell corporations that were controlled by associates of corrupt 1MDB officials. The funds were stolen under the pretense of having 1MDB invest in an oil exploration joint venture with a foreign partner. On paper, the $1billion was to be 1MDB's in what purported to be national resource rights. But this was not a legitimate investment for 1MDB or the Malaysian people. Instead, the funds transferred to the shell companies were used for the personal enrichment of the corrupt officials and their associates. They used the money to pay gambling debts at Las Vegas casinos, rent luxury yachts, hire an interior decorator in London, and spent millions on properties some of which is subject to this seizure and forfeitures. Among them was a jet purchased at the price of $35 million.

IRS Criminal Investigation Chief Richard Webber: 1MDB was originally established to drive strategic initiatives for the long-term economic development of Malaysia. Instead, it . . . was siphoned . . . for personal investment, not for the good of the Malaysian people and not for the achievement of their goals.

The case is another example of the ability to follow money through complex money laundering schemes and the web of opaque transactions and fraudulent shell corporations. In October 2015 . . . [a]pproximately $238 million was wired to Red Granite Capital in Singapore, an entity controlled by Reza Aziz. . . . This money was used to fund Red Granite Pictures operations including the production of the film "The Wolf of Wall Street." Additionally, the misappropriations were used to acquire $100 million in relics in the US, United Kingdom and elsewhere for the benefit of Aziz, including . . . [a] Beverly Hills mansion, a Park Laurel condo in New York City, and a townhouse in the United Kingdom.

   . . . .

This case represents a model for international cooperation in significant cross-border money laundering matters and sends a message that criminals cannot evade law enforcement authorities by simply laundering money through multiple jurisdictions and through a web of shell corporations.

Same Reality, Different Perception: Najib's RM 2.6B – Generous Donation Or Grand Corruption?

September 3, 2015

In the 1950s the Americans were alarmed with the shrill anti-Western rhetoric of leftist-leaning Indonesian President Sukarno. To neutralize him, they concocted a scheme to blackmail the man by portraying him as other than a true nationalist.

On one of his frequent visits to America, the CIA secretly set-up Sukarno to be in the company of high-priced hookers, and then clandestinely filmed him in his frolics. Sukarno must have felt that he was already in heaven with some of his 72 "virgins!"

The plan was to screen snippets of the tape in the movie houses of Jakarta. Surely in pious Muslim Indonesia such scenes would enrage the audiences such that they would take to the streets demanding Sukarno's downfall.

Thus far everything went according to the well-rehearsed script, one that would be repeated in different places and with different players.

Imagine the horror of the local CIA station agents in Jakarta when the audiences instead roared their approval of their President when snippets of the films were screened!

"Yeah! *Itu jantan kita!*" (He's *our* stud!) they roared as Sukarno, like the bunny powered by the Eveready battery kept going and going (or coming and coming)! "It's about time one of us gets to screw them, they did that to us for years!" they cheered with unconcealed lust.

The Indonesians saw reflected glory and pride in their leader's virility, fantasizing a part of themselves in him.

My long preamble here is to put forth a simple proposition. While the reality may be the same, the perceptions may be radically different. The world and many Malaysians may view Najib's RM2.6 billion "donation" as corruption on a grand scale, but to red-shirted Malays and their UMNO Putra patrons, it is but a measure of an Arab's high regard for their man.

Pardon my comparing Najib with Sukarno. Najib is no Sukarno in leadership talent or oratorical skills; he is however, in priapic proclivities.

It is not coincidental that Najib's spinmeisters would have the donation come from the Middle East, the land of the Prophet. To Muslim Malays, the Arabs and their desert are blessed. In Saudi Arabia even the flies on your food are halal. As for the ensuing diarrhea, well, that's Allah testing you.

This truism–differing perceptions of the same reality–extends in nature. A rotting carcass is revolting and haram but to vultures, a heavenly gift. Does the fastidious diner have moral superiority over the scavenger vulture?

Dispensing with the relativism, let us examine Najib's bonanza from a practical and more consequential perspective. Najib claims that the money was reward for his "exemplary" leadership, and to ensure that it be continued. In practical terms, to fund his re-election.

One fact or precedent is now established from that assertion. Malaysian leaders and elections can be bought, or at least influenced by foreign money and individuals. That is significant, and pivotal. Today, a generous Arab; tomorrow, the CIA! Next could be China or Singapore. Before long, a non-Arab Middle Eastern state! With the *ringgit* fast becoming worthless, topping that RM2.6 billion "gift" should be easy.

Money is not the only means of influence peddling. The Americans, Singaporeans and others are becoming more sophisticated. They are not crude, careless, or stupid like the Arabs as to write a massive check or drop off a bundle of cash.

Consider that many children of Third World leaders end up at top American universities despite not having super SAT scores. Likewise, many Third World leaders are invited as visiting fellows and professors to those esteemed campuses. They lap up the accolades! If those refined tricks fail, there is always the White House visit or a presidential golf game.

When all fails, there is the old trick that was played on Sukarno, or variations thereof on playing with those leaders' vanity.

Consider Singapore; Malaysians covet invitations to address institutions there, a reflection of their influence. The Republic today is far different from the early days of Lee Kuan Yew when its leaders took every opportunity to snipe across the causeway. Today Singaporeans are active partners in the development of the southern corridor. They choose their partners prudently, preferring for example, the Johore royal family. The same shrewd calculation applies as to whom they invite to be guest fellows and speakers at their august institutions.

China too is learning fast. The Chinese are now partnering with the Johore royal household to develop some swamps at the tip of the peninsula. With the sultan on your side, there would not be too many intrusive questions. Your application will glide through the approval process.

It is worth reminding that not too long ago the same royal family sold off the entire island of Singapore. With this propensity to sell, what else would they dispose of next?

Yet another perspective to Najib's bonanza is to analyze its opportunity cost. Granted we do not know how or where he spent the money; Najib is still trying to spin that one out. Nonetheless even a devalued RM2.6 billion could buy you both Australia's Anna Creek and the Texas King Ranch (world's and America's largest respectively), with plenty left over. If you were to run both outfits in other than the manner of Sharizat family's National Cattle Feedlot, there would be plenty of jobs and halal meat for generations of Malaysians and others.

Apart from the lucky few around Najib who benefitted directly from him, what purpose would there be for the others to view his loot as reward for his performance instead of an act of grand corruption?

I can understand (though condemn) Najib's ministers and UMNO warlords for being his ardent cheerleaders. They could not otherwise afford those luxuries; these characters have no marketable skills or professional accomplishments. Their flair for "sucking up" is appreciated only by their insecure and untalented superiors. To these unabashed supplicants, even Najib's crumbs are worth scrambling for. Absent that and they would be back into their old kampung mode.

Those whom I feel most sorry for are the young red-shirted *pemudas* (UMNO Youth members) and the pink-frocked UMNO *puteris* (princesses). Surely their *maruah* (morality) is worth much more than just the few hundred *ringgit* for their free trips to the capital city, plus their complimentary colorful attires and perhaps a sarong *pelekat* or two.

I would support them if they were to demand their share of the booty. Not as direct handouts as that would quickly end up in the hands of those retailers at Low Yat Plaza but to create enduring programs to train them as plumbers, mechanics, and electricians, or to improve the schools and universities.

They could then benefit from those initiatives and do something meaningful with their lives, quite apart from contributing to society and having a bright future. That would be a legacy worth bequeathing to their children and grandchildren. Those values and sense of self-worth are worth cultivating. *Itu maruah Melayu tulin!* (That's genuine Malay dignity!)

Maruah shapes our perception of reality. Malay *maruah* says that when we receive money or favors for which we are not entitled to or have not worked for, that is corruption, not donation. Those who claim otherwise have no *maruah*.

Other 1MDB Wannabes

FELDA – The Next 1MDB

July 18, 2018

FELDA (Federal Land Development Authority), the massive plantation development scheme that was Tun Razak's brainchild and crown jewel of his rural development program, threatens to rival the massive scandal of 1MDB in terms of massive corruption, grand larceny, and inept management.

Consider that its new head (now former, with UMNO's rout in the May 2018 elections), one Sharil Samad, admitted that title to the prime property on which its head office is located was transferred to a developer without his or his agency's knowledge! This character claims to have an MBA but his private venture up till then was to run a laundromat, and not a successful one. He could not even clean garments and yet he presumed to be able to clean up a governmental agency. Najib Razak had picked him to replace the scandal-ridden Isa Samad (no relation) who earlier had been found guilty by UMNO for "money politics."

FELDA is now a large, diversified agro-based GLC having morphed from its origin as a modest federal agency. It boasts revenues (2017 figures) in excess of RM17B. The profit picture is another story and best reflected by its stock prices which languished at a third of its initial offering price (IPO). When FELDA was listed in 2012 as FGV (FELDA Global Ventures), it was the largest in Asia and globally second only to Facebook.

For a reality check, if you were to visit FELDA's settlements today and compare them to the 1960s or 70s, nothing much would have changed. The settlers' standard of living has not improved. If there is any economic enterprise on those settlements, they would be under the control of FGV. The social and economic dynamics of those settlements resemble the old company town, except that the company here, FGV, is not in the least benevolent.

There is one significant change which the settlers are not even aware of, or if they are, cannot appreciate the full financial and other ramifications. Whereas before they had title to their land (about 16 acres each), today that has been subordinated to FGV as part of the IPO. When FGV shares tumbled, those settlers' assets went with it.

Those settlers as well as FELDA managers do not understand such sophisticated financial instruments as dividends, stock offerings, and capital gains. FGV should have emulated Nestlé and invested in its settlers instead and not be enthralled with pseudo high finance. FELDA is uniquely positioned to execute that as its leaders and managers are Malays, as are the settlers. As such there would be no cultural barriers in appreciating their problems, unlike Nestlé's European managers had with their African growers.

FELDA has done little to stimulate entrepreneurial activities among its settlers. It has not encouraged them through funding or training to be FELDA's vendors, suppliers, or subcontractors, nothing beyond harvesting the palm nuts and tapping their rubber trees. Those too have now been taken over by illegal immigrants. Yes, a government agency hiring illegal immigrants. Only in Malaysia!

I would have expected that with the huge profits FELDA often brags about, the schools and clinics in its settlements would be among the best to give those settlers' children a flying head start, as with those of Nestle's African cocoa growers. Instead FELDA schools perform below average. Regrettable considering that the mission of these GLCs is "national development foundation," with Bumiputras the target. FELDA has only recently set up a residential school exclusively for the children of its workers. Over half a century later, and only one school!

FELDA brags ad nauseum about the few successful "*Anak* FELDA" (children of FELDA). They are outliers, not the norm or consequence of enlightened policies.

As for the settlements, few have electricity or piped water, much less a clinic. Again, compare that to what Nestlé is doing for its African cocoa growers. Those Malay managers and executives at FELDA ought to be ashamed of themselves and their lousy performances with respect to treating those settlers.

FELDA has introduced little innovation to make the settlers' lives and work more bearable and less dangerous. Oil palm is harvested in the same old, crude, and dangerous manual ways as it was in the 1960s. FELDA has not introduced hydraulic lifts (like the ones telephone repairmen use to fix overhead lines) to make the harvesting of palm nuts more efficient. Those workers still use pitchforks and bare hands to collect those nuts. Not only do the pitchforks damage the nuts, their sharp shells often scrape the workers' hands giving rise to painful tumor-like growths (granulomas). Those chores are archaic and literally backbreaking; they should have been mechanized a long time ago.

Only through such innovations and mechanizations could you increase your workers' productivity, not endlessly exhorting them to "work harder!" or "be more efficient!"

FGV is the largest employer of unskilled laborers, meaning, illegal immigrants. Instead of investing in the skills and productivity of its workers, as well as modernizing its plantations to be less dependent on unskilled workers, FGV took the easy way out by importing them, with all the attendant social problems.

There is also little research done on maximizing the use of land, as with growing flowers and vegetables or raising livestock in between the palm trees to supplement the settlers' income.

FELDA has many subsidiaries. All look impressive until you examine their activities; few materially advance the settlers' plight. Those many subsidiaries are but crass opportunities for politicians and civil servants to earn extra-lucrative directorship fees by being appointed to their boards, all at the expense of the poor settlers.

With the resources it has, and freed from the micromanagement of the civil service, FGV could have built superb schools and other facilities to benefit the settlers and their children.

These GLCs as exemplified by FGV have failed in their primary mission of developing Bumiputra human capital. They succeed only in duplicating existing governmental programs and adding to the costs. They do not bring in any added value despite the tremendous resources, financial and otherwise, expended on them. That is good enough reason to get rid of them.

Time To Sell Or Liquidate Malaysia Airlines

August 27, 2014

Of the many functions of government, owning or running an airline is not one of them. Instead, taking care of the health, welfare, and security of its citizens should rank way up there.

Once you have done an excellent job in those essential areas and still have extra time, talent, or resources, then you could *consider* running an airline. A humble and conscientious leader would never be satisfied when it comes to serving the public, for no matter how excellent a job he may be doing, there will always be room for improvement. The Finns have the finest schools, yet their leaders are consumed with improving the system. That is what progress means.

In short, there is little time or need for government to dabble in business, as with running an airline.

Malaysia once again contemplates pouring billions to rescue Malaysia Airlines (MAS). Apart from consuming never-ending amounts of scarce and expensive government resources, MAS receives an inordinate degree of attention at the highest level of the Najib Administration. I would have preferred that those leaders be concerned with deteriorating schools and universities, or the awful delivery of public services.

Not being a vendor, customer, employee, or shareholder of MAS (that's 95 percent of Malaysians and 99 percent of Malays), I could not care less if the formerly blue-chip company is sold or liquidated. I am however saddened that the University of Malaya is now third-rate and falling fast. I am even more dismayed that there is no comparable bailout plan to rescue it or the education system in general.

The future of Malaysia or Malaysians (especially Malays) does not depend on MAS. Nor does the fate of the company reflect adversely or otherwise on the caliber or future of Malays, Malaysians, or Malaysia. Malaysian schools and universities on the other hand do determine the future of the country and society.

Malaysia does not need MAS to project her image abroad. Besides, the image MAS now projects is of the worse kind. Malaysia also does not need MAS to bring in tourists. The other airlines including Air Asia do a fine job at that, and at no cost to the government. Malaysians do not need MAS for their international travels. You can choose from a dozen airlines to fly out of Kuala Lumpur.

There can only be one prudent decision on what to do with MAS now after all the repeated expensive and unsuccessful bailouts as well as the umpteen reorganization exercises. Sell it or declare bankruptcy with a view of total liquidation.

MAS Now But A Shell Company

After its "successful" WAU (Widespread Asset Unbundling) maneuver a decade ago, MAS today is but a shell company, burdened with tons of liabilities. Even its brand is now tarnished. That leaves only its traffic rights as assets. I reckon there would be few takers for its slots in Buenos Aires and Mexico City.

Malaysians should not be squeamish about or be ashamed of bankruptcy; it is an integral part of business. No enterprise is guaranteed to be a success.

Swiss Air, once dubbed the "Flying Bank" because of is solid finances, went bankrupt in 2002. Nobody would conclude negatively from that the business acumen or executive talent of Swiss Air managers. The more relevant lesson that Malaysia could learn and adopt from the Swiss airline bankruptcy is this. The company's entire top management was prosecuted for alleged criminal misconduct. They were found not guilty; nonetheless they were made to go through the wringer. A thought should MAS file for bankruptcy.

Japan Airlines, another government-linked company, also filed for bankruptcy. Today it is flying high after its reorganization. The venerable Pan Am, the very icon of a once glamorous industry, too was done in. As for the legacy US airlines (Delta, United, American), all have at one time or other filed for bankruptcy. Neither Japanese nor American pride was dented. Life (and business) goes on.

Malaysians need an airline, a safe and reliable one without regard as to who owns or runs it. If MAS is liquidated, other airlines would fill in the void. That is the law of the marketplace. Government intervention would only distort this reality, and then only for long. Despite Air India, also a GLC, Emirate Airlines is the *de facto* official airline of India because Air India is so poorly run.

Instead of spending the one and a half billion ringgit buying the rest of MAS shares, and many billions more to "rehabilitate" the airline, Khazanah should sell the company and use the resources to enter a new line of business, such as private education and healthcare. There is a great need for both not only in Malaysia but also the region.

If I were running Khazanah, I would direct MAS management to settle quickly with its insurers over the recent loss of its two planes and distribute the proceeds as dividends. Then promptly declare bankruptcy. That way it would have recouped part of its bad investment.

American Airlines posted its biggest quarterly "profits" from the insurance settlement of its DC 10 that crashed on take-off from O'Hare in 1979. With MAS today, thanks to that "brilliant" WAU scheme, both MAS planes that crashed were probably owned by another company, with MAS merely leasing both back. Meaning, the insurance payments would go to that company instead of MAS!

In a statement referring to the proposed MAS reorganization, Najib said, "Only through a complete overhaul of the company can we deliver a genuinely strong and sustainable national carrier." He went on to say that renewal involves painful steps and sacrifices from all parties.

What Malaysia needs desperately is for Najib to overhaul *his* administration. Getting rid of MAS would be a great first step in that direction. Najib is incapable of undertaking that. He just does not have what it takes to lead Malaysia.

Najib's leadership, like MAS shares, is but penny stock quality. The airline is an apt metaphor for Najib, except that Najib was never blue chip.

Similar Scandals, Different Treatment

March 18, 2012

To assert that the Malaysian mass media is nothing more than the propaganda arm of the ruling Barisan coalition is no revelation. The personnel in the mainstream dailies, the national news agency Bernama, and the government broadcasting channels like RTM are less journalists and editors, more political hacks and spinmeisters. They are, to borrow

National Laureate Samad Ismail's word, *carma* (contraction for *cari makan*, lit. seeking a livelihood; fig. hired hands) variety.

Less appreciated is the fact that they are hired hands not of the Barisan government but whatever faction that is currently dominant or trying to be so. One can surmise the tensions and dynamics of the current swings of the political pendulum within Barisan, specifically UMNO, from perusing the headlines. Perusing is exactly the right word, for there is nothing much worth reading in those dailies.

Consider the contrasting treatment in the mainstream media of the two currently unfolding financial scandals. The first is the National Feedlot Corporation mess ("cow-gate") that is now ensnaring the husband and family of Women's Minister Shahrizat Jalil. It had also led to her resignation from her cabinet post. The other is the ostentatious engagement party for Prime Minister Najib Razak's daughter and an equally expensive birthday bash for himself that he allegedly tried to tag on to the Treasury, and thus taxpayers.

Both scandals were first exposed in the Internet through the diligent investigations of Rafizi Ramli, chief strategist for Pakatan Rakyat. With the first scandal, the mainstream media were quick to pick up on and embellish the story; on the second, there was no mention at all. One can safely conclude that the respective primary players in both scandals, Shahrizat with the first and Najib for the second, are from different factions within UMNO. No marks for guessing which side is on the ascendance.

Rafizi is no rabble rouser throwing off wild accusations here and there. His first exposé of the "cow-gate" was initially dismissed by no less than the Chief of Police. Today the principal player, Shahrizat's husband, is charged with criminal breach of trust. She in turn was caught up in the ensuing turbulence.

With Rafizi's track record, you would think that those investigative journalists in the mainstream media would be eager to pursue his leads. At the very least their curiosity should have been piqued. For them to ignore the story of the alleged publicly funded engagement and birthday parties meant that they are journalists only in name, and that they are being told what to write.

In terms of monetary value, Najib's birthday bash and his daughter's engagement party, both totaling at about "just" half a million *ringgit* are but small change compared to the cow-gate's RM250 million price tag. Cow-gate in turn pales in comparison to the multi-billion-*ringgit* Port Kang Free Zone Development debacle, or the "commission" paid on acquiring the second-hand French submarines that would not submerge.

While the price tag may vary, the underlying mindset of contempt for taxpayers' money remains. To these leaders the concept of integrity or the diligent exercise of fiduciary responsibility is foreign. At best they are but slogans uttered during election campaigns and then conveniently ignored.

This weakness is not unique unto Malaysian politicians. In some countries these wayward politicians would be caught and brought to justice while elsewhere they would continue business as usual, their greed feeding on itself. There is no limit to their avarice. Their "success" would then be celebrated, and they would become the new role models. That is where Malaysia is headed today.

What struck me most about this latest scandal, involving Najib's birthday and daughter's wedding party, was the utter lack of class. Najib has made more than a few UMNO Putras rich through his giving away many lucrative contracts. Surely at least one of them would be generous or grateful enough to host those parties.

Alas that is the problem with greed; there is literally no boundary to it. Najib's many rich friends are still expecting to sponge off him! Likewise with Shahrizat's husband; if he had spread the bounty around just a wee bit as, for example, to include the head of *Utusan*, Bernama or *The New Straits Times* to be on the board of directors of his Feedlot Corporation, Rafizi's accusation would never have gone beyond cyberspace.

Greedy and unscrupulous politicians alone would and could not be Malaysia's downfall. It would take more. There would have to be a general failure of institutions and leadership at all levels to allow such abuses and corruption to go on and be tolerated. Toleration soon degenerates into encouragement, and thus a new cultural norm is established.

This is what happens when institutions have been allowed to deteriorate. They are no longer able to function as effective defenders of citizens' interests. We expect members of the fourth estate to be aware of their awesome responsibility to keep citizens informed. We expect these journalists to be on the vanguard of this sacred task. Alas they too have been taken in; they have prostituted themselves to those in power.

There is an honorable place in this world for cheerleaders, spinmeisters, or even court jesters and others who see themselves doing the bidding of those who hired them, but reporters and journalists they are not. If those in the mainstream media feel that they are but *cari makan* (seek a living), then I suggest that they join the advertising or public relations industry. If they are talented enough in that endeavor there would be plenty of rewards. They do not need to soil and degrade the hallowed traditions and functions of the fourth estate.

This degradation of the mainstream media is not a recent phenomenon, nor is it subtle. And it shows. RTM has only a few hundred followers on its Twitter. As for *The New Straits Times*, if not for its highly subsidized distributions and subscriptions, its circulation would be down in the dumps. If not for the government-paid announcements and advertisements, plus the paid press releases of government-linked corporations, so too would the paper's revenue.

Just as the shifts in fortune among the politically powerful are reflected in their coverage of the mainstream media, so too is the dysfunctional leadership among them. We saw this played out during the early days of barely under-the-surface rivalry between Mahathir and his then-deputy, Anwar Ibrahim. Their supporters took their cue from how their patrons were covered in the mainstream media. *The New Straits Times* rivaled *Pravda* in this regard. This was repeated when Abdullah Badawi took over; then it was Mahathir's turn to be at the receiving end.

There is no honor among UMNO leaders. Theirs is a world of hyenas; of winner takes all, right to the last morsel. Mahathir did it to Tengku Razaleigh when the latter lost a closely contested leadership contest back in the 1980s. Mahathir did it again later, this time at a more vicious level, with Anwar Ibrahim. Then Abdullah Badawi tried to do it to Mahathir and learned to regret it.

You would expect the women of UMNO to show some gentleness. Yet there was Shahrizat and Rafidah still at it with their cat fight, now more openly and much uglier.

There is plenty of blame to go around for the present pathetic state in Malaysia. This callous acceptance by citizens of wrongdoing among their leaders did not develop overnight. Malaysians have been taught, and taught well, to accept these misdeeds as anything but, aided by those cheerleaders and spinmeisters in the mainstream media.

Raking In The Bounty Of FELDA's IPO

February 26, 2012

In the run-up to the Initial Public Offering (IPO) of FELDA Global Ventures Holdings (FGH), there was little, in fact no discussion on how the exercise would benefit FELDA settlers. Surely that should have been the foremost consideration. The only criterion upon which to judge the wisdom or success of any FELDA initiative, including this proposed IPO, would be assessing its impact on the settlers.

Instead the focus has been on bragging rights, as with trumpeting FGH to be the biggest IPO for the year, among the top 20 on the KLSE, and the world's biggest plantation company. Such milestones are meaningful only if achieved as the consequence of business activities and not through fancy paper-shuffling exercises. Apple recently surpassed Microsoft in market capitalization, but that was the consequence of Apple's much superior products. Contrast that with the earlier 'achievements' of such now-defunct financial giants as AIG and Lehman Brothers that were based on fancy "financial engineering" instead of solid products or services.

Far from delineating the potential benefits that would accrue upon the settlers from this IPO, its proponents dismissed the critics, imputing evil motives on their part. There are legitimate concerns that this exercise would prove to be nothing more than yet another fancy scheme for the politically powerful to cash out on a lucrative but underpriced government asset. Malaysia already has many ready examples of such greed.

Consider the National Feedlot Corporation (NFC) "Cowgate" mess involving a much smaller sum of money. Despite the presence of high government officials on NFC's board to safeguard the government's interest, NFC's senior managers still managed to subvert those subsidized loans to purchase luxury condominiums totally unrelated to the company's activities. This oversight failure reflects both the incompetence of the government's representatives in discharging their fiduciary responsibility as well as the lack of integrity with NFC's management.

Such despicable omissions and spectacular failures are not unique to NFC; they are endemic in government-linked corporations. Malaysians thus had good reasons to believe that this FGH's IPO would be no exception once the money starts rolling in.

It does not escape the public's attention that the man helming FGH, and thus whose hands would be at the till once the billions start pouring in from the IPO, is one Isa Samad, a former UMNO Vice-President. Not any VP, one who was found guilty by his party of "money politics" and subsequently suspended. UMNO is no paragon of virtue. To be found guilty by it would be akin to being called a slut by hookers, meaning, disgustingly gross and way beyond the pale.

It would be easy to blame Isa Samad. The bigger question, and one that has yet to be answered, is why did Prime Minister Najib choose such a shady character to helm this major corporation? That is as much a reflection of Najib as it is on Isa.

Peruse FGH current corporate structure. It has nearly over a hundred subsidiaries, associated companies, and joint ventures, many with overlapping functions, markets, and products. Those units are created less in response to market demands or commercial needs, more to create opportunities for senior civil servants to be appointed to the many governing boards, and thus garnering extra income in the form of directors' fees and allowances. No wonder these GLCs lack effective oversight, and government departments are shoddily run! You would think that their regular government jobs, diligently executed, would keep them fully occupied.

More sinister is that these GLC directorships are an effective trick to trap the loyalty of top civil servants. Be too critical of the idiotic ideas of your political superiors, and you risk being left out on those lucrative post-retirement board appointments. With Isa Samad, it is also a case of Najib buying Isa's silence, for reasons best known only to the pair.

Corrupting A Noble Initiative

FELDA was the crown jewel of Tun Razak's imaginative rural development scheme. It was to provide land to otherwise landless villagers, the equivalent of the land-grant homesteading to early American settlers in the Midwest. The other reason was to encourage Malays to undertake an internal migration of sorts by uprooting them from their tradition-bound villages to begin a new life unencumbered by prevailing non-productive cultural practices.

With the expertise of and financing from the government, those villagers would develop hitherto virgin jungles into productive rubber and palm oil plantations, with those settlers eventually getting title to their holdings. At about 14 acres each, those units were economically viable. To make sure that those lands would survive the next and subsequent generations and not be endlessly subdivided, the settlers had to agree to dispense with their usual Islamic inheritance practices. Meaning, the property would be inherited by only one of the children.

The surprise was the absence of howling protests from the ulama to this clear departure from Islamic inheritance practices. Everybody saw the wisdom of the move–to maintain the economic viability of these holdings by avoiding their fragmentation upon the death of their owners.

Returning to the IPO, if it were to enhance the condition of the settlers, then it should be supported. FELDA is meant to serve the settlers, not the other way around. Isa Samad had it backwards when he dismissed the concerns of the settlers on the IPO as voiced through their cooperatives.

In response to the settlers' concerns, Isa suggested a portion of the proceeds be placed in a "Special Purpose Vehicle" to meet their needs. He did not provide the specifics, risking this SPV degenerating into yet another honey jar to be grabbed by the politically powerful bears.

There are many ways of leveraging these GLCs to improve the lot of Bumiputras. The focus of GLCs should be on investing in people–human capital–not companies. Companies are subject to business cycles; they can also be ruined by incompetent and corrupt managers. All you would be left with then are worthless stock certificates. Where is Bank Bumiputra today? Malaysia Airlines is in no great shape either, despite the billions expended through SPVs and other accounting gimmicks.

Invest in people instead; the skills and knowledge they acquire would stay with them to benefit society through good and bad times. Why not sell these GLCs and put the proceeds into an escrow account for the sole purpose of investing in and developing Bumiputra human capital?

Bringing that to FGH, I would commit a third of the IPO proceeds to a special fund to develop the human capital of those settlers and their children, as with improving their schools and bringing in qualified teachers especially in English, science, and mathematics. If you want the children of those settlers to be other than *penorakas* (homesteaders), the best route would be to give them superior education. Their schools and teachers should be among the best; today they are among the worst.

Use the funds from the IPO to enrich the curriculum as with providing music classes. I would go further and provide free musical instruments as with Venezuela's successful much-emulated El Sistema Initiative. New York is modeling a similar Harmony Program with its low-income students, and this week those students had the thrill of their lifetime when their orchestra was conducted by Placido Domingo. Meanwhile, Gustavo Dudamel, the young conductor of the Los Angeles Philharmonic Orchestra, is a product of El Sistema, a tribute to Venezuela's investment in human capital.

On another level, why not use the IPO funds to mechanize the operations on those plantations? Today palm nuts are still harvested in the same labor-intensive and back-breaking ways as they were 50 years ago. There is little innovation or mechanization. Why can't FELDA engineers design harvesting machines and trucks with hydraulic lifts like those used by utility repair workers to fix broken lines? Only through such mechanization could the workers' safety and health be assured, and their productivity enhanced.

This IPO should improve the lives of FELDA settlers and their children. That should be the sole criterion. Anything less and it would not serve their purpose and thus should be abandoned.

American-Style Crony Capitalism

August 24, 2008

Beware of lecturing others. You may have to learn that same lesson yourself, and sooner than you may think or expect!

On September 1, 1983 when the Soviets shot down a Korean Airline 747 jet from New York to Seoul after its brief fuel stopover at Anchorage, there was outrage especially in America, and rightly so. How could those Russians be so barbaric? How could they not recognize a jumbo jet on a clear moonlit night?

Barely five years later, an American missile cruiser shot down Iran Air Flight 655 on a clear morning, also killing hundreds of innocent passengers.

As an aside, the Soviet general who ordered the shooting was disgraced while the American commander was honored upon his retirement.

In 1997 with an economic contagion destroying much of Asia's recently gained prosperity, the 'Washington consensus' demanded, as the price for its much-needed assistance, greater transparency, end of crony capitalism, and "shock therapy" to wean citizens off subsidies.

A decade later, with America reeling from its humongous sub-prime mortgage mess that threatens its (and the global) financial edifice, there is little indication that America is willing or able to learn the very lessons it dogmatically preached earlier to Asia and the rest of the world.

Asian leaders, especially former Malaysian Prime Minister Mahathir, could be excused in being gleeful at America's present [2008] economic plight. Alone among Third World leaders, Mahathir bravely defied the then prevailing wisdom and stood up against the 'Washington consensus.' The result of that unique and unfortunate economic 'experiment of nature' is now obvious for all to see and learn. Malaysia in defying the conventional Western wisdom, emerged earlier and stronger than the other Asian countries that followed Washington's stiff prescription.

Mahathir has a right to be smug for many of the measures Washington took in managing its 2008 economic mess were straight out of his 1997 economic playbook. There was the massive bailout of huge government-linked companies (Freddie Mac and Fannie Mae), the earlier 'rescue' of Bear Stearns (a major investment bank), and FDIC's (a regulatory agency) nationalizing a major bank, Indy Bank.

This being the 21st Century, and with that came some new vocabulary for the new-fangled financial age. Granting massive and generous credit lines to the two financially troubled giant mortgage companies was not a "bail out" as Mahathir was accused of doing a decade earlier in Malaysia but merely providing the necessary "liquidity backstop," to use Treasury Secretary Paulson's phrase. Taking over Indy Bank was not nationalization but "regulatory supervision."

Back then, suffering Asian countries were forced to end subsidies for food and other essential goods as per the wisdom of the Washington consensus. Meanwhile in America despite the severe 2008 crisis and the need for belt tightening, the tax-deductibility of mortgage interests (otherwise known as subsidy for homeowners) remained sacrosanct. No politician would even dare touch that, despite the current mortgage mess. At least back then with the Indonesians, the subsidies were for basic staples and benefited the poor.

Like Malaysia a decade earlier, America purposefully kept its interest rates low and unhesitatingly went into massive deficits to keep its economic pump primed, even at the risk of igniting inflation and devaluing its currency.

Malaysia also anticipated the same potential negative effects then and wisely devalued its currency formally; America left it to the marketplace to determine the value of her dollar. There is orderliness and predictability to the former; the latter would be at the mercy of and subject to the herd mentality inherent in the marketplace. Yes, it was this same herd mentality that created the housing bubble in the first place.

When Mahathir devalued the currency, kept interest rates low, and injected much-needed capital into government-linked enterprises (otherwise known as bailouts), he was accused of being reckless, anti-capitalistic, and ignorant of marketplace realities. When America and Paulson did essentially the same thing, he was being "prudent" and "responsible," to calm a jittery market and maintain its stability.

Cynicism aside, I hope (and the world too) that Secretary Paulson would be successful.

The Relevant Lessons

Before Malaysians savor their *schadenfreud* (glee in the misfortune of others), remember that America was (and still is), among other things, Malaysia's biggest trading partner and source of foreign investments. Whatever that would cause America to sniffle, could wreck a suffocating pneumonia upon Malaysia.

Schadenfreud aside, there is much that Malaysia could learn from the current American financial mess, and for America to tweak the lessons that Malaysia so painfully learned during its tribulations a decade earlier.

The Malaysian situation in 1997 was eased considerably in that the economic crisis was her only albeit heavy burden. America today faces the far more serious challenges of simultaneously fighting not one but two expensive and bloody wars abroad.

Paulson's remarks that the bailouts would cost "at most two month's war in Iraq" betrayed his callousness on the plight of hundreds of thousands of Americans evicted from their homes through foreclosures, and the consequent devastations on their loved ones. He also dishonored the sacrifices of the hundreds of thousands of civilians and soldiers in that war, Americans as well as Iraqis.

Quite apart from the huge expense, the wars diverted (still does, over two decades later) attention and resources of American leaders and institutions. The economic crisis was challenging enough even without the two ongoing wars (Iraq and Afghanistan). Ending both wars would simultaneously ease the global oil market and remove a huge financial burden, two steps that could only help the financial strain, quite apart from the humanitarian considerations.

Had Malaysia still been fighting its communist insurgency in 1997 or had to contend with ethnic unrest as with 1969, that would have slowed if not aborted the recovery. Economists in their analyses of the slower recovery in the other Asian countries ignore this important element. Indonesia was slow in recovering as she was bogged down fighting a bloody secessionist movement in Aceh; the Philippines, its Moro Independence movement; and Thailand, its rebellion in the south.

Malaysia also had a strong leader then; Mahathir could and did push whatever stern measures that was needed, and the populace complied, albeit grudgingly. Had Abdullah been in charge, he would be flip-flopping from one policy to the next, and Malaysia would still be mired in the mess. To say that President Bush was weak would be a gross understatement; besides, the Democrats (not President Bush's Republicans) controlled Congress. Any initiative would have to satisfy both parties and their respective lobbyists, meaning, it would more likely be diluted to the point of becoming ineffective, with the taxpayers carrying the final tab.

Malaysia could take comfort in that the blights of crony capitalism and political corruption in their infinite variations are universal. In America, the transfer of money from interested parties to politicians is lobbying and 'political contributions;' in Malaysia, outright corruption. The intent is the same in both.

Presumably when the transfer of money is receipted and duly claimed as 'business expense,' it all miraculously becomes legitimate.

America may swallow its capitalistic pride and adopt barely concealed socialistic remedies in managing its current crisis, nonetheless it did not lack for strong dissenting views. Those were expressed vigorously in open congressional hearings, the editorial pages, and various academic symposia.

There would be lawsuits, civil and criminal. Rest assured that accounting and other shenanigans would be uncovered, and appropriate punishments meted out. The Enron scandal of 2001 took down the venerable accounting firm of Arthur Andersen, together with some hitherto powerful corporate figures. More than a few were jailed.

Of more enduring significance, new legislations were adopted to prevent future recurrences. The consequence of the Savings and Loans scandal of the late 1980s saw the demise of that entire financial sector.

Contrast that to the many financial debacles in Malaysia, from the London Tin fiasco to the collapse of Bank Bumiputra. No one was held accountable. There were no parliamentary hearings or royal commissions, and Malaysian academics have showed minimal inclination to study them.

In the haste to be gleeful in criticizing the American style of crony capitalism, Malaysians overlooked these other important lessons. They missed a splendid and rare learning opportunity. It is always dyspeptic to acknowledge one's mistakes and to learn from them, but ultimately that is the best safeguard against repeating them. That is the crucial lesson Malaysia should take from America, regardless of whether America is preaching it or not.

Najib Razak
World's Greatest Kleptocrat

Najib's Ingrained Politics Of Lying

May 3, 2018

"The politics of lying," as Najib dismissed Mahathir's claim of tampering of the jet that would have flown him (Mahathir) to Langkawi last Friday, April 28, 2018 to file his election nomination papers. This from a man who has yet to explain how the hundreds of millions from Saudi Arabia ended up in his *personal* account instead of the Treasury.

Nor have Najib's ministers and party leaders bothered to enquire. They were neither inquisitive nor perturbed so long as they got a piece of the loot, if only the crumbs. Likewise, for UMNO apparatchiks; a few millions thrown their way, enough for a condo in KL or Singapore, would reduce them into Najib's puppy dogs, barking at anyone they deemed incurring Najib's disfavor. Or a parrot, to pick another metaphor, as they repeated and amplified whatever he said.

Najib has never given out any paycheck in his life, not even to his gardener or driver. They were all paid for by the government. As such he does not appreciate the value of money, or anything else for that matter. Like many of the Malay elite, Najib is wont to conspicuous displays of his wealth, as with acquiring Rolls Royce and mansions. Or gaudy shows of obscene ostentations and extravagant gifts, as at the recent wedding of his daughter.

A few, like Najib's stepson Reza Aziz, ventured out further to impress the world, as with acquiring luxury properties in London, Manhattan, and Beverly Hills. Malays may be impressed and not bother to ask where the money come from but not the professionals at the US Department of Justice.

DOJ investigated this stepson, and seized those assets and others, claiming that they were bought with money stolen from 1MDB.

There was a time not too long ago and certainly within my memory when even Malay sultans lived in wooden stilt "palaces" without electricity or indoor plumbing. Today they and other *nouveau riche* Malays *berlagak* (swagger), as we say back in the village. Apart from luxury properties in Western metropolises, they vacation on fancy yachts in the

Mediterranean, all at taxpayers' expense. Never mind that Malaysian beaches are much more enchanting and the waters considerably warmer!

That says a lot about Malay culture. The society is just emerging from feudalism. As such Malays generally have little appreciation for the value of money. Further, Malays have been but bystanders in the modern money economy of Malaysia. Rich Malays with rare exceptions gained their wealth through "rent seeking" activities. The sultans for example, do nothing productive or creative; they squat at the apex of this huge special privileges heap.

In that regard the Malay elite differs from those of the West. The Gates, Bezos, and Zuckerbergs do not need to flaunt their wealth. They are richer than most countries! Instead they donate their wealth. Consider the Dukes, Stanfords, as well as the Rockerfellars and the stellar universities that bear their names.

The Albukharys, Halim Saads, and Daim Zainuddins being the rare exceptions, how many rich Malays including and especially the sultans have worthy causes? The Sultan of Johor, Malaysia's richest, does not even endow a professorship let alone a university.

Back to that jet's tempering and Najib's politics of lying, I believe the pilot more than the Chairman of Aviation or the Chief of Police. The pilot would literally pay with his life as well as that of his passengers if he were to make an error in his assessment. For the Police Chief and Aviation Chairman, it is never a mistake to *bodek* (suck up) your superiors. As one former favored Bumiputra, Tajuddin Ramli, (the man who nearly destroyed Malaysian Airlines) put it, you don't say no to the Prime Minister! On the contrary you would be rewarded, and very generously too, as Tajuddin was.

Ever the *bodek*, Tajuddin now does not say no to Najib. Now Tajuddin campaigns for him.

Like all thieves and crooks, lying is in Najib's nature. His ministers and civil servants in turn are gullible. They believe him. I would hate to have them negotiate for Malaysia. Look at 1MDB; it paid over 6 percent for its bonds at a time when I could secure a mortgage at a mere 2.5. Malaysia is being fleeced by her own greedy and corrupt leaders.

The *rakyat* (citizens) pays for that extra cost. A 0.001 difference in interest rate on a billion-dollar loan equates to millions during the duration of the loan. Even an industrial economics graduate from a provincial British university like Najib should appreciate that.

Najib's supporters use Mahathir's excesses when he was Prime Minister as the excuse to support Najib. Mahathir had the Bank Bumiputra and London Tin fiascoes, they rationalized. Why the double standard with Najib? He in turn took that to be his license to continue plundering Malaysia.

Najib's latest campaign video had him confess to his many mistakes and weaknesses, all attempts to gain voters' sympathy. As a last desperate resort like the rogue that he is, Najib invoked Allah's name, with clips showing him praying. At least he did not resort to the cheap Abdullah Badawi's theatrics, as with having him lead the prayers. The hypocrisy then would be too nauseating.

Admitting and confessing alone would not do it. Najib must explain the hundreds of millions that was in his *personal* account, and the billions in debt he imposed upon Malaysia. Most of all he must explain the deaths of Altantuyaa (the brutally murdered Mongolian model), Hussain Najebi (founder of Am Bank), and Kevin Morais (public prosecutor). May their souls rest in peace. Najib has been silent on those deaths. Those are compelling reasons why voters should boot him out in this election [GE 14, May 9, 2019].

Greed, Incompetence, And Utterly Devoid Of Integrity: Banality Of Najib's Leadership

April 27, 2018

When the day of judgement comes to Malaysia, which it inevitably will and I hope soon (as with this May 9 2018 General Elections), Malaysians would be shocked into disbelief to discover the banality of Najib Razak's leadership.

How did such a character ascend to the highest office in the land? I cannot accept that Malaysians are that stupid to have let that happen. Yes, there are plenty of dumb and gullible ones, but overall Malaysians are sensible folks. Yet there he is, Najib as Prime Minister for the past long, nine embarrassing and totally wasted years.

Najib did not get there on his own effort. That much is certain.

Others had paved the path for him right from the very beginning. Now that he is Prime Minister, Najib does not know how to clear the path ahead, much less which direction to take the nation. He is clueless. Time to get another leader. Time to disabuse Najib of his delusion of entitlement.

It is not difficult to imagine what his fate would have been had he not been a "bin Tun Razak." At best a junior functionary in his backward state of Pahang. Likewise, had he not been born in a deeply feudal Malay culture of rural Pahang in the early 1950s but modern Kuala Lumpur of today, his taking over his father's hereditary title of "Orang Kaya Indera Shahbandar" would have been a non-event.

In the kampung that title conferred instant aristocratic aura. It roughly translates as "Rich, Exalted Lord Mayor." Rich and exalted at least by local standards, with vague reference to the mythical prince of classical Malay literature, Inderaputera.

I would have thought that being suave and the product of a British public school he would have found that title a little quaint, and the elaborate installation ceremony comical, *a la* an African tribal rite of passage. Yet there he was lapping it up, like that prepubescent Tibetan kid who was anointed to be the future Dalai Lama.

Najib's seeming suaveness is what my folks back in the old village referred to with undisguised sneer as "*moden culup*," a veneer of or pseudo modernity.

Najib would not have inherited that title had his father lived to his expected lifespan. Razak's premature death also hid his dark side, and Najib shined in the reflected glow of his father's halo.

One of Razak's many dark sides was his secretiveness. He concealed his mortal illness from his family and the nation. Even on his final but futile trip to London for his medical treatment there was an elaborate ruse to camouflage it, and thus deceive Malaysians and the world.

That could not have been undertaken without the complicity of many, like his pilots and physicians. As a result, his death stunned the nation. Judging by his reaction to the tragic news, even his deputy, Hussein Onn, was kept out of the loop. What a way to treat your second-in-command.

With the outpouring of grief, sympathy was, as expected, showered on Razak's young family. Najib, being the oldest son, was the main beneficiary. His fast and smooth glide to the top thus began.

Najib's first enabler was Prime Minister Hussein Onn who selected him at the age of 23 to take over Tun Razak's old parliamentary seat. Reflecting the enormous reservoir of public sympathy, Najib won unopposed. Hussein went further; he appointed Najib to be a minister soon after.

A Sorry Ending

From there, Najib's trajectory was fast and steep. The prodigal prince from the jungle of Pahang could do no wrong. Everyone wanted to be on his coattail or be seen greasing his path. Everyone, from political leaders to the religious and royal.

Earlier there was Tengku Razaleigh Hamzah, himself a protege of Razak. Tengku, then head of Petronas, took Najib under his wings. Tengku however, was cautious and did not put Najib in a critical position, instead in "government relations." He could not possibly bungle much in that department.

Najib's gratitude to Razaleigh? In a subsequent close contest in 1987 between Razaleigh and Mahathir for the UMNO presidency (and thus prime minister of the country), Najib switched his support to Mahathir at the very last minute, denying Razaleigh what would have been his widely expected victory.

Mahathir, too, was Najib's enabler. As Prime Minister, Mahathir boosted Najib further, later using him to dislodge Abdullah Badawi. Najib was only too willing to be Mahathir's tool. Today Mahathir is Najib's nemesis. Unlike all those other enablers, Mahathir at least recognized his mistake, albeit late, and is now desperate to remedy. Let us hope he succeeds.

Other minor but no less consequential enablers include the current Attorney-General who gave Najib a pass on the 1MDB mess. The AG, Apandi Ali, was a Najib political appointee and a former UMNO apparatchik. No surprise there. More reprehensible are the behaviors of the permanent establishment including the top civil servants.

It was widely believed the Chief Secretary Ali Hamsa had a hand in the retirement of the former AG who had apparently was ready to file papers for Najib's arrest over the 1MDB mess.

There are others, the most unapologetic being his party. UMNO is now United Mohammad Najib Organization, as one wag put it, ready and ever willing to do his bidding. What a sorry ending to an organization that was instrumental in bringing independence to Malaysia.

Beyond individuals and institutions, there is that old standby and most effective enabler of all–cash. Packets of *ringgit* are openly passed out during UMNO's elections. Now that scourge is infecting the general elections.

The *ringgit* is literally being dispersed at campaign rallies like beads and candies at a Mardi Gras parade. Unlike UMNO members who scooped up the cash with unrestrained glee, voters are now increasingly asking the pivotal question: Where is all this money coming from?

Malaysians could not care less of the future of Najib or his party. Instead, they are concerned about their fate as well as that of their children and grandchildren.

Malaysians long to have a leader who is competent, trustworthy, and with a modicum of integrity. The realization of that aspiration begins with Najib's removal in the upcoming election.

Reject Najib And His Dedak-Fed Enablers

April 22, 2018

Prime Minister Najib Razak is painful to listen to; I have long ago tuned him out. His shrill voice grates, he raises it often when he tries to make a point. Instead, all he succeeds in doing is to sound like a hooker who has been spurned. His frequent and irritating hand gestures make him look like a monkey in heat. He mangles his rojak "Manglish" to the point of being incomprehensible. Those would be hilarious if caricatured by a consummate comedian. Najib however fancies himself a mesmerizing orator with a great stage presence. Such divergence of fantasy from reality!

Those irritating habits are not enough to ignore him. After all, he is Prime Minister. The reason I tuned him out is less his inability to discern fantasy from reality rather that the stuff coming out of his mouth nauseates me. What he utters is also dangerous to Malaysia. His actions give support to the rabidly racist "red shirts" in his party. Way back when he was UMNO Youth leader, he was notorious for his racist taunts, as his infamous brandishing of his *keris* dripping with tomato sauce, to symbolize Chinese blood. He soiled, literally, a hallowed and cherished icon of Malay culture.

Compared to those, his telling Malaysians and the world that the billions he received from Saudi Arabia that ended up in his personal bank account was a generous "gift" would seem benign and ordinary enough, more so in corrupt Third World Malaysia.

I do not fault Malays in the kampungs for believing him on that one. Not that they are gullible. Far from it! Rather they harbor and cherish the old Malay values of respect and trust in leaders. Malays are tolerant of their leaders to a fault. As with everything else, there is a limit to that.

What I find incredulous is the gullibility of his ministers and officials. Even the sultans bought into Najib's spin, or to be more accurate, Najib bought them! Kampung folks call that *dedak*, the rice husks they feed to their chickens. Throw some into their pen and they would rush in. Then all you had to do was close the barn door behind you and you had secured those birds.

Najib's *dedak* comes in many guises; for his ministers, continued appointments; senior officials, promises of post-retirement lucrative GLC directorships; and party apparatchiks, headships of statutory bodies or an ambassadorship to Timbuktu. For the sultans, a few lucrative contracts thrown their way and they would then outdo the similarly *dedak*-fed ulama in quoting hadith on the importance of loyalty to leaders.

Back to that earlier generous Saudi "donation." At first Najib claimed that to be "reward" for Malaysia's fight against ISIS. Then when reminded that ISIS was formed much later or that he had once urged his UMNO Youth members to emulate them, Najib backed down. Those millions then morphed into an outright "gift." Even Najib did not believe that for he later claimed he had returned it. I wonder his donor's reaction to that!

The man cannot keep his story straight. He is a habitual liar.

Gift or donation, that transaction triggered massive legal proceedings in no fewer than five jurisdictions, including the mother of all lawsuits, the American DOJ civil asset forfeiture under its Kleptocracy Asset

Recovery Initiative (KARI). Switzerland and Singapore have jailed a few of the involved principals. The DOJ suit euphemistically referred to Najib as "Malaysian Official 1," the top culprit.

Unlike many in Malaysia including his current nemesis Mahathir, my low expectations of Najib began much earlier. If not for his many enablers, Mahathir and Tengku Razaleigh in particular, men indebted to his late father, Najib would today be at best nothing but a middling civil servant in one of the many backward districts in Pahang.

Unlike Najib's many enablers, I discerned Tun Razak's many sinister sides in Najib from much early on. So too his kampung constituents back in Pekan, for Najib had a near-death political experience there in the 1999 election when he squeaked in by a mere 241 votes out of a total of over 26,000. The number of rejected votes far exceeded his majority. The influx of "late" postal votes from the army base nearby tipped the balance for him. At that time Najib was Minister of Defense.

Najib's father Tun Razak is today hailed a national hero, his body rests in the Heroes Mausoleum at Masjid Negara. Less acknowledged is that he enlisted in the Japanese Army during The Occupation. Today his son Najib carries on that traitorous tradition. Najib (and UMNO) collaborates with China's Communist Party, forgetting that it helped its Malaysian counterpart during the brutal Emergency years.

Tun Razak's hypocrisy was also well hidden. He claimed to be a nationalist and a champion of Malay language. He exhorted Malay parents to enroll their children in Malay schools. Meanwhile he sent all his to English schools, and in England to boot. I wonder where he found the money for that; his minister's pay would not be enough for that.

Najib inherits his father's hypocrisy. He exhorts everyone to be frugal and adjust to the high cost of living triggered by his GST. Meanwhile he and his family jet worldwide and vacation on luxury yachts in the Mediterranean, at taxpayers' expense of course. His stepson, whose father was but an army officer, owns luxury condos and mansions in Manhattan and Beverly Hills. He did, at least until the KARI lawsuit forfeiture.

Most unpardonable as well as dangerous of all is this: Tun Razak was instrumental in the ugly race riots of May 1969 following a drubbing his coalition suffered in the very divisive just-held general elections. This upcoming May 9th [2018] general elections have already degenerated into an even uglier and more divisive battle, except that the polarization this time is among Malays in contrast to the interracial one, specifically between Malays and Chinese, in 1969. This coming election could prove even uglier and more vicious.

Najib's father divided Malaysians; Najib divides Malays. Malaysians, Malays as well as non-Malays, cannot let him do that. Malaysians must never, ever let the country descend into another orgy of bloodletting.

Najib is a leader with unbounded greed, devoid of trust, lacking in competence, and most of all, without an iota of integrity. He is *pemimpin tampa maruah dan tak beramanah* (amoral and untrustworthy leader). Voters must reject Najib and his Barisan coalition. Do it for the country! Finish the job Pekan voters attempted to do and nearly succeeded in 1999.

Snatch The Match From That Monkey Najib Before He Burns Down The Village

April 14. 2018

It would take more than just a monkey with a match to burn down a village, despite the dwellings being made of wood and having flammable thatched roofs. Those homes have withstood generations of indoor wood-burning stoves and nightly mosquito-repelling ambers beneath their floors. There would have to be more, as with a long spell of dry hot weather and mountains of ignitable garbage strewn around.

Yet when that kampung does get burned down, everyone would be shocked. The immediate reaction then would be to blame the idiot with the match, and the fury heaped upon that poor soul would then be merciless.

Consumed with vengeance and with little inclination or intelligence for reflection, the necessary probing questions would never get raised. Such as who gave the idiot the match or why was he not supervised. Few would notice much less ponder why the strewn garbage had been allowed to accumulate and thus pose a fire as well as health and other hazards.

The kampung that is Malaysia has not burnt down, at least not yet. Malaysians are still smug and remain blissfully unaware of the long dry spell and the tinder dried debris that has been stacking up. Nor do they realize the danger posed by the idiot running around with a match in his hand, threatening mischief. God knows, he has wrecked enough damage upon the village already.

Being in the tropics, Malaysians are used to hot weather, but the current hot political climate is very recent. The 1969 "incident" excepted, political riots and turmoil are not yet the norm. Malaysia has also been thankfully spared such scourges as the assassinations of leaders and politicians, the staple of Third World politics elsewhere.

If Najib and his Barisan coalition were to prevail in the upcoming general election on May 9, 2018, regardless how slim their victory, that would be akin to giving the village idiot a match, and then encouraging him to continue playing with it amidst the flammable debris around and the high-voltage political atmosphere.

The flammable debris are the nation's failing institutions. Malaysians are also now deeply polarized, lending to the current supercharged political climate. The last time Malaysians were so stridently divided was during the 1969 election. Then the ruling coalition's defeat in a few states and its loss of a supra majority at the federal level triggered a horrific race riot that killed thousands and maimed many more. Parliament was suspended and the nation ruled by decree. The scar of that national tragedy has now thankfully been sealed with a thick scab. It is unlikely that it would be rubbed open again despite the mischievous attempts by many.

The polarization then was interracial, between Malays and Chinese to be specific, and the outbreak of violence localized only to Kuala Lumpur. Today the schisms and polarizations are widespread but not *inter* racial despite crude attempts by many to make it so, rather *intra*-racial, among Malays, to be specific. Only East Malaysia is spared. As such Malaysians, more so Malays, do not or refuse to recognize or even acknowledge this new threat. Therein lies the danger.

Yet the evidences are glaring. I have never seen more ugly or blatant displays of vicious and visceral hatred directed at Najib and Mahathir. The two leaders themselves have set the pace and tone. Others too like the sultans and ulama have taken sides. Their revulsion, as well as that of their followers, is so open. Such gross and uncouth displays are so *un*-Malay. I fear that should something untoward were to happen to Najib or Mahathir, that would trigger a vicious civil war among their fanatic followers, meaning, Malays.

Throughout history, the most savage conflicts are *intra-* rather than inter-racial. Witness the ongoing carnage in the Middle East. I am referring not to the Arab-Israeli dispute but the continuing savageries among the Arabs. The Korean Peninsula is still a tinderbox, ready to explode and taking down the world with it. Then there was the earlier Chinese civil war. It would be a futile exercise to venture whether the Chinese suffered more under the Japanese or during their own civil war. It would not be an exaggeration to assert that the Japanese Occupation at least interrupted the brutalities the Chinese had inflicted among themselves.

What is so volatile about the current threat facing Malaysia is the absence of any restraining element to buffer or dampen this intra-Malay schism. The nation's institutions–from the sultans and the Election Commission to the armed services and the police–have failed the citizens. The sultans and Agung are not the "protectors" of Islam and Malay customs as they claim, or as tradition and the constitution would have it. They are partial to UMNO Malays, thanks to Najib's "cash is king" lure.

The Chief of the Armed Forces had to retract his earlier statement proclaiming his troops' and officers' loyalty to Najib. That General forgot his oath of office, to serve king and country. Likewise, the Registrar of Societies; she did her "job" in a single blow (pardon the pornographic pun) by denying the registration of Mahathir's new party, a powerful opposition force. Meanwhile that clown prince and sultan wannabe in the southern tip of the peninsula thinks he can just *titah* (command) his fantasized "Bangsa Johor" as to which party to vote for! His father the Sultan of Johore had gone even further.

I would have expected Malaysian minorities to buffer or dampen this dangerous intra-Malay rift if nothing else for their (non-Malay) own self-interest. Instead they are sucked in by their own miscalculations into this perilous undertow.

A sliver of hope is Sabah and Sarawak. Perhaps because everyone there is a minority, Malaysians in the two states are an inclusive and tolerant lot. They have gone beyond; they have not let their ethnic and cultural identities define or limit them. It is sad that their exemplary collective stance is lost on their fellow Malaysians on the peninsula.

The fact that UMNO, a national party otherwise, does not have a beachhead in Sarawak, explains why the particularly virulent racist virus that has infected UMNO's body and mind in the peninsula has not spread east across the South China Sea. I hope East Malaysians will keep it that way and maintain their immunity against this deadly virus.

Malaysians have a crucial task in this upcoming [May 9th, 2018] General Election. They must snatch that dangerous match away from that idiot Najib and his band of mischievous UMNO monkeys. He and they have done enough damage to Malaysia. Stop them before they burn the whole country down.

The Legacy Of Tun Razak's Oldest Son

June 18, 2017

The dismissive attitude of Malaysian officials to the latest US Department of Justice's (DOJ) civil forfeiture lawsuit targeting expensive assets allegedly acquired with funds illicitly siphoned from 1MDB is misplaced. Their stance is an embarrassing display of their gross ignorance.

Yes, civil lawsuits in America are as common as mushrooms after a rainfall. Nonetheless this DOJ action is the largest (in dollar value) such forfeitures to date. This second set of lawsuits targeted assets allegedly given to Hollywood celebrities, as well as to the spouse of "Malaysian Official 1" (MO1). The two categories are separate though the latter believe that she is in the same class as the former.

Najib apologists and enablers point out with unconcealed smugness that the defendants to the lawsuits are not individuals, specifically Najib or his associates and relatives, rather those assets.

They are right, but such sophistry reveals a fundamental ignorance of the American judicial system. Those targeted assets do not exist *in vacuo*; someone or somebody *owns* them. *They* in effect are the defendants.

By targeting those assets and not their owners, DOJ is spared the task of identifying their rightful owners. That can be an arduous and expensive task, what with multiple shell companies involved in dizzying number of foreign jurisdictions. Instead, all DOJ does now is wait for the owners to come out of the woodwork to identify themselves and lay claim to those assets by challenging the lawsuit. Otherwise they would lose those assets, or at least their share.

One of those owners is Jho Low. He claimed to have bought those assets with his family's wealth. That at least was believable as he came from a wealthy clan in Penang. Sure enough, his family's assorted trusts have contested the lawsuit from faraway New Zealand!

Then there is one Reza Aziz, identified as the "stepson of MO1." Where did this son of a nondescript Malaysian army officer get his wealth? From his mother, the daughter of my parent's contemporary as village schoolteachers in Kuala Pilah? Visit her dilapidated ancestral home back in my kampung, and her current flamboyant lifestyle would make you puke. As for Reza's stepfather Najib Razak, that man had spent his entire adult life in government, with its measly pay.

Reza Aziz concocted the idea that the money (some hundred million!) was a "gift" from a benevolent Saudi Sheik. Even the wealthiest corpulent Sheik would not be so extravagant with his favorite toy-boy, yet this Reza Aziz character wants those seasoned DOJ prosecutors to believe his story! Even his American accountants did not believe him.

One other owner has also come forward. Hollywood celebrity Leonardo DiCaprio has not only surrendered the gifts he had received "from the parties named in the civil complaint" but went further and cooperated with DOJ investigators. That cannot be good news for Jho Low or Reza Aziz.

Don't bet on the other "owners," specifically the alleged recipient of that seized pink diamond (MO1's spouse) returning their gifts.

Najib supporters trivialize the DOJ's lawsuit, citing its lack of "action" after its first filing last year (2016) as proof of political intent. To them, these series of forfeiture lawsuits are yet another albeit more sophisticated American attempt at regime change abroad. Such commentaries reveal a pathetic lack of the basic understanding of the US justice system.

This asset forfeiture is a *civil* lawsuit. Unlike criminal ones where the axiom "justice delayed, justice denied" is adhered to, civil suits can and do drag on for years. They go to trial only when all parties are ready, and all extraneous issues as with ownership claims settled. The fact that these forfeiture lawsuits drag on should not be misinterpreted in any way to favor one or the other party.

There is also the possibility that criminal charges could be filed against specific individuals during the discovery phase or during the trial.

There is only one certainty. Once a lawsuit is filed, those assets are effectively tied up. They cannot be sold, mortgaged, or altered in any way without the court's consent. DOJ has in effect total control of those assets, meaning, DOJ is their new *de facto* owner.

These forfeiture lawsuits will not be settled out of court. Those prosecutors have a point to prove, and with unlimited resources to pursue it. That reality prompted owners like DiCaprio to cooperate with DOJ.

This will not be like a Malaysian trial where prosecutors could be illicitly paid off or where defense lawyers openly brag about having judges in their (lawyer's) back pockets. Some of the defendants have hired some of the best legal minds including those who had once worked in DOJ and had successfully prosecuted many high profile kleptocrats. It will be far from a walk in the park for DOJ lawyers.

DOJ does have something in its favor. In a civil suit, unlike a criminal trial, the burden of proof is lower, only the "preponderance of evidence" and not the "beyond reasonable doubt" standard of a criminal trial. The burden of proof also shifts from the plaintiff to the defendant. Meaning, the owners must prove that the funds they used to purchase those assets were untainted. It would be difficult to convince an American jury that a Middle Eastern sheik would willingly part away with hundreds of millions to a Malay boy no matter how pretty he looks, for nothing in return.

Regardless of the outcome, this trial would expose to the world all the ugly sordid details of the 1MDB shenanigans. Once those are out, not many would be proud to call themselves Malaysians. They would be downright ashamed for having elected a leader with such unbounded avarice, and then letting him get away with it for so long.

As for MO1, his spouse and stepson, they are beyond shame. With the millions if not billions they have already stolen, they could handle the setback. For Malaysians, they would be saddled for generations with 1MDB's humongous debt. Quite a legacy for the son of the late Tun Razak! As for the Tun, what a legacy to have bequeathed Malaysia with his ethically challenged son.

RUU355 U-Turn Exposes Najib's Mischief And Vulnerability

April 3, 2017

Many applaud Prime Minister Najib's recent U-turn on RUU355, the legislative amendment to "strengthen" the *syaria*. That circus, which is far from over, exposes Najib's mischief and vulnerability. Lauding him for withdrawing the government's sponsorship of that bill is akin to praising a pyromaniac who had tried to start a fire but failed. Najib should be condemned, not praised, for his dangerous game of stirring religious discord.

Whenever Islam enters the discourse in Malaysia, all rational discussions evaporate. Leaders and followers, Muslims and non-Muslims alike, descent with gusto into the gutter of religious and underlying racial bigotry. I would have thought that such a realization would have cautioned leaders to be more circumspect when treading on matters religious. On the contrary, as revealed by Najib's latest and very crude mischief, they are only too eager to fan the fire to serve their political ends.

With over 60 years of corrupt and incompetent UMNO-led administration, Malaysia is littered with debris and garbage, literal as well as figurative. Any idiot with a matchstick could start a conflagration with ease. Imagine a mischievous one, if Malaysians let it be. It is time to grab the matchstick away from Najib's reach.

RUU355 began as PAS Hadi's private member's bill. Clueless on matters of statecraft, PAS leaders, well exemplified by Hadi, resort to simplistic and gimmicky maneuvers as with introducing "Islamic laws" and making Malaysia an "Islamic state."

For his part, Najib was desperate to be a latter-day Malay hero championing *syaria*. Or at least seen as one. He also sensed an opportunity to create mischief by driving a wedge in the opposition coalition; hence his eagerness to take over the bill's sponsorship. Later, caught and surprised by the unanticipated strong opposition from the now emboldened non-UMNO Barisan partners, specifically those from Sarawak, Najib had to backtrack.

Clever only by half, Najib now finds himself on the unfamiliar terrain of having to make difficult choices. He opted for throwing PAS under the bus, hoping that his support among conservative Malays would not be too adversely affected. The risk of losing his crucial Sarawak partners, and with that the fall of his government, was much greater and more immediate. Earlier, Najib had hoped to endear himself to PAS followers and entice their party away from the opposition in time for the election.

With Najib's vulnerability now exposed, expect more challenges and shifts in the wind, and for him to be jerked around like a yoyo. It would be quite a sight! As for PAS, it is but the flighty woman jilted by her hitherto ardent suitor and now not welcomed by her previous partner. Not a pretty sight for a far-from-desirable old maid.

For Malaysians, the choice is simple. Deny Najib the privilege of leading Malaysia.

If I were a non-Malay, I would support RUU355 with unrestraint enthusiasm. I would do likewise for all Islam-centric legislations, including the introduction of *hudud*. My assertion here is not meant to shock or raise eyebrows, nor is it a clumsy attempt at sarcasm or literary spoof, rather a matter of pragmatism if not blatant opportunism.

As a Malay, I am terrified at this crude fascistic attempt to make Islam an instrument for repression. It pains me to see my faith debased as a political and social tool to control the ummah. Greatness can never emerge from a controlled and repressed society. Islam thrives only when there is freedom and justice. Oppression promotes neither.

Malaysian ulama and Islamic scholars have failed the ummah here. They have subverted what should be a political debate into a test of faith. Oppose RUU355 and you are destined for Hell, they contend. How infantile!

There are many reasons (most are selfish and self-serving) why non-Malays should support the expansion of Islamic institutions. One benign rationale would be so as not be seen interfering with the wishes of the majority (Malays) so long as those initiatives do not impact non-Muslims adversely. The constitution protects and spares non-Muslims from *hudud*. You could say that they do not "deserve" such "divinely" derived laws!

Non-Muslims should for example push for public executions and whippings, following Afghanistan's example. Turn those into revenue-producing events, with "premium" front-row seats commanding hefty prices, and market them as showcasing the "beauty" and "superiority" of Islamic laws.

Sell ads to whip and sword manufacturers, much like oil companies advertise at Formula One races. Such public executions and whippings could rival major spectator events like boxing to draw foreign tourists. Pardon my sarcasm for these suggestions.

It would also be in the self-interest of non-Muslim Malaysians to encourage Malays to be obsessed by and consumed with matters religious and the pursuit of the Hereafter. With more young Malays preoccupied with studying revealed knowledge and prophetic traditions, there would be that much fewer to pursue STEM. Meaning, less competition for non-Malays wishing to become doctors, scientists, and engineers.

With young Malays opting for Al Azhar and Pakistani madrasahs, there would be less competition among Malaysians aspiring for the Oxfords and Harvards. Not that the Malay community is a formidable competitor on that front.

For non-Muslim politicians, embracing pro-Islam postures would be a sure way into the hearts of Malays and thus capturing their votes. Those politicians would become instant darlings of the Malay community, fast eclipsing the likes of that *mualaf* Ridhaun Tee, and without having to change name or religion. You do not have to suck up to UMNO or PAS politicians either! All you do is don a white *kopiah* (or hijab for a woman) at Muslim functions, and of course support RUU355 and similar legislations.

Non-Malays should be heartened that the Padang Merbok pro-RUU355 rally drew thousands of Malays. It went well past midnight. Not even the early evening rain dampened the mood. They came from as far north as Perlis and Kelantan, giddy with the excitement of doing God's work, as they had been led to believe.

Imagine the acres of paddy fields untilled that day and the next, the thousands of rubber trees not tapped, and hundreds of fishing boats idle in port. You do not need to be an economist to see the impact; all negative. Perhaps minimal; they are marginal participants in the modern Malaysian economy, consumed as they are with the Hereafter.

As one of the few non-Malays present at that rally noted, the only non-Muslims affected by RUU355 would be casino operators. Few Malaysians, Muslims or non-Muslims, have much sympathy for them.

I compliment that non-Malay for his deep understanding of Malay culture and values. It is a sad commentary that individuals like him are a rarity today. Not so a few generations ago.

For example, following the failed Malayan Union, a coalition of populist Malay organizations under PUTERA, together with the primarily non-Malay trade union group AMCJA, put forth a proposal for self-rule.

A central feature of that proposal would have liberalized conditions for citizenship. The leftist Malay leaders in PUTERA enthusiastically embraced that simply because those new citizens would be called Melayu, not Malayans. Non-Malays, being pragmatic, too accepted that. They could not care less about the label so long as they were granted citizenship.

Malays were without difficulty seduced into relaxing the citizenship requirements in return for the Melayu label. Never mind that those would-be *culup* (a veneer) Melayus were not Muslims and could not speak Malay or give a hoot about Malay mores and customs!

Thank God the British rejected the PUTERA/AMCJA idea and instead imposed the Federation Agreement.

To Malays, the label is all important. Do what you want with the content, in line with our culture's premium on *peraga* (appearances). It was true then and it is even more true today. Label something as Islamic or *hudud*, and Malays would swallow it without question. Likewise, anything from the land of the Prophet is holy. Even the flies in Mecca are *hallal!* It is not a surprise that Najib's receiving millions from a Saudi sheik would be viewed as *borkat* (divine bounty) by Malays and not, as the rest of the world sees it, blatant corruption.

Two centuries ago, the British nearly succeeded in destroying the Chinese civilization by giving the masses what they craved for—opium. In the process the Brits made tons of money and controlled China. The Chinese elite, from the emperor and mandarins down to the farmers and peasants were aware of the danger opium posed but they could not prevail against the mighty British.

With Malays on the other hand, our leaders are the biggest pushers of the metaphorical opium today. Non-Malays should let that be, and let Malays be narcotized by religion. Then like the British in China of yore, non-Malays could control the economy and country even more and with ease. If Malays were to complain or be resentful, flatter them that a much bigger and better reward awaits them in the Hereafter.

That is a distracting issue. The key conclusion from Najib's latest U-turn on RUU355 is that he and the party he leads are now vulnerable. Najib is floundering. As any boxer will tell you, that is the best time to give your opponent your knock-out blow.

Tun Razak: Seeing The Father Through The Son

March 26, 2017

Last March 11, 2017 would have been Tun Razak's 95th birthday. He died in 1976, his sixth year in office and two months shy of turning 54. On April 3, 2017, his son, Prime Minister Najib, will enter his ninth year in office, more than enough time to judge his performance.

Najib seems so different from his father. Or is he? Could Najib be but a reflection of his late father?

Just to pose that question is to commit secular blasphemy in Malaysia. Many Malaysians, Malays especially, revere the Tun. He was buried at the Heroes Mausoleum at Masjid Negara. By contrast, the country's first Prime Minister, Tunku Abdul Rahman, *Bapak Merdeka* (Father of Independence), was buried in the very provincial capital of Alor Star.

"Many" does not mean all Malaysians. Among non-Malays, excluded from the largesse of Tun's landmark New Economic Policy (NEP), memories of him are less charitable.

As a young surgeon in Canada in the 1970s I came across William Shaw's glowing biography of Tun Razak. He was a legend at Malay College, and a scholar-athlete par excellence. He breezed through his law studies, completing it well before his scholarship term ended. He could have been a successful lawyer in London or a lucrative career with one of the many colonial firms.

Instead he chose to return and serve his country. The colonials recognized his talent and he could have been the first native Governor of the proposed but subsequently aborted Malayan Union. He was a rising star destined for great heights. Yet he gave all that up to join the fledgling UMNO, and with that, a very uncertain future. UMNO then, very unlike today, had no plump GLC directorships or lucrative government contracts to dole out.

Tun's story, as spun by Shaw, inspired me to return home to Malaysia. Then just days after I landed came the news of his unexpected death in London. Sudden and shocking! I was devastated. So too was the nation. The grief was deep and the loss palpable.

Razak's political legacy is NEP, and biological, Najib. It's too early to tell about Najib. This much is indisputable. He has through 1MDB burdened Malaysia with a humungous debt to be borne by Malaysians for generations. The full liabilities are not yet known. With most of the debt in foreign currencies and with the *ringgit* fast becoming worthless, it would only get worse. Crippling cuts to hospitals' and universities' budgets are just the beginning.

Also indisputable is this. America's Justice Department has filed its largest asset forfeiture lawsuit under its corruption and money laundering laws. "Malaysian Official 1," *aka* Najib, is alleged to have siphoned off a staggering over US$4 billion from 1MDB.

Najib is both corrupt and incompetent, a lethal combination. Now desperate to hang on to power, Najib adds a volatile mix to Malaysian politics—religion. He now sports white *jubbah* and *kopiah*, *a la* the Bedouins. He unabashedly apes his predecessor in leading congregational prayers, an imam wannabe, with camera crew in tow of course. This from a man with Bill Clinton's sexual proclivities but minus the compensating intellect.

Those desert accoutrements are harmless, more juvenile. Far more dangerous is his cavorting with extremist Islamists. Earlier, Najib exhorted UMNO Youths to emulate ISIS. Now he eggs on PAS Hadi with his mischievous RUU355, the so-called Hudud Bill. In plural Malaysia, that is playing with religious fire, a potential hell on earth.

Razak too co-opted PAS following the 1969 race riot. While he acted from strength, Najib is from weakness. Make that desperation.

These observations on Najib prompted me to reassess my hitherto hero, Tun Razak, spurred by the village wisdom, *Bapak borek, anak rintik*. Literally translated, frizzled roosters having spotted chicks; idiomatically, like father, like son. We do not become the characters we are out of nowhere. Our parents shape, influence, and develop our beliefs, morals, and assumptions.

As a kampung youngster back in the 1950s, I remember Minister of Education Razak exhorting Malays to send their children to the new Malay secondary schools that he had just established. Many fell for his sway, dis-enrolling their children out of English schools. The consequences of that initiative, and his education policies generally, are now plain.

I was a temporary teacher at one of those new Malay secondary schools back in 1963. I was appalled at the atrocious quality of the textbooks and the total lack of preparation for the new system. The price for that folly? Generations of Malay children are permanently educationally handicapped.

My saddest moment visiting my old village today was seeing my former English school friends whose parents had switched them into the new Malay stream on Razak's exhortations. They were stuck in the kampung; their education had failed them. Their only comment on seeing me was, "Your father was wiser than mine!"

What was my father's wisdom? We should not listen to what our leaders say, rather follow what they do.

What did Razak do for his children? He sent them to English schools, and in England to boot! Hypocrisy would be too mild a term for that!

Today his son Najib is asking Malaysians to be frugal and civil servants not be corrupt. Laughable! Many in UMNO today are taking my father's advice. They do not listen to him but follow what he does! While Najib, his family, the Lows, and a few like that Goldman Sachs bonds salesman get hundreds of millions if not billions while those UMNO *kutus* are satisfied with a few devalued *ringgits* and some leftover contracts as rewards for their sucking up to Najib.

Malays are not *mudah lupa* (a forgetful lot), as Mahathir famously claimed, rather *mudah selesa* (easily satisfied).

Returning to the shock of his death, Razak hid his lethal cancer from his family and country for years. Even his last desperate flight to England seeking medical treatment was undertaken in an elaborate ruse. A leader not trusting his people. Razak deceived not only Malaysians but also his loved ones.

Our prophet counselled us to lead a life as if we would live forever (meaning, plan long term), but be prepared as if you will die tomorrow (keep your affairs in order so as not to leave a mess). Razak failed to prepare his young family as well as the nation. With five young sons, and a wife unprepared, that was the height of paternal and spousal irresponsibility.

In his memoir, Tunku lamented how Razak went through elaborate machinations to topple Tunku, or at least forced him to resign following the May 1969 riot. If only Razak had been straightforward and confided his wish to Tunku, he would have stepped aside sooner and willingly. There was no need for Razak to undertake those dirty, unseemly backroom maneuvers. Despite being comrades in arms for over a quarter of a century, Razak still did not take Tunku in his (Razak's) confidence.

That was the late Tunku's assessment of Razak's character.

There is a picture of a young Razak in a Japanese Imperial Army uniform. His apologists spun that as his being a 'secret agent' for the British! Only with imminent Japanese surrender did he switch sides. There should be a special word to describe such Benedict Arnold duplicity. "Coward" and "traitor" would not do justice.

Young Razak was no Lieutenant Adnan. The late Lt. Adnan wore his Malay Regiment uniform with pride in defending his Tanah Air against the Japanese. Adnan gave the ultimate sacrifice—his life; a *wira sahih* (genuine hero).

Note the parallel between Razak's Japanese uniform and Najib's Bedouin trappings.

Najib also has a political father in Mahathir. He mentored Najib and more than just greased his ascent. Najib is Mahathir's most obscene political legacy. The redeeming grace is that Mahathir now recognizes his error and is desperate to rectify it. It must pain him to spend his retirement years on this onerous but necessary dirty duty.

Muslims believe that Allah punishes us in this world to spare us a more horrible one in the Hereafter. That belief is a salve to our current travails. As to what awaits us in the Hereafter, only He knows. That aside, I pray for Mahathir's success in getting rid of Najib, not for Mahathir's personal salvation but for Malaysia's.

As for Razak, may his soul rest in peace. His early demise spared him the agony of witnessing what he had bequeathed unto Malaysia through his oldest son, Najib.

Dancing Dragons Have No Partners, Only Prey

November 6, 2016

With Prime Minister Najib Razak merrily dancing with the Chinese dragon, it is worth reminding him and his admirers that dragons have no dance partners, only prey.

Najib is using the old and dangerous game of playing the major powers against each other. During his latest visit to Beijing he railed against the Americans for lecturing him on lapses in his leadership, specifically his corruption and trampling on his fellow citizens' human rights. Najib then went on to poke America's eyes by putting out a joint declaration with his Chinese counterpart calling for no outside interference in the brewing South China Sea crisis.

Only the deluded would believe that Najib had an equal or any say in that joint communique. His only contribution was to agree. Najib was there to beg China to bail out his 1MDB, as well as to borrow money. Beggars do not get to choose.

The world is full of tragic examples of once stable nations now in tatters because their leaders thought they were smart or adroit enough to play one world power against the other. Egypt's Nasser had the Russians finance his ambitious Aswan Dam, and banked on them to help Egypt against Israel. The humiliation of the Six Day War still haunts the Egyptians. His successor Anwar Sadat reversed course and cozied up to America, and in the process won the approval of the ultimate values gatekeeper of the West, the Nobel Committee, which awarded him the Peace Prize. At least Sadat brought peace to his people, albeit only too briefly. Egyptians today are still being whipsawed from one extreme to the other.

In dealing with others, local or foreign, small or great powers, we must be guided by our internal compass, our values. Others may or may not share our *qiblat* (lit. direction towards where Muslims pray; fig, compass or objectives). Malaysia has for example no desire to emulate China on how it treats its minorities or dissidents. Nor does Malaysia wish to be treated like Tibet or China's western Muslim provinces. Although I must admit that at times wishing that Malaysia would adopt China's treatment of its corrupt officials–public execution.

Najib thinks that he looks elegant and puffed up dancing with the Chinese dragon. To me, he is more the painted lady on the dance floor of a Vegas whorehouse. We know who is paying for Najib's services, on the dance floor and afterwards. Najib is paid well to act like an equal and enthusiastic partner, but we know what his role is, as well as the price tag.

It is well over RM140 billion, the amount Najib sought from the Chinese to bail him out. Regardless, a high-priced hooker is still a hooker.

Najib would like us to believe that China is investing in Malaysia, and he has convinced many. The reality is that Malaysia is borrowing those hundreds of billions. That money would have to be repaid. The only positive aspect is that some of the money would be for financing infrastructures like the East Coast Rail and Trans Sabah Gas Pipeline, not for skyscrapers and fancy headquarters for civil servants.

Left unanswered is how much those projects would have cost had there been competitive international bidding. Nor do we know the financing terms. The 1MDB bonds cost several hundred basis points above the prevailing market rates. Another unknown is how much of the Chinese money would be shifted to Najib's personal account *a la* the Saudi investor and 1MDB in gratitude for Najib's 'leadership?'

Beijing was generous to Najib. I am reminded of the rich towkay in a Malay village, charitable to his customers, extending them easy credit. Soon he owned the entire village. As we Malays say, *Menang sorak, kampung tergadai* (win the applause but end up mortgaging the village).

China is an important country, quite apart from it being Malaysia's biggest trading partner and sharing an extensive and contested maritime border. That relationship should be based on mutual respect and in accordance with international laws and norms, acknowledging that China is a major power while Malaysia is not. Being deep in hock to China is not a good start to achieve that kind of relationship.

The sparkle of Najib's golf soiree with President Obama in Hawaii during Christmas of 2014 was brief. Najib is discovering to his sorrow that America has robust independent institutions. You may be Obama's golfing partner, but if you indulge in illicit activities, its media will expose you and Attorney-General prosecute you. Malaysian officials may be bought with cheap titles and trinkets, not so America's.

The Malaysian media is Najib's lapdog, not so foreign ones or the local social media. Thanks to *The Guardian*, *The Wall Street Journal*, *Sarawak Report*, and others, Najib is being subjected to unaccustomed scrutiny. Local social media amplify and extend the reach of those foreign news sources to the average Malaysian.

There are a few certainties to Najib's leadership. One, it *will* end. As for when, how and under what circumstances, the *bomohs* have as much credibility as the experts. With his echo chambers well amplified, Najib feels invincible. As a reminder, so did Saddam and Ghaddafi not too long ago; they were even more ruthless and in power for a far longer period than Najib. Two, the massive debts through 1MDB and now the Chinese loans incurred by Najib will burden Malaysians for generations. Three, Najib's rank corruption. Regardless of the outcome of the current US Department of Justice's 1MDB asset forfeiture lawsuit, it has already put a black mark on Malaysia.

Najib's future does not interest me. As for the debt load, at least that is quantifiable; not so the soiling of Malaysia's name. The plastic glitter of Najib dancing with the dragon star, like his earlier soiree with Obama, will also be short-lived. The dragon will not be denied its prey. Najib, and Malaysians, may yet feel the true impact of a tsunami, the Chinese version.

Luqman Al-Hikmah Versus Najib Al-Kebas

September 4, 2016

Luqman Al-Hikmah (Luqman The Wise) is revered in Islam, with a Surah (31) in the Koran named after him, chronicling his sage advice to his son.

Those are wise words for anyone, anytime, and anywhere.

Legend has it that once as a slave, his master ordered him to slaughter a sheep and bring its best parts to him. Luqman did. He brought forth the animal's heart and tongue. Intrigued, the next day the master asked him to bring the worst parts. Luqman brought him again the heart and tongue.

When asked, Luqman explained that when a sheep is halal, the heart and tongue are the sweetest parts. When it is haram, the two are the worst. Likewise with leaders; halal leaders' words (the consequence of their tongue) and deeds (heart) inspire and bring out the best in their followers.

They in turn would make the world better. In contrast, the words and deeds of a Hitler would agitate his followers and bring out the worst in them. They in turn would wreck the world, theirs and ours. Brandishing a ketchup-soaked *keris* and stretching out a stiff-arm salute are but different deeds from the same heart of a haram leader.

With individuals, the same attribute may be venerated in a pious person but detested in the corrupt. Prime Minister Najib values loyalty above everything else in his staff and ministers. Loyalty is the finest attribute you can heap upon a leader, but only when he is halal, meaning honest, competent, and does not betray the faith and trust followers have in him. When he is not, then that loyalty is not only misplaced but also your most hideous attribute. You betray not only yourself and your values but also your fellow citizens' and theirs. That loyalty is haram.

In Malay culture the iconic hero Hang Jebat put it best, "*Raja adil raja di sembah; Raja zalim raja di sanggah*" (Venerate the just king and censure the unjust ruler).

Najib is confused about loyalty and what it stands for. His staff, ministers, and supporters too are confused on whether their loyalty is to the country and its enshrined principles, or to a leader and his unbounded avarice. Had UMNO members been loyal to the person of Datuk Onn as leader back in 1951, Malaysia would still be a British colony today. Although he fought against and prevailed over the Malayan Union, Onn opposed *merdeka* (independence for the country).

As Prime Minister, Najib should be loyal not to his party, ministers, or supporters but to the oath of office he took in front of the King, and to the constitution he swore to uphold and defend. Loyalty to anyone or anything else is misplaced and may even be treasonous.

In defending his hideous corrupt act with 1MDB, Najib points with pride to the BR1M grants to the poor given by the company. Caliph Bakar too gave every man, woman, and child twenty durham annually, long before economists advocated guaranteed minimum income. Credit Najib for implementing a good idea. Lest it be forgotten he has also burdened Malaysians with the Goods and Services Tax. GST is the least progressive of taxes, meaning, the poor bears a disproportionate burden.

The 2016 budget for BR1M was RM4.9 billion; the government estimates raking in RM5.6 with GST. The ledger does not favor the *rakyat*, especially the poor.

If 1MDB had funded BR1M, as Najib had intimated, consider that the American DOJ alleges an estimated over US$4 billion (in excess of RM16B) have been corruptly siphoned off from that sovereign fund. While Najib gave away RM4.9B in BR1M, Malaysian Official 1 had *kebas* (swiped off) over RM16B from 1MDB. The ledger again favored him to the tune in excess of RM11B.

Unlike Luqman Al-Hikmah, what Malaysia has instead is a Najib Al-Kebas (the swiper). Loyalty to Al-Kebas would be the worst attribute in a Malaysian.

Najib fessed up to swiping off hundreds of millions into his personal bank account. It was a "gift" from a Saudi sheikh, he claimed. For Malays, anything from the Holy Land is halal, even its flies and maggots.

Would Najib have received the gift had he not been Prime Minister? Obviously not. Which means that the donation was to his office. Najib admitted as much when he said it was in appreciation for Malaysia's fight against ISIS. Najib did not fight ISIS alone, Malaysians did. The money then should have gone to Treasury, not his personal account.

Even in the days of generous foreign aid no nation ever received such a windfall, except for Israel from America.

When Najib's 'explanation' did not sell even to UMNO members, he concocted yet another spin. It was a political donation. That satisfied UMNO "wise" ones, the likes of Shahril Samad and Ahmad Maslan with their MBAs, chartered accountant Wahid Omar, and lawyers Nazri and Azalina. Shahril and Maslan admitted to receiving a million or two from Najib. Crumbs really, but that satisfied them. Wahid was rewarded with the Pernas chairmanship. Nazri and Azlina are still ministers. For these characters, loyalty is but a commodity with a price tag. Rather cheap, fitting their characters.

Ponder this. Today Saudis can buy Malaysian elections by financing the party they favor. Tomorrow, Americans to Pakatan? How about China or Singapore to DAP? UMNO is Saudi's current favored flavor. Tomorrow, PAS?

Why not put up Malaysian elections to the highest foreign bidder? That would simplify things and remove the charade. It would also be clean and transparent, with the *rakyat* benefitting from the cash. Do likewise with UMNO elections and distribute the loot to the members. At least they would get something. As of now, Najib *kebas* (swiped) them all, with only the crumbs falling to the lesser chiefs. Ordinary members are still waiting for the leftovers, if any.

Legend also has it that Luqman advised his son to be wary of women with heavy makeup. In today's parlance, those who resort to plastic surgery and anti-ageing potions. They will end up spending everything you have, he cautioned. When Luqman died, his son ignored that advice. He partied and chased women with heavy makeup. Within a year he was bankrupt.

If as Najib says that he fears only Allah, then heed His advice as revealed through Luqman Al-Hikmah.

I risk flattering Najib and his supporters by mentioning him in the same breath with Luqman Al-Hikmah. Najib Al-Kebas has more in common with Luqman's son. If Malaysians were to be spared the fate that befell Luqman's son, then they ought to get rid of Najib Al-Kebas.

Lowering The Bar On Najib's Already Mediocre Leadership

August 7, 2016

I am baffled at the continued praise and support for Prime Minister Najib in the face of the mounting 1MDB mess. To be sure, those came only from Malays, specifically those in UMNO, plus a few scattered voices elsewhere. They are lowering the bar for Najib's already mediocre leadership.

Najib is but a Third World corrupt kleptocrat robbing billions belonging to the people of Malaysia, to quote the US Department of Justice (DOJ). Meanwhile those toadying Malays continue blathering "let justice take its course" or "innocent till proven guilty." Those are the standards of a criminal trial, but for leaders we must demand and impose a much higher criterion, as "without even the hint of impropriety."

Those praises for Najib come in various contortions. Consider the absurd statement from PAS Hadi Awang who ventured that DOJ must produce four witnesses or that the accusation against Najib could come only from Muslims. Which cave did Hadi emerge from?

The evidence of Najib's impropriety abounds, not just in the DOJ filings or complicated charts tracing the cross-border flows of illicit money as reported in *The Guardian, Wall Street Journal* and elsewhere, rather by the simple and obvious fact that 1MDB has saddled Malaysians with billions worth of debt and little to show for it. The proposed Tun Razak Exchange site is still empty while power plants once locally owned are now in foreign hands.

Najib denies that he is the "Malaysian Official 1" referred to in the DOJ documents. I wonder who could that top Malaysian public official related to Reza Aziz be? Najib also denies being linked to the DOJ's lawsuit. Poor Najib! Despite his expensive British boarding school education, Najib could not comprehend the difference between the legal term "defendant" and the everyday meaning of "linked."

This 1MDB mess is now being investigated in no fewer than six jurisdictions. Singapore has already frozen the assets of Jho Low, Najib's financial confidant. Switzerland terminated the license of its bank involved in the transactions. It would take great effort on Najib's part not to know that. Perhaps his staple of reading does not extend beyond UMNO newsletters *New Straits Times* and *Utusan Melayu.*

The behaviors of Najib's courtiers and political whores, like his ministers and party chieftains, do not surprise me. They are paid to pleasure the man. The Rahman Dahlans and Khairy Jamaluddins remind me of Saddam Hussein's cartoonish Information Chief "Bagdad Bob" just before the fall of that city. The American tanks could be heard and seen rolling in the background, but he kept insisting otherwise in a televised press conference. Those UMNO boys fancy themselves heroes defending their leader, but the world sees them as cretins, or worse.

As for Najib's nonchalance, I am certain that Saddam Hussein felt the same way right to the very moment before he had to flee to that rat hole in the desert; his Bagdad Bob had earlier assured him that everything was fine. Muammar Gaddafi probably felt likewise moments before he was caught and butchered by his fellow Libyans.

Najib's personal fate does not concern me; Malaysia's does. If Najib were not to get off the stage on his own volition and soon, the price for him as well as Malaysia would be high. Malaysia must be spared such a fate. Leaders in the mold of Najib, like Saddam and Gaddafi, have an unwarranted sense of invincibility, surrounded as they are with their flatterers.

It annoys me only a tad to read the toadying comments of the Khairys, Rahmans, and Nazris. What upsets me most is that these characters are seen by non-Malays as the best of what the Malay community could produce.

What pains me even more are comments by the likes of Tunku Aziz, former Chairman of Transparency International and member of the Anti-Corruption Advisory Committee. Does he think keeping the Auditor-General's Report secret increases transparency? Then there is Bernama Chairman Azman Ujang who quoted an obscure Malaysian-born Australian lawyer's opinion that the DOJ's filing was flawed! Azman must have undertaken quite a search to find that character!

The shocking silence of Malay ulama and intellectuals too disturbs me. Surely there must be an honest, competent, and not *dedek* dependent economist in the Majlis Professor Negara (National Professors Council) who could enlighten us on the implications of 1MDB's massive debts and the associated opportunity costs.

There were notable exceptions of course but few and far between. Dr. Asri (MAZA), the Perlis mufti, chastised his fellow ulama for their silence. Mustapha Kamil, Group Managing Editor of the *New Straits Times* finally reached his limit and quit. Former Law Minister Zaid Ibrahim continues to warn Malaysians of the danger that the Najib's leadership imposes upon Malaysians. Law Professor Azmi Sharom is another brave soul. For that he was charged with sedition. Thus far they have not been able to nail him. Rest assured that Azmi will not be nominated any time soon to the Professors Council.

Those mute *carma* (contraction for *cari makan*; lit. looking for food; fig. hired hands) professors and ulama, as well as the Tunku Azizs and Azman Ujangs must remember that although Najib may have appointed them, their salaries are being paid for by taxpayers. Their duty and loyalty should thus be to the public. They should remain true to their calling.

I could sympathize with their support of Najib if those characters had been showered with gravy on the same scale as that Malaysian Official 1's stepson Reza Aziz, Jho Low, or that Goldman Sachs' bond salesman. Instead those Malays are getting only the crumbs, and for that they are willing to soil their reputation. Meanwhile those who had received the juiciest morsels were too busy enjoying their loot to comment.

There is only one certainty; Najib's tenure will end and Malaysians will be saddled by his legacy. The questions our children and grandchildren would be asking then would be: Were you part of the solution when that happened? If you were not, then you were *ipso facto* the problem.

Post-Najib Unity Transition Administration

September 1, 2015

Despite his bravado, Najib Razak's days as Prime Minister are numbered. Last weekend's massive BERSIH 4 demonstrations are only the latest and most public expressions of citizens' disgust and contempt for him.

I hope Najib would be spared the ignominious fate of many corrupt Third World leaders. The visceral hatred for him not just as a leader but also a person is palpable. The sentiment is worse for his obscenely ostentatious wife. Judging by the extraordinarily tight security around him these days, Najib too is aware of that.

If Najib were to suffer a Marcos, or worse, a Ngo Dinh Diem, that would plunge Malaysia into an abyss. If Najib were to execute an Assad of Syria, that is, retain power at all costs, then I shudder to imagine the images of his last days, as surely that would come. I saw enough gory details of Gaddafi's demise.

Regardless of Najib's fate, prudence calls for Malaysia to be ready for a post-Najib administration. Those arguing for patience have it wrong. Nothing in the constitution precludes the removal of a sitting prime minister between elections. It has been done.

If Najib's successor were to be chosen in the manner of recent past, meaning, by UMNO power brokers, that would only ensure another mediocre pick. Najib is worse than Abdullah (who would have thought that possible!); rest assured that Najib's successor chosen thus would be even worse. This Ahmad Zahid character, Najib's current deputy, is fast living up (or down) to the low expectations many have of him.

Mahathir has apologized for his role in picking Najib, and Abdullah before that. It is not productive to continue blaming Mahathir; he retired over a decade ago. Malaysia should be able to recover from his blunders by now. At least the man recognizes his error and is trying to rectify it. Mahathir succeeded in ridding Malaysia of Abdullah; let us hope he could also do the same with Najib.

It is not enough to dump just Najib. His entire cabinet too must go, plus half a dozen top heads in the permanent establishment. To redress Najib's legacy of endemic corruption, I propose granting temporary amnesty to corruptors who confess. To discourage future such acts, I propose a permanent body to scrutinize all gifts and public contracts awarded to the top 100 public officials. They would also have to declare their assets annually to this body.

Anything less would condemn Malaysia to "business as usual." The nation cannot afford that.

Transition Prime Minister and Unity Cabinet

Najib's successor should be chosen through consensus by the parties now in Parliament. That would be the only way to get a unity leader. That individual would have to be ratified by Parliament. As UMNO has the largest number of representatives, it is only right that the Prime Minister should be from that party, meaning, one of its current MPs. Nonetheless the cabinet should have nominees from all parties.

The new Prime Minister and his ministers should commit to three stipulations. One, they should not be a candidate in the next general election; two, give up their party positions (if any) in the interim; and three, agree to stay out of government for at least a year immediately following their tenure. That would tamper the enthusiasm of many of the current career politicians. A positive effect.

On assuming office, reduce the cabinet to about a dozen ministers, as with Tunku's original team back in 1955. The current bloated one is inefficient, designed less to pick the best candidates, more to bribe compliant and none-too-bright supporters. Former Parliamentary Accounts Committee Chairman Nur Juzlan tasked with investigating 1MDB, now a junior minister, is Exhibit A in this regard.

This first stipulation would ensure that ministers focus on their cabinet responsibilities and not be consumed with jockeying to be candidates in the next election. Without this stricture those new ministers would begin their next political campaign right away, mocking the unity theme of the cabinet.

The second—decoupling cabinet appointments from party positions—could prove to be a worthy precedent for future administrations. The duties of a minister are onerous enough without the added burden of party obligations. This stipulation would also widen the talent pool beyond career politicians.

All Najib's current ministers would have to go with him. They have either explicitly or implicitly by their silence endorsed Najib's corrupt ways. They do not deserve to lead the nation. Firing them would impress upon these new ministers that while they may serve at the pleasure of the Prime Minister, their ultimate paymaster and thus clients are the citizens.

One standout candidate for Prime Minister is Tengku Razaleigh. He commands instant respect at home and abroad. Untainted by the many sordid UMNO scandals, he is also highly regarded by the opposition as well as ordinary citizens. At age 78 we can believe him when he says that he would not stand in the next election, as he informed Najib last week. He is robust physically and mentally. No other candidate could come close to Razaleigh in stature, integrity, or competence.

If reluctant leaders make the best ones, then the Tengku is the embodiment of that principle. With his accomplishments he does not need yet another accolade.

Fire Key Leaders in the Permanent Establishment

One least-noted but very revealing aspect to the present 1MDB scandal is the less-than-admirable to downright despicable performances of many heads in the permanent establishment.

The Bank Negara Governor, hitherto distinguished by her sterling professional reputation, was reduced to saying that her duties were done with the handing in of her report on 1MDB to the Attorney-General. She was not in the least interested on whether her findings would be acted upon, using the familiar Jamaican excuse, "It's not my job, *mon!*"

She felt no compulsion to protect the integrity of her institution. She also failed in her obligation to the public, her ultimate paymaster.

It gets worse. Chief Secretary Ali Hamsa, the top civil servant, announced the *retroactive* retirement of Attorney-General Gani Patail while he (Gani) was in the final stages of investigating Najib's scandal. Not to be outdone, Hamsa's new appointee as AG, Apandi Ali, announced even before being sworn in that Najib was cleared of any wrongdoing with respect to the massive 1MDB scandal!

If you want to *bodek* (suck up), at least do so in a credible way to spare yourself and your master needless embarrassment. In case the point is missed, Apandi, a retired judge, was a former state UMNO treasurer. A political hack, essentially.

Meanwhile the number one and two at the Anti-Corruption Commission (MACC) chose to be on elective medical leave during the midst of the crisis. To top that, Inspector-General of the Police (IGP) Khalid Bakar made himself the subject of international ridicule when his request to Interpol for the arrest of the *Sarawak Report* editor was rebuffed. In an unusual departure, Interpol asserted that its Red Alert is meant to nab terrorists and dangerous criminals. The smack to the IGP's face was heard around the world.

The IGP tried to keep that rebuff secret. The first blunder was bad enough, but a second one so soon! Sheer incompetence and lack of professionalism personified in Khalid Bakar.

At a minimum Chief Secretary Ali Hamsa, IGP Khalid Bakar, MACC Chief Abu Kassim, and new Attorney-General Apandi Ali should be fired and then be prosecuted for obstruction of justice with respect to the 1MDB investigation.

There are many capable Malaysians who could replace those four, and others. With Malaysians now deeply polarized, it is unlikely that any local replacement could command the confidence and respect of the populace. The new administration should thus initiate a global search to get the best talent without regard to nationality.

An important task for these new appointees would be to groom their local successors, to impress upon them the importance of protecting and enhancing the integrity of their institutions. They should not be handmaidens to their political superiors. This is especially critical now as Malaysian public institutions, even religious ones, are hopelessly corrupt and politicized.

Najib was embarrassed enough to withdraw his previously arranged address to an international conference on anti-corruption. The urbane and sophisticated audience would laugh him off. Not so at local mosques.

There he was in his long white *jubbah*, *a la* the Grand Ayatollah, Najib leading a congregational prayer with the compliant local media in full force with cameras on hand. Next the man would go for *umrah* and announce that he had a vision that the RM2 billion "donation" was *rezeki* (bounty from Allah), and the donor a descendant of the Prophet!

Samuel Johnson had it slightly off; religion, not patriotism, is the last refuge of scoundrels, at least the Malay-Muslim ones.

Amnesty for Corruptors and Asset Declaration

Corruption is now endemic in Malaysia; it is the norm at all levels. The only reason Najib's RM 2 billion "donation" raised a raucous was the sheer colossal amount (even in today's devalued *ringgit*) and the utter brazenness of the man.

It is difficult to gauge the extent of or aggregate loss from corruption. Its corrosive consequences are of course beyond quantification, from collapsed buildings endangering their occupants to watered-down academic standards depriving the young their rightful opportunities.

Tackling corruption at this stage is a formidable undertaking. One suggestion would be to grant amnesty to encourage corruptors to come forward. That would give some insight as to the extent of the blight as well as its infinite variations. There is no limit to human ingenuity in disguising corruption, from friendly "wagers" at golf games to the funding of Hajj pilgrimages. Nothing is sacred to the corrupt.

Amnesty would also create a prisoner's dilemma between the corrupting parties that could potentially be exploited. If one side confesses and the other does not, you now have the evidence to prosecute the other party.

To reduce future opportunities for corruption, there should be a permanent body to scrutinize all gifts and contracts given to the top 100 public officials and their immediate families. This 100 would include the sultans and governors, cabinet and chief ministers, top civil servants and heads of major statutory bodies, as well as Federal Court judges. They all would also have to declare their assets annually to this body.

There are many excellent models of such bodies out there; there is no need to reinvent the wheel.

Meanwhile BERSIH 4 and other protests against Najib must continue until the man is out. However, dumping only Najib without the other needed changes would only condemn Malaysia to business as usual with his successor. The nation can ill afford that.

Labi Gone, Next Labu!

August 12, 2015

Remember Labu and Labi, the two bumbling idiots in P. Ramlee's 1962 comedy movie of the same title?

Today we have a political version of that duo. With the latest cabinet reshuffle, Labi, *aka* Muhyddin, is gone. Next should be Labu, better known as Najib Razak. The leadership of Malaysia is too important to be entrusted to these twin jokers.

In a twist of irony, this latest exercise eases the process. By firing his deputy, Najib has set an important precedent–decoupling cabinet positions from party leadership. It has been the tradition, and only that as it is unsupported by the constitution, that leaders of the ruling party should also lead the country.

By having someone other than the party's deputy leader be the Deputy Prime Minister, that sets the stage whereby the Prime Minister too could be someone other than the party's President. That is the only silver lining to this latest reshuffle. That excepted, Najib's new cabinet remains a yawner. The elusive "wow" factor still eludes him.

In picking his new ministers Najib is taken in by the glint of pebbles, mistaking that for the sparkle of diamonds, or in my kampung expression, *pasir berkilau disangkakan intan*. No surprise there as Najib himself is a pebble. He values loyalty over smarts, pebbles over diamonds. Expect Malaysia to be continually grinded down.

One new minister gushed that she knew of her appointment through the radio! Obviously Najib had not vetted her. Even a housewife would be more careful in picking her *kangkung* to cook.

The new appointees were so eager that they were oblivious of the darkening clouds hovering over their leader, desperate as they were for personal advancement. May they be struck by the same lightning and be drenched in the same downpour. That would spare Malaysia from their personal ethics and pebble-stone quality.

By "promoting" four members of the parliamentary committee investigating 1MDB, Najib tried to sidetrack and emasculate that committee. I would have thought that completing a crucial national investigation would be the committee's highest priority and patriotic mission as its chairman had earlier professed and promised. As I said, these characters are pebbles, not diamonds.

If Najib thinks that he would stymie the investigation, he is mistaken. Already the Deputy Chairman has vowed to continue. Now the committee has more opposition members, including its Deputy Chairman. Najib may rue his "brilliance" in promoting those committee members.

Muhyiddin No Hero

Muhyiddin's protestation over 1MDB was neither forceful nor strategic in content, setting, or timing, despite the hullabaloo it triggered. His mild and belated attempt at being a Hang Jebat after over six years as a compliant sidekick *a la* Hang Tuah to Najib was awkward. It was, to borrow his phrase, "*lebih daripada meluat*" (beyond nauseating).

Beyond nauseating because it was self-serving. Consider the content. "I told him [Najib] to let go of his post in 1MDB, but he didn't want to listen!" protested poor Muhyiddin. Imagine had he said, "I could not get an unequivocal denial from the Prime Minister! On the contrary he admitted to having that account!"

In Muhyiddin's retelling, he is "the first minister to take a stand on 1MDB." He bragged about being vocal in cabinet and UMNO Supreme Council meetings. Then he complained that he and his cabinet and Supreme Council members had been kept in the dark about 1MDB!

You cannot have it both ways. A fellow cabinet as well as Supreme Council colleague rebuked Muhyiddin, noting that he had chaired some of those meetings.

The setting too was inappropriate. Muhyiddin should have picked a more influential audience as in a formal press conference preferably with foreign correspondents being present, not his party's divisional meeting. He could then have answered the ensuing inevitable tough questions.

As for the timing, imagine if Muhyiddin had also submitted his resignation. His stock would have soared. By letting himself be sacked, Muhyiddin's subsequent ranting was seen more as the whining of an ex-wife about her former husband. Worse, it made Najib look strong. Now *that* took some doing!

Muhyiddin did better in his later press conference. Although it was somewhat chaotic, nonetheless he exuded great confidence, a portrait not of a man who had been fired rather one who had had a great burden lifted off his broad shoulders. One wonders what is that great burden!

He would have appeared more in command had he dispensed with the prop of his wife beside him and the throngs of hangers-on behind. You do not have to major in Theater to appreciate these subtleties of effective stage or visual presentation.

Going by Muhyiddin's account, it was Najib who was weak. Muhyiddin had to prod Najib as he could not utter the words to fire Muhyiddin to his face. Najib merely nodded. There was no "you are fired" Trump-style. If Najib could not handle his deputy one-on-one, I wonder how he would fare with world leaders.

Muhyiddin should have given his press conference first instead of that speech at his divisional meeting. The latter was more a sly maneuver to "suck up" to Mahathir.

Mahathir was instrumental in Najib and Abdullah becoming Prime Ministers. Muhyiddin was trying to ingratiate himself to Mahathir in the hope of becoming his third dud pick.

Malaysians should not let that happen. Yes, Mahathir successfully undid his first mistake and is now desperate to undo his second, with no sign of success in sight. If Mahathir again prevails, Malaysians should be grateful but not let him have this third pick. Malaysia has had enough of his mistakes.

Muhyiddin is no hero. This is the Minister of Education who claimed that our schools and universities are the best. He could not be more wrong if he thinks the current outpouring of support he gets in the social media as an endorsement of his performance. Those are more expressions of citizens' disgust with Najib, a variation of the enemy-of-your-enemy-is-my-friend dynamics.

Getting Labu Out

With Labi out, getting rid of Labu should now be easier. With 1MDB short of cash, bribing and influencing potential rebellious politicians would be that much more difficult. Nonetheless there are still other tools of persuasion, as Najib demonstrated with his latest cabinet reshuffle.

Those too, like cash, are finite. There are just not enough cabinet slots or lucrative GLC directorships to accommodate all UMNO MPs and the many more avaricious local warlords, not counting those MPs from Barisan's other component parties. Those from Sarawak and Sabah are "fixed deposits" support only if their "inducements" keep flowing.

Muhyiddin is from Johore where UMNO began. Without inducements it would be difficult for him to keep his supporters there and elsewhere in tow. He is also no Tenkgu Razaleigh or Anwar Ibrahim. The chance of another Semangat 46 or Keadilan emerging to challenge UMNO and Najib is slim.

Muhyiddin's firing, cabinet reshuffle, "promotions" of parliamentary investigating committee members, "retirement" of Attorney-General Gani Patail, and the spectacular arrests of supposed "leakers" are all deliberate distractions. There would be no "leakers" had no crime been committed. They are arresting the good guys while the bad ones are running free if not rewarded.

The central question remains. Did Najib Razak siphon funds from 1MDB into his personal account? In short, did he steal public funds?

Having failed in their attempts at denials, Najib's pebble boys and girls are desperate for novel spins, the latest being "political donations" and "trust accounts." I shudder to think that foreigners are buying Malaysian elections. What would these pebble brains think of next? Najib had a royal flush in Vegas?

Ignore these new distractions. The greatest challenge remains to get the truth on 1MDB out and the culprits brought to justice. That should be the duty and priority for all, ahead of personal interests and loyalty to individuals or party.

Najib's Nixon Moment

July 26, 2015

The Special Task Force and Parliamentary Committee investigating 1MDB are missing the crux of the matter. They are distracted by and consumed with extraneous and irrelevant issues, either through incompetence or on purpose, as being directed to do so.

The consequence is that what was initially a problem of corporate cash-flow squeeze has now degenerated into a full-blown scandal engulfing not only Najib's leadership but also the national governance. The only redeeming feature is that for once a national crisis does not parallel the country's volatile racial divide, despite attempts by many to make it so.

Torrents of ink have been expended on commentaries pertaining to that tattooed Swiss national now in a Thai jail, the suspension of the publication *The Edge*, Najib's threatened lawsuit against *The Wall Street Journal* (WSJ), and the blocking of the *Sarawak Report* website. These are but distracting sideshows. Even veteran and hard-nosed observers and commentators are taken in by these distractions.

The central and simple issue is this: Did Prime Minister Najib divert funds from 1MDB to his private account as alleged by *WSJ* and others?

The issue is simple because it requires only a brief "Yes" or "No" response. If the answer is "Yes," then all else pales in comparison.

If the answer is "No," then we could proceed to such secondary issues as how much debt 1MDB has incurred, the extent of the government's exposure, and whether the company could service its loans or even generate any revenue, as well as the related question of who leaked confidential bank and other sensitive financial information.

Thus all, whether pro or anti Najib, should be asking him to answer that simple central question whether money from 1MDB (essentially public funds) was diverted to Najib's account. That is the Malaysian Nixonian equivalent of "What did the president know and when did he know it?" of the infamous Watergate scandal of the 1970s.

Queries that do not confront this central issue serve only to distract matters. Likewise, the commentaries. Those succeed only in exposing the biases and political leanings of their writers. We all can be spared that, as well as the obvious sucking-up gestures by Najib's flatterers.

If Najib were to remain silent, then the parliamentary committee and special task force must focus their investigations to answering that basic question. They do not need the cooperation of the Monetary Authority of Singapore to do that. Nor do they have to travel to Thailand and interview that tattooed character or subpoena that moon-faced chubby fellow who was so taken in with Paris Hilton.

Arresting low-level employees like the company dispatcher would only divert resources and distract the staff. Instead there should be a laser-like focus on ascertaining the central truth. All other matters as who leaked the incriminating information are secondary.

This allegation of illegal diversion of public funds is made not by some *kucing kurap* (fig. sleazy) anti-government blogger or a disgruntled UMNO operative deprived of his lucrative government contracts, but by *WSJ*. The only way to rebut the damning allegation is to show that the documents laid out were false by producing your own evidence to the contrary.

Alternatively, sue the publication. When the *Financial Times* alleged impropriety on the part of Tengku Razaleigh regarding the Bank Bumiputra fiasco of yore, he sued the publication, and won. It was the rare occasion when that influential publication was humbled!

If Najib were to sue *WSJ*, the ensuing depositions would uncover the truth. Lawsuits are expensive and protracted. All these hullabaloos would end, and confidence restored fast if Najib were to answer with a simple "No" to the central question *and* if his answer were indeed the truth and could be substantiated as such. Then he could sue *WSJ* and everyone else.

Tengku Razaleigh called upon those Malaysians who know the truth on this matter to come forward. There are only a few who are so privileged. They owe it to their fellow citizens to do so. As he so wisely put it, "Not telling the truth is not an option."

Malaysia should not be held hostage to their honesty and integrity, or lack of either. Instead Malaysians must do their part to make sure that the central truth be exposed.

I am heartened by the reactions of our corporate leaders. Nazir Razak (Najib's younger brother) and Tony Fernandes, both widely admired and highly accomplished, have condemned the suspension of *The Edge*. They went beyond; they *praised* the paper!

I applaud Nazir for another reason. What he did was another not-so-subtle rebuke to his oldest brother. He did it earlier as when he and his other brothers (minus Najib of course) reminded everyone that their father died leaving only a modest estate. In our culture, Nazir's action took great courage. He did it in the finest Jebat tradition of fidelity to principle and country, over kin and leaders.

We need others to do likewise. The Bar Council has taken an exemplary lead; likewise, the Raja Muda of Johore and a former Mufti of Perlis. When exposing a crime is treated as a crime, the former Mufti reminded us, then we are ruled by criminals. The young prince upbraided politicians who are more loyal to their party than their fellow citizens.

This 1MDB scandal threatens to not only bring down Najib but also damage Malaysia's credibility, much like Nixon's Watergate was to him and to America. It took the courage of Nixon's closest allies in his own Republican Party to convince him to do the honorable thing. As a result, America was spared an unnecessary crisis, and a generous nation later forgave Nixon. With that, his monumental legacies, as with his engagement with China, remain intact.

Najib does not have any positive legacy despite his over six years as Prime Minister, longer than Nixon was as President. Nonetheless Najib could still save his skin if he were to do the honorable thing–tell the truth.

If he does not, then it is up to those closest to him to do the honorable thing–tell him the truth. The chance of that happening is remote as UMNO is bereft of courageous individuals who could see beyond their party (and its lucrative patronage system) and to tell it straight to Najib's face.

Deputy Prime Minister Muhyiddin's belated protest is too little, too late. It is also self-serving. Now if he were to resign in protest, *that* would be something. Meanwhile as a member of Najib's cabinet, he and the other ministers are collectively responsible and should be held jointly accountable for the 1MDB mess.

The only person who could force Najib out would be Barisan's Sarawak Chief Minister Adenan Satem. His support is critical to Najib. Thus far Adenan is satisfied with squeezing the maximum out of Najib in his hour of crisis to benefit Sarawak. Adenan should remember that Sarawak, like the rest of the country, would progress only if the central government is competent and honest. An inept, corrupt, and distracted central government would be detrimental to all, Sarawak included.

It is time for Najib to do a Nixon moment, or made to do so. If Najib were to do it voluntarily, then he could control the timing and to some extent, subsequent developments as with choosing his successor. Nothing in the constitution mandates that his current Deputy be the one.

If he were to pick Tengku Razaleigh, a man of proven leadership and impeccable integrity, not only would that meet widespread approval including within Parliament, Najib would have secured for himself a significant legacy. He would also better his nemesis, Tun Mahathir, in one respect. The Tun chose two duds as his successors and in the process wasted a precious decade for Malaysia.

Najib's personal fate does not interest me. He could suffer a Marcos for all I care, but if Malaysia were to degenerate into another Philippines because of Najib, then those who remain silent or don't take a stand now must bear a heavy responsibility. How would they answer their grandchildren's lament?

May Allah bless those many brave and righteous Malaysians who have done and continue to do their part, and at great risk. I salute them! We must remain focused on the central issue: Did Najib embezzle those 1MDB funds?

Failure Of Leadership And Institutions

Reflections On Merdeka Day: Mahathir's Halfway Leadership

August 31, 2019

During the polio epidemic of the 1950s ingenious engineers created the iron lungs and saved many lives, while skillful surgeons crafted nifty operations and salvaged countless paralyzed limbs.

Those advancements, though impressive, were what physician Lewis Thomas referred to as halfway technology. True technology came when Salk and Sabin produced their vaccines. Halfway technology is not only expensive but also does not address the basic problem.

The same with leadership. There is the true version and then there are the many halfway varieties. Halfway leadership too does not solve problems; it in fact compounds them. It is also expensive both in terms of the direct damages inflicted as well as in the lost opportunities.

Malaysia was blessed with a few true leaders during her first half. Tengku Abdul Rahman inspired the multiracial population hitherto (and still is though less so) suspicious of each other, on a single pursuit—the country's independence—and successfully *negotiated* for it. Malaysia was thus spared any "glorious" war of independence. And Malaysians today are unabashed admirers of their former colonizers.

Economist Ungku Aziz leveraged the powerful religious aspiration of Hajj to make Malays save. In the process he ushered them into the modern economy, making Tabung Haji one of the region's biggest financial institutions. Chief Justice Tun Suffian elevated the country's judiciary to be the envy of the region.

During Malaysia's second half, Mahathir's leadership dominated from 1981 until he retired in 2003. Then in May 2018, at 92, he toppled the ruling coalition that he once led. Its leader, Najib Razak, was Mahathir's protégé and chosen successor. The irony!

A visitor today would be impressed on landing at Kuala Lumpur's gleaming international airport. The smooth, undulating freeways into the city, beautifully landscaped, would make you feel as if you are still in the First World. The glut of five-star hotels adds to that aura.

Impressive those may be, they are but halfway developments, showy artifacts of modernity. They cannot hide the stark realities that often intrude, like hideous acnes through thick makeup. Malaysian schools and universities for example, are an embarrassment. Minister of Education Mahathir initiated the decline in the late 1970s. Later as Prime Minister, he greased the slide.

Mahathir was also instrumental in the state's massive involvement in Islamic affairs. Today the religious bureaucracy exceeds that of the Papal one in budget, personnel, and most pernicious of all, power. While the Pope could only *influence* Catholics, Malaysian state-employed ulama *control* Malays, in activities as well as thoughts.

This huge and sinister religious serpent that Mahathir created is now striking back. Witness the current raging and unnecessary controversies over a radical, Indian-Muslim dropout physician-turned-preacher Zakir Naik, and the introduction of *khat* (Arabic calligraphy) in schools. Both do not contribute to the economy. On the contrary, they come in the way of improving it.

This huge Islamic beast sucks up precious resources that could otherwise be used to tackle pressing social problems. Those appalling pathologies disproportionately inflict Malays. In their pursuit of Heaven, those religious types believe in first making Muslims endure Hell right here on earth.

As for Tabung Haji, it had to be bailed out recently. For the judiciary, a high-profile attorney was once caught on videotape aggressively lobbying on the phone then Chief Justice Ahmad Fairuz. Among that lawyer's clients was Prime Minister Mahathir.

Mahathir tolerated corruption; a necessary lubricant for a creaky bureaucracy, he rationalized. That attitude, and the culture it nurtured, produced today's unbridled venality, with former Prime Minister Najib and a dozen of his ministers and aides now facing criminal charges of corruption. Mahathir absolved himself of any responsibility.

Mahathir was and still is a halfway leader. He is ensnared by what the young Nigerian writer Chimamanda Adichie termed "the trap of a single story." Mahathir's self-fabricated sole narrative remains unchanged: Malays are stupid and lazy; Chinese, wily and greedy.

Nor could Mahathir overcome that subtle and crippling Malay cultural trap of *terhutang budi* (debt of gratitude). His earlier support for

Najib had nothing to do with the latter's talent (Najib had none) but an expression of that old sentiment of *terhutang budi*. In early 1970s Najib's father, then Prime Minister Razak, resurrected Mahathir's crumbling political prospects.

At 94, Mahathir has not much time. He ignores his most crucial assignment—to ensure a peaceful and predictable transition of power. He is back to his trademark destructive trait—fomenting unnecessary confusion and divisive uncertainty as to his successor.

True leaders believe in their followers. When their initiatives fail, those leaders would reexamine them and formulate new ones, not blame their followers. Mahathir revels in stereotyping and blaming his followers.

In his book *Robert Kuok, A Memoir*, the author quoted Deng Xiaoping at their only meeting. "Mr. Kuok, they all say I am the one that is bringing this huge and rapid development in China. They are wrong. When I opened the door for China, they were all pushing me from behind. They are still pushing me."

A variation on Lao Tzu's theme—when a true leader's work is done, the people would say, "We did it ourselves!"

What Deng did not reveal, as evident from Ezra Vogel's biography of the man, was that there were many who opposed Deng's opening of China. His wisdom was in *not* listening to or heeding them. That is true leadership, discerning and then encouraging the wise instincts in their followers and ignoring those less blessed.

Mahathir panders to and exploits the raw emotions and base instincts of Malays. His championing Islam is not to emancipate Malays, as the Prophet did to the Bedouins of the 7th Century, but as a political tool, and a dangerous one. Mahathir exploits issues of Malay special privileges. He feeds the illusion of success and reflected glory among Malays by selling the opulence of their sultans and UMNO elite, their rent-seeking spoils sold as "entrepreneurial success."

Mahathir Version-2 is no enhancement. He is still obsessed with iron lungs and weakened limbs. He does not see the need for a vaccine, much less work on one. Today's slew of UMNO leaders indicted for corruption is only one malignant manifestation of Mahathir's halfway leadership. Another, his once much-hyped Vision 2020, is just that—hype. Not a word from him now. It was never a vision, only a slogan.

Mahathir's last hurrah was in ejecting Najib and his Barisan coalition in this last 14th General Elections [2018]. Malaysians are grateful but that gratitude is not without bounds. Mahathir is determined to breach that, thus betraying the trust Malaysians gave him in that election. He is back to his old spiteful self, provoking controversies and then blaming others for stirring them up.

Mahathir wants to burden Malaysia with another Najib-caliber successor in Azmin Ali. Time to stop Mahathir. Besides, if he could not achieve his goals when he led the nation for 23 years and when he was much younger, there is little hope for him now that he is nearing 95. Time to disabuse the man of his Messiah delusion.

The man should exit gracefully. Entice him with whatever it would take. Award Mahathir whatever title he craves and shower him with all the luxuries he desires. At his age, a lifetime corporate jet privilege and rent-free penthouse suite at his favorite Petronas Towers would be much cheaper than the damage he is inflicting and continues to inflict on Malaysia. If those do not work, not-so-gently remind him of the sorry fate that awaits the many Third World leaders who overstayed.

Malaysia deserves a true leader as she enters her 63rd year of Merdeka.

Temple Riot Reflects Failure Of Leadership And Institutions

December 2, 2018

The November 26, 2018 Seafield temple riot in Selangor was yet another needless example and tragic consequence of the failure of Malaysian leadership and institutions.

You would not know that from Interior Minister Muhyiddin's smug satisfaction and misplaced confidence when he announced its "cause"—a group of unemployable Malays being paid a measly RM 150-300 each to storm the temple. Muhyiddin was confused between, what Joseph Conrad wrote in *Lord Jim*, the fundamental *why* and the superficial *how*.

Buoyed by that delusion, Muhyiddin went on to assert that the riot was not racial. Only an idiot would utter such nonsense. It was. Just listen to the ugly epithets and seething rage before, during, and after the riot.

The idiocy continued. Mahathir announced that henceforth all houses of worship must have local authorities' approval. Meaning, up to now they did not. Again, failure of leadership and institutions.

Mahathir blamed the foreign developer's ignorance of local racial sensitivities. Quite the contrary! If the developer's intent were benign, he would have hired Indian youths from the estates, or cheaper still, illegal Banglas to do the eviction. That was vintage Mahathir, blaming foreigners.

Malaysia's incompetent leaders and failed institutions allowed problems to fester until they pitted neighbors and communities against each other.

Consider stray dogs, a major public health issue what with rabies still a problem. In America, dogs have their shots and identification chips implanted in them. Owners must also carry plastic bags to pick up the poop when walking their pets. Also, those dogs should always be on a leash. Those sensible rules escape Malaysian authorities. When stray dogs are rounded up, that becomes racial, what with dog owners mostly being non-Malays and dog catchers, being public employees, mostly Malays.

Seafield was a straightforward eviction problem. Only through much conniving and even greater malice did it become racial.

Things have not always been this way. When I was young, the streets would be littered with fake paper money and neighborhoods assaulted with raucous gongs during Chinese funerals. That is still true in Malaysia. In Singapore, Lee Kuan Yew put a stop to all that. No one else, most of all a non-Chinese or a colonialist, would or could have dared to do that. That simple fiat was effective and ignited no racial animosities. Everyone saw its wisdom.

Drive by a mosque on a Friday noon in Malaysia. You cannot; the streets would be plugged with cars parked haphazardly. Yet no Imam had ever advised his congregation to be considerate to other road users. Nor would a Malay mayor dare order towing those vehicles, or that mosques should have adequate parking.

In the late 1950s there was a potential major strike at Malayan Railway that threatened to degenerate into an ugly racial showdown, what with the engineers and workers being mostly Indians and their managers, being recently seconded civil servants, Malays.

To the Malay managers, those Indian workers were getting uppity and should be shown their place. To the Indians, those incompetent civil servants masquerading as executives needed to be taught a lesson or two on workers' rights.

It took the wisdom of Ungku Aziz to see the incendiary potential of what to most was but another industrial labor dispute. He had no formal government position, but he used his considerable influence as a respected economist to frame the dispute differently, an economic issue that would impact *all* Malaysians. He ignored the obvious racial angle and educated both parties, as well as the public. The strike was averted through his efforts.

Today, few remember that incident, akin to a plane that had landed safely after averting a potential mid-air disaster. That Seafield tragedy grabbed headlines and reopened raw racial wounds because those in charge were incompetent, like the pilot who failed to recognize and correct an earlier simple inflight issue, causing the crash.

Malaysia today desperately needs her Ungku Aziz. We also need a Lee Kuan Yew among the Indians to tell them that they cannot build temples on land they do not own. The nation would also need a Malay Lee to tell those unemployable youths that they would have a better future, as well as for Malaysia, not by being hired hooligans but by acquiring skills.

Looking ahead to December 8, 2018 and the planned protest against ICERD, a competent Interior Minister would direct his Police Chief (or the latter would have done it on his own) to infiltrate anti-ICERD organizations and have FRU conduct visible anti-riot exercises. Meaning, be prepared! This being Malaysia, do not count on that. All those security personnel were *menunggu arahan* (awaiting instructions).

A few Muftis have come out against the protest. I applaud their wisdom and courage. Special praise for Kelantan's Shukri's enlightened views, considering that his state is ruled by PAS, a vociferous anti-ICERD champion. Those few Muftis went beyond just advising; they gave good reasons based on our scripture.

They also understood the fundamental *why* of racial riots, whereas Muhyiddin only the superficial *how*. If only these other Malaysian leaders have a modicum of those Muftis' courage and wisdom, Malaysia would be better served.

Mahathir Should Scour The Field For His Ibn Jabal

November 11, 2018

The current favorite political speculation is on Mahathir's choice of a successor. At 93, Providence may not give Mahathir the luxury of an unhurried pace, and Malaysia can ill afford a leadership chaos or uncertainty.

Mahathir can learn much from our Prophet Muhammad, s.a.w. One narration has the prophet sounding out his young companion, Mu'adh Ibn Jabal, for the governorship of Yemen, a pivotal appointment. It goes something like this (approximate rendition):

Prophet, s.a.w.: "How would you govern?"
Ibn Jabal: "According to the Book of Allah!"
"What if you do not find it there?"
"Then in your sunnah!" (traditions and practices of the prophet)
"What if you do not find it there either?"
To which Ibn Jabar replied, "Then I will strive for my own judgement."

The prophet was most pleased by that response.

Every time I hear this hadith cited, regardless of the speaker, audience, or venue, the discourse would be long on Ibn Jabal's vast knowledge of the Koran and his ability to discern halal from haram, together with embellished accounts of the prophet's love and praises for the man. Many of the accounts, if we can believe the narrators, bordered on the homoerotic.

Then there would be the recitations of the various versions with their excruciating details, as if the prophet's utterance of over 14 centuries ago had been recorded verbatim.

Rarely would one hear of the hadith's wisdom, or how it could be applied to contemporary challenges. The fetish, then and now, is in displaying one's Arabic fluency and memorization prowess.

Another tradition has it that the prophet had earlier sought out other candidates. When Abu Bakar volunteered, the prophet remained silent.

Then Omar Khattab offered himself. Again, the prophet fell silent. When Ibn Jabal responded, the prophet was most pleased.

A measure of Abu Bakar and Omar Khattab is that both would later succeed the prophet. Yet he bypassed them. You could say that the prophet practiced meritocracy and fast-tracked Ibn Jabal. This insight of the hadith, as I see it, is rarely recognized or recounted.

Note, the prophet did not inquire whether Ibn Jabal had paid his zakat or gone to Hajj. The prophet was interested only in that one quality most crucial in a leader—his judgement. That insight too is often missed.

Had Mahathir heeded this in his first go as Prime Minister, Malaysia would have been spared much grief. So would he! Now in his second time around I hope that he would be more diligent. Scour the field wide for his Ibn Jabal and bypass his Abu Bakars and Omar Khattabs if need be. Mahathir's potential Ibn Jabal may not even be in the cabinet.

Ponder that hadith again. Imagine, the prophet reminding Ibn Jabal that he may not find all the answers in the Koran or *seerah*! Tell that to those whose rote response to today's complex problems is to endlessly chant, "The Koran and *seerah* have all the answers!"

We degrade the Koran when we reduce it to a how-to manual; worse, a talisman or a Muslim's lucky rabbit foot. Soak a verse of *Surah Yaseen* in your tea and that would protect you from illness. Chant this *Ayat* 72 times and your debt would magically dissipate, or there would be no need to be vaccinated. Plaster a Koranic verse on your dashboard and that would protect you even if you were to text while driving. That simple!

They chose to ignore this other prophetic tradition: First tie your camel securely, only then pray it does not escape.

Martin Luther observed that a Christian cobbler would best demonstrate his piety not by making shoes decorated with fancy crucifixes but by making them cheap and durable so the poor could afford them. Likewise, a Muslim engineer would best demonstrate his *iman* (faith) not by carving Koranic verses onto fancy arches but by being diligent in his calculations and meticulous in his construction so the bridge would not collapse with the first rainstorm.

Today the Koran and hadith are being exploited to end a discussion rather than illuminate it. "The Koran (or hadith as narrated by Bukhari, Muslim, Termidhi, etc.,) says . . . ," an alim would assert with arrogant certitude, as if his interpretation is the only valid one. Koran and hadith should stimulate discussions, not close them.

Then there are those who would dispense entirely with hadith. To them, Prophet Muhammad, s.a.w., was but a human fax machine, a robotic intermediary mouthing whatever God had placed in his vocal cords. Once you received your message, the fax machine is superfluous.

Hadith scholar Jonathan Brown put it best. When we read the Koran, we implicitly put on the lens of the holy prophet. Like lens, hadith enhances and clarifies the Koran, as well as helps us focus on it. We could only achieve that if we are not preoccupied with and distracted by such extraneous matters as the chain of narrators or argue endlessly on the authenticity of what was uttered a millennium-and-a-half ago.

If the prophet had to remind Ibn Jabal that the answer may not always be in the Koran or hadith, we too would be wise to follow that prophetic precept.

Back to Mahathir, he would do well to focus on finding and nurturing his Ibn Jabal. Everything else pales in comparison. Seeing that he blew it—and on such a horrendous scale—with both Abdullah Badawi and Najib Razak, the wise course would be to deny him the privilege of a third pick.

Mahathir Should Focus On *Not* Creating Another Najib Razak

September 2, 2018

Prime Minister Mahathir's grand opening speech at the Kongress Masa Depan Bumiputra Dan Negara (Congress on the Future of Bumiputra and the Nation) on September 1, 2018, was a severe disappointment. It was as if he was in a time warp. There he was, hectoring his admirers and others who would listen to him with the same old refrain, if not the same old tired phrases. It was as if he had been awakened after 15 years of siesta and he was back to where he was when he left office in 2013.

He resurrected his old, ugly, hackneyed stereotypes about Malays. Listening to him it felt as if he was reading excerpts from his old *The Malay Dilemma*, first published in 1970. He forgot that he had been given the rare responsibility and manifest privilege to lead the nation for well over two decades. That ought to have been enough time for him to remedy whatever it was that ailed Malays.

Now that he is given a unique second chance, he sticks to the same old prescription that has now been proven to be not only ineffective but has made the problem even worse.

The man lacks humility or any sense of introspection to even consider that just maybe the fault lies with him, or his policies and their implementations. A brilliant policy badly executed would fail just as a bad policy carried out faithfully.

It would not occur to Mahathir to even ponder the possibility that the assumptions of his policies could be erroneous, or if correct, his remedies were inappropriate if not wrong. After all, he is brilliant. As one of his early admirers noted, he was the first Malay to qualify as a doctor without having to sit for any supplemental examination. That ought to count for something! Beyond that, he succeeded in dethroning the hitherto thought formidable Najib Razak to become the world's oldest chief executive of a nation. Even Mahathir admitted that he doubted whether he would succeed in doing that.

Make no mistake. Malaysians ought to be grateful to Mahathir for getting rid of that crude, corrupt, and incompetent Najib. If not for Mahathir, that rogue would still be plundering Malaysia, and the millions hoarded in Najib's personal residence would not have been uncovered.

Before that gratitude gets too deep into Mahathir's head, he should be reminded—and often—that he, Mahathir, more than anyone else was responsible for Najib's rise to the highest office in the land. And before Najib, that equally inept Abdullah Badawi. As such, Mahathir is responsible for Malaysia's wasted precious past decade and a half.

Again, let it be stated lest Mahathir might forget (after all he is a Malay and forgets easily, quite apart from his advanced age), the rot and corruption of Malaysia began long before Najib. He merely brought both to a whole new, low obscene level.

My plea to Mahathir is simple. Please, do not bother trying to save Malays. You have given that noble mission your best shot and for over two decades. Just move on. Time to give others the chance for that difficult mission.

Meanwhile I pray and hope that Mahathir focuses on *not* bequeathing unto Malaysia another Abdullah Badawi or Najib Razak. That is an awesome responsibility and a monumental task. The next Najib Razak might be slightly smarter and could prove even more difficult to dislodge. That would doom Malaysia forever.

Sad to note that thus far I have not seen any evidence that Mahathir has learned the painful lessons with Abdullah and Najib. *That* should worry all Malaysians.

End The Outrageous "Double Dipping" By Top Public Officials

June 3, 2018

The revelation by Transport Minister Loke that the Malaysian Aviation Commission (Mavcom) Chairman Abdullah Ahmad earns about RM85K a month, while a shocker, is not a secret. It is a long-held practice for top officials to earn more than their official salaries. Abdullah Ahmad is not alone. Far from it!

This practice proliferated under Najib, one of the many manifestations of his cash-is-king schemes to buy the loyalty of senior public officials. He of course received much more in return through their loyalty and cooperation, as evidenced by the loot hauled from his private residences after he was booted out in the 2018 elections.

Prime Minister Mahathir, who earns less than a quarter of what that Mavcom Chairman gets, has ordered Chief Secretary Ali Hamsa to review the remunerations of top public officials as well as heads of GLCs and statutory bodies.

There is no need for such a review. Instead, Mahathir should just ban them from having extra income beyond their salaries. They are being paid to devote their time and effort exclusively to their current positions. Theirs is not a 9 to 5 job; they have no business assuming added responsibilities except in an *ex officio* (by virtue of their positions) capacity. For that they already have generous allowances to cover the extra expenses incurred, as with travelling and lodging.

Ali Hamsa is also the wrong person to undertake such an important review. Foremost is the issue of conflict of interest. He is as guilty as that Mavcom Chairman. Hamsa should begin by declaring how much extra compensation he was paid in addition to his regular salary as Chief Secretary to the Government by virtue of appointing himself to be on the various GLC boards. The disgraced former Treasury Secretary Irwan Serigar was on Khazanah's and Bank Negara's Boards, as well as others not yet revealed. He must have raked in substantial additional income ib the form of director's fees.

Ali Hamsa, Irwan Serigar, Abdullah Ahmad, and countless others are guilty of double dipping into the public purse. The poor rakyat bears the burden of such rampant, lucrative, and possibly illegal practices.

Ali Hamsa is also ill-qualified to undertake such a review for another reason. He has spent all his career in the civil service. He knows nothing of the culture or value of talent in the competitive private sector. He has been *receiving* not giving out paychecks all his life; he has no appreciation of the challenges in having to meet a payroll.

Scrutinize the corporate structures of many GLCs and statutory bodies. They have myriads of subsidiaries and associated companies. The reason is simple: management greed. With more corporate entities, more board of director's positions and fees! Ever wonder why those GLCs and statutory bodies lose money?

If companies like Petronas need outside directors, the Professor of Petroleum Engineering from the University of Malaya would be a far superior choice than a retired government bureaucrat. All the latter would do is graft the stultifying civil service culture onto the company.

Appointing that professor as director would also be a way to augment his otherwise meager academic pay. That might just be the inducement for him to stay on campus instead of joining the private sector, which would be a loss to his students who would be the country's future petroleum engineers. The professor would also gain real world experience, again to the benefit of his students. Similar consideration with Tabung Haji. Why not appoint the local Professor of Economics or Accounting to its board? That would be far superior than having that *mamak* with a PhD or MBA from Preston University! Unlike the Ivy League Princeton, Preston awards degrees based on "life experiences!"

Another common and lucrative double-dipping scheme occurs when retired civil servants or former public officials are appointed to statutory bodies or GLCs. The number one culprit in the news today is Isa Samad. He is notorious for other reasons. For this discussion, while he is drawing a substantial pay as the head of SPAD (the Malay initials for the federal public transportation agency), he is still getting his pension as a former MP and a Federal Minister, as well as that of a State (Negri Sembilan) Chief Minister, and as a state legislator. Beyond that he is also getting one for being the former head of FELDA. These entities may have different names, but their paymaster is the same–the rakyat.

Such "double dipping" should be banned. If a retired civil servant or public official is appointed to a GLC or statutory body and getting a salary, then he should not draw the pension of his previous job. He should be considered as continuing to work for the same employer but in a different capacity. If he were to start his own business or be employed by a private company, that would be a different matter. In that case he should be entitled to the government pension of his old job plus his new pay.

There would be two other immediate positive effects of such a policy. One, those civil servants would now be less likely to be seduced by their political masters as is the current culture. They would now be more likely to be independent if not outspoken in disagreeing with their political superiors. That could only be good for the country's administration.

The other positive effect would be to encourage more Malays (most civil servants are Malays) to enter the private sector either as employees, directors, or to create their own businesses. That would increase the rate of Malay participation in the private sector far more effectively and efficiently than starting expensive and often money losing GLCs. They would then be more like Rafidah Aziz with Air Asia. Or they could set up their own professional practices as Aziz Abdul Rahman, former Managing Director of Malaysia Airlines, with his own law firm.

In the 1960s Tun Razak lowered the retirement age (it was 55 then) so enterprising young civil servants could retire to start their own businesses. That initiative spawned many Malay-owned businesses. This was also the practice of the Italian government and resulted in the blossoming of entrepreneurial activities spurred by young retired civil servants who had the safety net of their civil service retirement income.

This double dipping by senior civil servants and public officials costs the nation a hefty bundle. With Malaysia's debt now exceeding a trillion ringgit, the nation can ill afford such outrageous wastages. Time to ban double dipping outright. There is no need for further unnecessary studies.

Devolution And The Rise Of Sarawak's Adenan Satem

August 28, 2016

Do not anticipate any positive change in Malaysia coming from the center, not from the current corrupt and incompetent UMNO leadership under Najib Razak. Instead expect it from the periphery, and the personality to watch is Sarawak's Chief Minister Adenan Setam.

This rise of the periphery is a worldwide phenomenon. Witness the successes of the Scottish Nationalist Party, and the Brexit referendum. Devolution in the United Kingdom is a backlash against globalization; with Malaysia, a weak and distracted center.

Adenan's rise is facilitated both by his political prowess as well as Najib's precarious position. Najib is inept in dealing with state leaders other than those from within his UMNO party. With them, Najib could bribe or bully his way.

A measure of Najib's lack of sensitivity to Sarawak's concerns is that not a single university in the country has a Department of Iban Studies. Petronas, which gets the bulk of its oil from Sarawak, does not even have a Sarawakian on its Board of Directors or senior management. Now Adenan has imposed a moratorium on work permits for West Malaysians in Petronas. It is significant that he spared non-Malaysians from that stricture.

Unlike his predecessor, the crude and greedy Taib Mahmud who exploited his leverage to enrich himself, Adenan uses his to extract greater autonomy for Sarawak. He acts as if he already has that, declaring English to be on par with Malay in schools and the state's administration, in defiance of Federal policies. The surprise is the silence of UMNO chauvinists and Malay language nationalists. That can only happen with specific directives from Najib.

Adenan has banned UMNO from Sarawak; there is no legal basis for that. Again, no challenge from Najib. If UMNO were to defy that, Adenan and his party would quit the ruling coalition and Najib would fall. Note Adenan's ease in castrating UMNO *jantans*. Not a peep of protest from them. They bear and grin, as instructed.

Sarawak and Sabah already enjoy considerable autonomy on immigration. West Malaysians need a passport or special permit to enter, a unique requirement in any country, save China. Adenan exploited that to maximal effect in the last state election, denying entry to opposition MPs from West Malaysia, a slap to Parliament's prestige. Again, the surprise was the silence of the Speaker, an UMNO man, to this unprecedented affront to his institution.

Adenan could act with impunity as his party is critical to Barisan. Through that he controls Najib. To Najib, Sarawak is his "fixed deposit." That euphemism cannot hide the political reality. Without Adenan's party, Najib and UMNO would topple. At present it is to Adenan's (and Sarawak's) advantage to stay with the ruling coalition. Najib will do everything to ensure that; his survival depends on it.

Autonomy is meaningless without changes in federal tax laws, a formidable obstacle. The federal government has near-exclusive taxing authority. Only minor items like land taxes are under state control. The oil royalty-sharing formula heavily favors the central government. Even if Sarawak could re-negotiate that, it is no windfall, what with the declining oil price. Despite its massive rain forest with its valuable hardwood, Sarawak still cannot forgo massive federal transfer payments.

One way to circumvent the tax hurdle would be to execute a secular zakat maneuver. Zakat is a religious tax based on assets, not income, and is under state jurisdiction, albeit applicable only to Muslims and is voluntary. It could be made mandatory and extended to all, non-Muslims included. Both moves would enthrall the Islamists.

Zakat contributions are treated as federal tax credits, not deductions. That would provide a neat way to circumvent federal income tax.

Sarawakians have minimal fondness for the federal government. They could be persuaded to pay zakat (and its secular equivalent for non-Muslims) instead of income tax as the benefits would accrue to them, as the money stays in Sarawak. Sarawakians would not be paying both, rather diverting income tax to zakat.

Adenan has adopted an excellent negotiating strategy with Najib by creating momentum with the easily agreed upon and costless items like increasing the number of Sarawakians in Petronas and having one on its Board of Directors.

With Najib's current weakness, Sarawak could drive a hard bargain for greater autonomy, including independent taxing power, to the point of being a virtual sovereign state. Once that happens, Sabah would be next in line to demand similar status. Sabah UMNO leaders would not dare defy the demands of their members no matter how much Najib bribes those leaders. From there, other states. Johor Sultan already stirs noises for Bangsa Johor (nation of Johor) and threatens secession. Kelantan wants its hudud. Najib supporting that ill-advised initiative could come back to haunt him.

Once the unravelling begins, it would be unstoppable. The prospect of a chief minister being on par with the prime minister is a giddy one to ambitious state politicians. Remember, the old Federation of Malaya was recent, set up only in 1948; Malaysia even more recent in 1963.

Consider the impact of autonomy on national policies like education and special privileges. Even with the current restrictions, note the ease with which the opposition DAP terminated special privileges for Malay contractors in Penang. Selangor under Pakatan's Khalid Ibrahim annihilated a whole class of UMNO rent seekers, and saw his predecessor, that dentist character Khir Toyo jailed for corruption.

Even if Najib were to balk at Adenan's demands, what's to stop Adenan from asking his party members in Parliament to submit a private member's bill, *a la* PAS Hadi's hudud, seeking greater autonomy and taxing authority for Sarawak? If Adenan were to do that, then watch both Najib and the opposition competing to accommodate Adenan in an epic *lu tolong gua, gua tolong lu* (fig. you scratch my back, I'll scratch yours) battle. He would be holding Parliament–and Malaysia–to ransom.

I support the principle that a government closest to the people governs best. There are however pitfalls to that assumption.

Sarawak shares a long unguarded land border with Indonesia. Most of Borneo is Indonesia; Sarawak being part of Malaysia is a political and geographic anomaly. It would not take much for the Indonesians to overwhelm Sarawak. If not for the British, they would have done that during *konfrontasi*. Besides, Jokowi is everything that Najib is not: honest, effective and charismatic.

As for Sabah, Filipino pirates could enter that state with impunity, and Philippines is resurrecting her claim to Sabah. A complicating factor is the traditional kinship ties between Sabah and Southern Philippines.

Adenan envies tiny independent Brunei. The lesson there is not the Brunei of today but earlier. In 1962 one A. M. Azahari toppled the sultan. If not for the British Gurkhas, the Sultan would have remained a refugee in Singapore. The son of Azahari may yet arise. This time there would be no Gurkhas to rescue the Sultan or the state Chief Minister.

I see great potential for Sarawak under Adenan Satem. He may be the transforming leader Malaysia needs while remaining within the ruling coalition. Today that coalition is Barisan. Tomorrow who knows. If Adenan plays his cards well, that would be good for him, Sarawak, and most of all, Malaysia.

Getting Rid Of The Monkeys Of Putrajaya

February 10, 2016

I was visiting my old village near Sri Menanti, Negri Sembilan, not too long ago and was struck by an unexpected but common sight—the absence of any fruit trees or vegetable plots around what few remaining houses there that were still occupied.

Such a scene would have been unthinkable during my youth. Then there were always nearly ripe papayas or bananas ready to be picked for breakfast, and enough long beans in the garden or chickens scurrying around to fill a cooking pot should unexpected guests arrive for dinner.

On querying my few elderly relatives still there in the serene kampung lifestyle, they replied that the *monyet* and *kera* (monkeys) have descended from the jungle and destroyed everything. They have become so brazen and aggressive that my relatives now fear for their safety.

That is one of the many consequences of our having destroyed the primates' natural habitat through illegal logging and replacing it with the hostile monoculture plantations of rubber and palm oil.

Like displaced people, those monkeys are forced into the kampungs to survive and unleash their frustrations. Meanwhile, those loggers and planters luxuriate in their new wealth oblivious of the burden they have inflicted on those monkeys and poor villagers.

Back in the city, I read the daily papers only to discover that marauding monkeys of another kind have also descended on and ravaged Putrajaya. The Year of the Monkey began early in Malaysia.

The havoc wrecked by the *kera* in the kampung is readily visible and the damages they inflict potentially recoverable. The critters, too, could also easily be scared away by letting those villagers have guns.

Not so with the primates of Putrajaya. The damage they inflict are not readily visible, appearing only on the computer terminals of banks and other financial institutions. Nonetheless the damage they inflict is much more devastating. Worse, it is being borne not only by citizens of today but also generations to come.

Already scholarships for some of Malaysia's brightest students are being withdrawn for lack of funds. They are the next generation of talent, their dreams crushed at the last minute through no fault of their own. And what a loss to the nation!

At least my relatives in the kampung are smart enough to be aware of the menace posed by those monkeys. By contrast Malaysians, more so the Malay elite, regard their chief monkey now marauding in the nation's capital and plundering the country's wealth as the Prince of Putrajaya, perverse though it might seem to the rest of the world.

Such obscenity and the perversion of Malay values are possible only because the elite holed up in Putrajaya and elsewhere have abandoned their souls.

They have gone beyond. They have unabashedly sold theirs. Their price is pathetically cheap. The leftover crumbs that fall their way after their chief monkey has satiated his gluttony.

When confronted with their chief monkey's continually changing and contradictory "explanations" to rationalize his gluttony, those little monkeys around him would insist that they have not sold their souls, rather that they have merely "loaned" or "sacrificed" them to their "beloved" chief monkey.

Well, monkey see, monkey do. When they see that their chief monkey was being "exonerated" upon returning the money it had earlier stolen, those little monkeys around soon got the message. That is, if you get caught stealing, then return the loot, or make a pretense of it. Then it would not be considered wrong or a crime.

That is the new ethics of those Putrajaya monkeys.

They also have a new religion. That is, if they steal something and not get caught, then the loot is halal. Likewise, if they are caught and then returned the loot, then they have not committed a *dosa* (sin).

With the loot that they have acquired, if they were to harbor any tinge of guilt or remorse, they could "cleanse" themselves by undertaking the hajj or umrah, just to be sure.

What a mockery of our great faith of Islam!

Today, our monkey chief has sold, oops, "lent" his soul to the Arabs; tomorrow it could be the Mainland Chinese. Who will be next?

The philosopher Hamka related a story of the prophet who encountered a sad young man in the mosque one day. When asked as to the cause, the young man replied that he was deep in debt and unable to repay it. He now feared for his life.

Whereupon the prophet advised the young man never to be fearful of another mortal. We should fear only Allah.

There are eight ways in which we put ourselves in fear of our fellow human beings, the prophet counselled the young man. For brevity as well as relevance, I will mention only the last one.

We put ourselves in the grip of others by being indebted to them. That is how the Ah Longs could instill fear and dread in their victims. Spare yourselves such a fate by not borrowing or being in debt. That is the lesson the prophet imparted on the frightened young man.

Nonetheless debts of money or material things are potentially repayable, and then you would be freed from the bondage and carry on with your life. You may have to work hard to achieve that, but at least it is doable.

There is one debt that can never be repaid, the prophet advised the young man, and that is the debt of gratitude.

An ancient Malay saying reflects this wisdom: *hutang emas boleh dibayar, hutang budi di bawa mati*. A debt of gold is repayable, but you carry your debt of gratitude to your death.

Former Prime Minister Mahathir Mohamad recently expressed his deep regret in having groomed the young Datuk Seri Najib Razak.

Mahathir greased the path for Najib because he (Mahathir) owed a huge debt of gratitude to Najib's father, Tun Razak, who "rehabilitated" Mahathir when he was in the political wilderness after being expelled from UMNO in the early 1970s.

It looks like Mahathir would carry to his grave not only his huge debt of gratitude to Razak but also the burden he has imposed upon the nation by being instrumental in Najib becoming Prime Minister.

Najib, in turn, owes a huge debt of gratitude to the Arabs for their generous "donations" before the last elections, and to the Chinese for currently bailing out 1MDB by buying rusty Malaysian generating plants.

I could not care less what burden Najib would carry to his grave, but I am concerned with the huge burden he has imposed and continues to impose on Malaysians of today, as well as on their children and grandchildren.

The *kera* in my old village could easily be gotten rid of by giving those villagers rifles. Getting rid of the monkeys in Putrajaya is much more problematic.

Leaders' First World Education, Third World Mentality

Review of Syed Husin Ali's *Memoirs of a Political Struggle*. Strategic Information and Research Development, Petaling Jaya, 2013. 273 pp.

June 8, 2014

The deserved universal condemnation and merciless ridicule of the Malaysian authorities' bungling of the Malaysian Airlines MH370 tragedy did not arise in a vacuum. From leaders' refusing to entertain questions at their press briefings to radar operators ignoring intruding beeps on their screens, this unconcealed contempt for the public, and the accompanying lackadaisical attitude, is the norm.

Malaysian leaders may have had First World education, alas their mentality remains stubbornly stuck in Third World mode. Their *bebalism* (obstinance) and *tidak apa*ism (could not care less attitude) make the Jamaican "It's not my job, mon!" a valid excuse by contrast.

To readers of the alternate media, I am not stating anything new here. Likewise, ordinary citizens who have had to deal with the various governmental agencies know this only too well. When these general inadequacies and gross incompetence in their infinite manifestations are put in print as in books, there is satisfaction, at least to their authors, that they are being documented for posterity. So that when Malaysia degenerates (as surely it would) into another Nigeria with its endemic corruption, or Pakistan with religious fanaticism, scholars would then have ample materials upon which to base their analyses. Till then, these accounts are a much-needed antidote to the fluff and gloss that typify Malaysian official reports.

We owe these authors, from ordinary citizens to seasoned journalists, and opposition activists to members of the establishment, a huge debt of gratitude when they record their experiences. Syed Husin Ali's reflective autobiography, *Memoirs of a Political Struggle*, is one such valuable addition, tracing the nation's social and political development beginning with the decade before independence. Despite the title, the book is more autobiography than memoir.

Once readers get past the pedestrian I-was-born-in opening, the scholar in Syed Husin gives us an unsentimental and detached view. As a politician, he details the many hypocritical ways of his peers. He relates an occasion when he was on a panel discussion with one Dr. Mahathir at the University of Malaya campus. Mahathir then was not yet prime minister but was headed that way through his rising popularity as head of UMNO Youth, the party's powerful wing.

Mahathir chided those "impure" Malay political activists. "Those of Arab descent," Syed Husin quoted Mahathir, "should not have any right to talk about political issues of this country."

Syed Husin's understated nonchalant riposte was, "I do not wish to talk about ancestry for otherwise I will have to talk about the rights of those of Indian descent."

Mahathir is of Indian descent though he never highlights that fact.

My purpose with this quote is not to showcase Mahathir's hypocrisy (readers can readily find their own far more consequential examples) or highlight Syed Husin's not-widely recognized wit, rather to point out one significant observation. That is, you will never find such a panel discussion on today's Malaysian campuses where contrasting positions would be presented. That is one the many destructive legacies of Mahathir.

Syed Husin is, quoting Anwar Ibrahim, "in a category of his own, unique in terms of moral conviction, and not in the business of saying things to please people." A sociologist, Syed Husin gave up his productive academic career to *turun padang* (get down to the field) and get involved in electoral politics. He is less successful in this second endeavor. Nonetheless with the victory of his party's coalition in the last general election, he was appointed a Senator from Selangor. A well-deserved appointment!

Syed Husin Ali had a First World education (London School of Economics PhD), but unlike many in the country similarly blessed, he maintained those First World qualities. As an academic he was not content resting on his sterling academic qualifications. His pioneering work on social stratification in traditional Malay society remains seminal.

In an enlightened administration, especially one that professes to champion the plight of poor rural folks, a man of Syed Husin's insight and talent would be co-opted to play a major role. Alas, UMNO is far from being enlightened, and its commitment to alleviating rural poverty is more an election gimmick, a scheme to enrich its operatives through the many "development" schemes. Funds meant for poor livestock growers for example, are siphoned by ministers or their spouses to buy luxury condos in Kuala Lumpur and Singapore.

Three qualities struck me about Syed Husin. One, his humility, integrity, and piety; two, his early socio-political consciousness, beginning right at primary school; and three, his thoroughly Malaysian experience and outlook. His rural upbringing in Batu Pahat, Johore, has much to do with his humility; his religious parents, his piety; and, being a former King Scout, his integrity.

When Anwar underwent surgery in Germany, Syed Husin visited him using his own funds. One of Anwar's operatives tried to reimburse Syed by handing him a bundle of $100 US notes, but he would have none of it. Unable to stop the man, Syed gave the money to his party's treasurer upon his return. On another occasion, when as a scholar he was given a UNESCO research grant, he returned to his dean the unused portion. That's integrity! Anyone else would finagle a way to present his paper at the University of Hawaii or Bali with those leftover funds.

Syed Husin grew up in colonial Malaya. To today's young accustomed to incompetence, cronyism, and influence peddling, that was an entirely different era. While he did not hide his nationalistic and anti-colonial streaks, nonetheless that did not stop the colonial authorities from selecting him to attend a scouting jamboree in Australia.

The other aspect to Syed Husin's path is that his schooling, extracurricular activities, and political activism all took place in an environment involving Malaysians of all races. That was why he was so offended by Mahathir's remarks at that panel discussion. Syed embodies the values and aspirations of a truly modern Malaysian.

Syed's leftwing leanings began early. In a society obsessed with labels, and where political sophistication rudimentary, it was not wise to be identified or labeled as a socialist especially when memories of the brutal communist insurgency were still fresh. Dispensing with labels, what is clear is that Syed Husin is committed to social justice, economic equity, and equal opportunities. What he abhors is leaders betraying their followers' trust. This betrayal comes in many guises—greed and its associated corruption, incompetence and its *bebalism* or *tidak apaism*, or plain stupidity and ignorance.

I wonder what his fate would be had Syed Husin dispensed with labels and joined UMNO like so many like-minded Malays. The Fabian socialists would surely approve of Tun Razak's generous redistributionist policies and massive state interventions in the economy. After all there was a time when the term *kaum kapitalis* (capitalist hordes) was an epithet hurled by the likes of UMNO's Syed Jaafar Albar and Syed Nasir. Today with the spoils of crony capitalism, socialism is a curse; likewise, social justice.

Had Syed Husin joined UMNO, would he be as corrupt as the rest or would he be like the snake that would not lose its venom despite crawling among vines, as per the Malay proverb? I believe he would be the latter, and the nation would have been richer for his contributions.

I detect a tinge of regret as Syed Husin recollects his struggles over these years. He tried hard to conceal his disappointments. As such there is no settling of old scores in his memoir, not even with his old jailors. Yes, he too was snared by Malaysia's infamous Internal Security Act. There is a touching picture of a smiling Syed greeting his old tormentor from the Special Branch. That's class! Contrast that to the vile-filled memoirs of many recently retired politicians.

Make no mistake. Syed Husin is capable of penning moving prose and be passionate in his writings. I remember reading his *Two Faces. Detention Without Trial* and slamming down the book in anger at the authorities' brutal and inhumane treatment of this great intellect and patriotic Malaysian.

This was his poignant ending to the short opening paragraph in *Two Faces*: "One minute I was a professor, the next I was a prisoner." I suppose his fate could have been worse. Consider Egypt's Morsi's cryptic last comment, "One minute I was president; the next, a prisoner."

A generation hence when dysfunctional countries like Egypt would be Malaysia's peers, citizens can look back and realize that there were committed and courageous Malaysians like Syed Husin who tried hard to stem the slide. And our descendants would glow in the reflected glory of his many heroic efforts.

The Distracting Bilateral Issue Of Maids

August 8, 2010

It is telling of the state of development for both Indonesia and Malaysia that when their two leaders met recently, the key topic was the issue with Indonesian maids in Malaysia. Malaysia wishes to import more while Indonesia wants better working conditions for her workers in Malaysia.

I would have expected the two leaders to discuss such consequential issues as joint development of the region as a tourism destination to rival the Caribbean, harnessing the power of satellite and wireless communication to leapfrog the development of both countries, or conducting joint maritime research for both ecological and economic purposes. Alas, none of that!

It is reflective of the abysmal state of human development in Indonesia that maids are her major "export." Likewise, it reflects the perverted status symbol of Malaysians that having a maid reflects a "luxurious" lifestyle.

It is beyond me why Malaysians think that way. Australians have a per capita income considerably much higher, yet I do not see them having a "maid crisis;" likewise the Japanese. Even in America where it is now the norm for both parents to be working, very few homes have live-in maids; most do with only daytime helpers. Granted, there are many childcare centers to take up the slack.

In America, those maids (nannies) get social security benefits (America's Employee Provident Fund—EPF) as well as workmen's compensation insurance (for work-related injuries). They are also governed by prevailing labor laws. Slavery is long gone in America.

While conditions for maids in Malaysia are far superior to the old American slaves, nonetheless the family-servant dynamics in Malaysia is closer to the owner-slave mentality of the Old South than to a modern employer-employee relationship.

I am surprised at the high level of engagement in this maid issue. If only a similar commitment were made in luring foreign academics and skilled workers, imagine the good it would do for Malaysia!

If Malaysia were to continue importing maids, then I would suggest imposing strict standards and paying them attractive salaries. We can begin by calling them "nannies" instead of the degrading "servants."

The minimum monthly salary should be RM800.00, with overtime rate twice that on a prorated per hour basis. Additionally, the employer would contribute towards the nanny's EPF. Those funds would become vested (meaning, the nannies could claim the benefits) only if they were to serve cumulatively for at least 40 quarters (equivalent of ten years), though not necessarily continuously or even with the same family. That is the rule with America's Social Security.

As for work hours, they must have at least an eight-hour stretch of undisturbed time in a 24-hour-day period, and an additional 24-hour in a seven-day period. They could choose to work during those times, but they would be paid overtime.

The employer would also have to pay towards health insurance and a "performance bond." The pooled money in the bond would pay for any maid caught in criminal activities. It would also cover the cost of the loss as well as deportation. The bond funds would also benefit the nanny should her employer for some reason is unable to pay her salary, as with the employer declaring bankruptcy.

It would cost at least RM1,200 per month to employ a nanny. Such a remuneration would make not only the Indonesian authorities happy (that is always a good neighborly gesture) but also those nannies. Heck, at that rate we may even interest locals to become nannies!

For those who think that such a pay rate is unrealistic, consider that the average expatriate family in Malaysia is already paying considerably more. The services provided to those families are considerably superior than what the local Ahmad and Ah Chong are getting.

To justify the higher pay, these maids must provide superior services. They must be trained to do that. They must take at least a three-month course learning basic hygiene and the rudiments of safe and healthy childcare. This would include basic nutrition, child safety, and child proofing the house, including training in first aid, cardiopulmonary resuscitation, and Heimlich maneuver.

The cost of training is beyond the reach of the potential typical maid from an Indonesian village. This is where the government, using funds from the performance bond, could finance these courses. They would be free if the attendee were to work in Malaysia for at least three years, enough time to recoup the costs of training. Such a scheme would benefit not only potential employers but also these young women. When they return to their villages, they could then take better care of their own children or grandchildren.

The government could ease the need for these foreign maids (and thus save on the associated social and other costs) by encouraging the setting up of childcare centers through various incentives.

More Fruitful Avenues for Cooperation

It is not my purpose to write on how to get better maids. My focus is on exploring areas of potentially fruitful cooperation between Malaysia and Indonesia. In my book *Towards A Competitive Malaysia*, I proposed greater economic cooperation leading to integration *a la* the European Union between Indonesia, Brunei, and Malaysia (a political IBM!).

While all three are still essentially developing and thus would be competing in the same arenas, nonetheless there are enough differentiating factors between them that would make cooperating more beneficial than competing. The potential areas for cooperation include energy (oil and gas), plantations, tourism, wireless technology, and natural products development.

All three countries are oil and gas producers. Individually they are no match to the slick "seven sisters" oil companies, but collectively the three countries could be a powerful countervailing force. While Pertamina and Brunei National Petroleum are still babes in the woods, Petronas has acquired significant international expertise.

With plantations, Indonesia has plenty of land in Sumatra and Kalimantan as well as labor, while Malaysia has the sophisticated experience. Brunei of course has the financial capital; at least what is left after its profligate sultan has his take.

As for tourism, the region could rival the Caribbean as a tropical paradise for rich cold-climate dwellers. It is just as arduous to fly from Frankfurt to Cancun or St. Bart as it is to Bali or Langkawi. As in the Caribbean, I envisage four or five major cruise companies serving the area.

The Malay Nusantara or Archipelago with its endless islands is an ideal place to test the limits of and potential for satellite and wireless technologies. Imagine if we open the whole area to global competition and let the likes of Nokia, ATT, Nippon Tel, and Siemens compete. Once we have reliable real-time communication from Sulawesi to Seremban, and from Lubbock to Langkawi, then watch intra-regional trade and other economic activities flourish.

Likewise, imagine if we liberalize the region's airspace to all comers, domestic and foreign. Who cares if the companies are foreign so long as they provide affordable, reliable, and efficient service? Those who could do, survive; those could not, leave.

With natural products, both Indonesia and Malaysia have vast tracts of ancient jungles that have yet to be explored. What is lacking is the expertise to exploit this invaluable resource and the political enlightenment to treat it wisely.

These are only some of the potential areas for cooperation. The issue of maids pales in comparison.

Indonesia's Susilo Bambang Yudhoyono holds a PhD in economics, while Najib Razak is generously described as a "British-trained economist." This makes it even more incomprehensible why they would be involved in dealing with such trivia as the "maid issue."

Tiada Maruah (Lack of Integrity) At The Very Top

August 1, 2010

Last week I wrote[2], "So we have two disturbing displays of less-than-exemplary behaviors if not outright lack of professionalism at the highest levels of the Malaysian civil service. One is the Chief Secretary not hearing both sides to the Lim Eng Guan (Penang's Chief Minister) and Nik Ali (a federal civil servant) squabble before rendering judgment, and the other, the Solicitor General failing to recognize a breach of professional ethics."

A few days later we had a third example, this time with Attorney General (AG) Gani Patail. Responding to allegations of improper behavior by one of his prosecutors in the Anwar Ibrahim's Sodomy II trial, Gani Patail simply reassigned her.

These displays of *tiada maruah* (lack of integrity) at the very top reflect something else. The civil service and political establishment reflect the best of Malays. Or viewed as such. Consequently, their shortcomings are viewed less as their personal failures, more as reflecting the cultural deficiencies of Malays. That makes me angry.

The AG justified his action "to remove any negative public perception of the prosecuting team." He did not address the substance of the allegation; he managed only the perception but ignored the reality.

Raja Petra Kamarudin (RPK) first made the explosive allegation in *Malaysia Today*. In a headline-blaring column titled, "The Bizarre Case of Sodomy 2," RPK, in his trademark style, named the specific prosecutor and rightly characterized the indiscretion as "a conflict of interest of the first degree."

The allegation appeared at the end of a long article and seemed more as an afterthought. You would have to read his entire piece to get at the stunning revelation. Those who gave up earlier would miss it. It was as if RPK was challenging his readers to be thorough and not be content with only the headlines and a few introductory paragraphs.

There was also a teasing coyness to the exposé; it was uncharacteristically brief. Beyond the mention of the name, there were no

---

[2] See following article, Chief Secretary Sidek's "Mother Hen" Folly

other details. It was as if RPK was laying a trap. Throw a teaser out, and then see those bastards falling all over themselves condemning him.

This time there was only silence. No hysterical accusations or righteous condemnations that RPK was purveying "half-truths," or as one novice politician put it, "only 40 percent facts and the rest made up."

My gut feeling is that RPK reveals way less than 40 percent of what he knows or has information on this evolving scandal. I had hoped that those UMNO jackasses would have resorted to their usual mouth-frothing denunciations of RPK. Then I could see him salivating like a lion that had successfully lured its prey to a trap where it could be pounced upon mercilessly.

Alas, no one walked into the trap. We have to be patient with RPK or hope that someone would aggravate him enough for him to reveal the sordid details, perhaps titillating snippets of the videotape of the amorous illicit encounter!

The Larger Issue

It took less than a week for Gani Patail to respond to RPK's revelation; unusually 'efficient.' This promptness, while laudatory, did not excuse his avoiding the heart of the matter–the truth to the allegation, if any. For if the allegation were other than the "only 40 percent facts," then the AG would have perpetrated a grave injustice on the young lawyer. Far from reassigning her, she should have been publicly exonerated, her integrity openly defended.

At the very least she should have been accorded due process. Even an accused murderer deserves that! The AG should be the last person to have to be reminded of this elementary legal tenet. Here we have the obscenity of the AG having a press conference first, with the poor prosecutor learning of her fate from the media. Simple decency demanded that the AG should have met with the alleged wayward lawyer first, to get her side of the story, and only then inform her of his decision.

If the allegation were true, then the AG has more than a serious disciplinary problem. There are the legal issues with respect to the Sodomy 2 trial. The alleged act was also criminal per *syaria*.

Gani Patail cannot abrogate his responsibility. It is not enough for him to simply declare, "... [A]ny personal matter, if it can have any implication in whatever form on the department, will be handled very seriously." He must demonstrate that.

If the allegation has substance, then the AG must remind himself that if she is not disciplined now, she would continue winding her way up the civil service. She could one day be a judge or even the AG!

I am not concerned here with the career trajectory of a young lawyer. Nor am I particularly perturbed at the ineptness of local top officials. I have seen enough examples elsewhere to put that in perspective. The Peter Principle (of being promoted beyond once competence) is after all universal.

I am concerned with the pattern of *tiada maruah* (lack of morality) leadership in the civil service and other essentially Malay entities for another reason. This being Malaysia, the racial element is never far from the public radar. Read the glut of bigoted comments on the social media and elsewhere to be painfully reminded of this ugly reality.

These *tiada maruah* Malays only feed this ugly stereotype. Of all people I would have expected them to be conscious of this, and thus make every effort to ensure that their behaviors would help tear down this unfair and ugly stereotype.

I am not in the least comforted by the fact that the Indian civil service is even more bloated and lumbering, or that the folks in Beijing are hideously more corrupt (note the recent scandal of tainted baby formulas) and disrespectful of basic human rights (witness their all too frequent summary executions). We are talking about Malaysia here, with her own rules, norms, and expectations.

The other communities too have their own peculiar blights. The scandals with MAIKA and Port Klang Free Zone Project are obscene reminders of that. To me that is neither an excuse nor consolation.

I feel for those honest, competent, and diligent public servants who are Malays. They give all they have but their good work is being overshadowed by these yahoos at the top. How did the likes of Gani Patail reach the top? Likewise, I keep wondering how such unimaginative, frankly corrupt, and not terribly competent people get to lead Malaysia. More importantly, why did we let them? The answers elude me.

We can only change the negative image of our community by changing the reality. Vote these corrupt and incompetent bastards out! Voting them in again would only encourage those sordid behaviors in them as well as others. That is exactly what has been happening. By repeatedly voting them in for the past 50 years, Malaysians are implicitly condoning if not encouraging their wayward ways.

By having capable political leaders, they will take care of the Napoleons in the public service, the little as well as the big ones. Meanwhile we must do everything we can to shame them. This essay is an exercise in that. Come the election, voters can punish them.

Those who love Malaysia, including those *Ketuanan Melayu* folks, would do well to undertake this urgent and critical mission of getting rid of these *tiada maruah* leaders and civil servants. Destroy the blight now or it will be the undoing of Malaysia.

Chief Secretary Sidek's "Mother Hen" Folly

July 25, 2010

Chief Secretary Sidek Hassan did not acquit himself honorably in so quickly defending federal civil servant Nik Ali Yunus in his very public and ugly squabble with Penang's Chief Minister Lim Eng Guan.

Sidek's swift reaction reflected more of a "mother hen" instinct of protecting its brood rather than the cool considered judgment of the head of an organization of professionals, as our civil servants would like us to believe them to be.

A state development officer (Nik Ali's designation) is far down in the federal civil service scheme of things, yet Sidek felt compelled to intervene. He did it in a rash and clumsy manner. At the very least he should have sought the views of both sides before rendering judgment. That would have been the mark of a true professional; it would also be the decent thing to do.

Sidek's quick reaction to this personnel crisis stands in sharp contrast to his lack of one to another far-from-exemplary behavior of a very senior civil servant. I refer to the utterance of Solicitor-General Yusof Zainal Abidin to the allegation that one of his lawyers was romantically involved with the key prosecution witness in Anwar Ibrahim's "Sodomy II" trial.

While not categorically denying the allegation, Yusof simply dismissed it, adding this astounding assertion, "What my team does in their own personal time is not my business. Usually, I don't check on their personal lives."

A Solicitor-General is high up on the totem pole of the civil service; only the most capable and senior would reach that lofty position. Yet we have this character failing to recognize the potential implications of a member of his team being romantically involved with a witness, especially a key one. To think that we have as Solicitor-General a lawyer who is unaware of the essence of professional ethics and elementary breaches of conflict of interest! This reflects poorly on the caliber of persons appointed to senior positions in the civil service.

Yusof's inept attempt at minimizing that lawyer's role in his prosecuting team was equally unprofessional. Yusof conveniently forgot that he was dealing with a lawyer, a professional in his department, not the office clerk. It does not matter whether that lawyer "was only brought in to help with taking notes, compiling data, evidence." A lawyer involved in such unethical activities ought to be disbarred regardless of where she works or what she does.

Lack of Professionalism at the Highest Levels

We have here two disturbing displays of less-than-exemplary behaviors if not outright lack of professionalism at the highest levels of the civil service. One is the Chief Secretary not hearing both sides to a dispute before rendering judgment, and the other, the Solicitor-General failing to recognize a serious breach of professional ethics in his staff.

Contrary to Solicitor-General Yusof's assertion, what civil servants do in private can and do have a major impact on the effectiveness of their official duties. If Malaysian top civil servants do not know this, as clearly demonstrated by Yusof's remarks, then Sidek has a monumental task ahead of him.

Back to the squabble in Penang; in defending the federal officer, Sidek chided Lim for being extreme in resorting to public criticisms of the officer. Sidek also asserted that there was nothing unprofessional for Nik Ali to retaliate openly by condemning the Chief Minister at an UMNO gathering.

Nik Ali was obviously ignorant of the internal channels available to him to express his dissatisfaction, hence his enlisting the help of a political party. With Sidek's rousing endorsement of Nik Ali's action, this could well prove to be the new and accepted way. I shudder to contemplate the consequences to the nation generally and the civil service specifically should that be the norm. Perhaps I am being naïve here for this may already be the set pattern; hence the sorry shape Malaysia is in.

For his part, Lim claimed that he had sought a private meeting with Sidek as far back as May to discuss the matter, but he (Sidek) cancelled it at the last minute. Had Sidek acted professionally, he would have realized that the request came not from an opposition politician but the chief executive of a major state. If Lim's assertion were true, then Sidek owes the public an explanation for spurning Lim. Sidek should have been more respectful of federal-state relationships.

It was incredible that Sidek did not find anything unusual or a breach of the civil service code for a federal officer to be addressing partisan party gatherings. His excuse was that he as Chief Secretary had to be present when Najib gave his speeches. Sidek could not differentiate between a political speech at a party gathering versus an official or policymaking one.

Sidek also failed to grasp the essential difference between Najib the Prime Minister and Najib the UMNO President. Yes, the Chief Secretary should be by the Prime Minister on official functions, but Sidek should not be seen or be in any way officially or unofficially associated with the President of UMNO. Sidek is a career civil servant, a professional and politically neutral. If he were a political appointee, that would be a different matter.

Sidek's incredulous assertion and crudely inappropriate behavior did not end there. As Chief Secretary, he manages matters to be discussed at cabinet meetings. That he saw fit to bring this to the highest level revealed Sidek's warped sense of priorities. I would have thought that the cabinet had other more pressing matters. It was pathetic to see both the Prime Minister and his deputy putting in their *dua-sen* (two-cent worth) comments on this lowly personnel matter.

As leader, a major part of Sidek's responsibility is to solve problems, not create them. He should also be able to anticipate them, and thus try to avoid or at least be ready. With the Penang issue, Sidek not only failed to solve it but he also aggravated it.

More deplorable, Sidek failed to anticipate the potential ugly racial undercurrent to this conflict. This is Malaysia and any conflict quickly acquires a racial hue unless intelligently and sensitively handled. Sidek's management of this crisis fails on both counts.

The outcome would have been far more favorable, and the nation spared a potentially destructive racial crisis, had Sidek been wise, restrained, and professional. In failing to have the earlier scheduled meeting with Lim, and not hearing both sides to the dispute between Lim and Nik Ali, Sidek flunked the most elementary test of leadership–nipping a problem in the bud, as well as being fair to all.

Now that different parties can be the governing as well as the opposition simultaneously at the federal and state levels, it behooves Sidek to provide guidelines on the proper relationship between civil servants and their political superiors.

Sidek must do this now, well before the next general elections. Failure to do so would risk Malaysia having to endure once again the ugly spectacle that was witnessed at Shah Alam following the last general elections when then Chief Minister Khir Toyo in cahoots with the state's top civil servants acted like a bunch of yahoos in destroying state's documents and properties with the change in political leadership. That was criminal. That they were not prosecuted again reflected the lack of professionalism in the Malaysian civil service.

While he is at it, Sidek should also draw up guidelines on how our diplomats abroad should handle visiting Malaysians, specifically lawmakers from other than the ruling party. These Malaysians should not be ignored, as is the current practice. They are Malaysian lawmakers regardless of their party affiliations. Our diplomats should learn from their British and American counterparts in Malaysia and see how they treat visiting Labor MPs and Republican members of Congress.

There was another unpleasant dimension to the Shah Alam spectacle of 2004. Selangor was not the only state that saw a change in political leadership; there was also Penang. Unlike Selangor, the transition in Penang was smooth and civilized. In the former, the change was between Khir Toyo and Khalid Ibrahim; the latter, Koh Tsu Koon and Lim Eng Guan. This being Malaysia, one cannot escape from drawing a racial conclusion to this difference. I am embarrassed to state this, but it is obvious though not talked openly in polite social discourse.

Sidek needs to scrutinize the performance of his top officers. He should not tolerate such inept and unprofessional conduct as displayed by the Solicitor General. That would be more productive than intervening in the problems of his junior officers.

Like his political superior Prime Minister Najib, Sidek talks endlessly of "transforming" the government. He would have a much greater chance of success if he were to first transform himself. Begin by quitting being the "mother hen" for his junior civil servants and start being professional.

Genuine Obsessions With Fake Qualifications

April 25, 2010

The kerfuffle over the college credentials of Kamalanathan *a/l* (anak/lelaki–son of) Pancanathan, the Barisan candidate in the recent Ulu Selangor by-election, reveals less of the man but more on the Malaysian fascination with paper qualifications. This obsession with credentialism is an intellectually lazy way to judge someone; you let those papers and certificates do it for you.

Who cares if you have a doctorate from Oxford, for if you cannot speak and read our national language then you have no business to be in Parliament or the state Assembly, where bills are debated and businesses conducted in Malay. You cannot possibly be effective if you are not fluent in Malaysia's national language.

At the same time with Malaysia inextricably linked with the greater world and English being the global language, legislators and others who presume to lead the nation should be equally facile in that language. Anything less and they would not be serving their clients honestly and honorably.

I do not expect average citizens, least of all potential political candidates, to appreciate or acknowledge this reality. I do expect party leaders, both in Barisan and Pakatan, to be sensitive to this and factor it heavily in their selection of candidates to represent their parties.

At one level it is amusing that Malaysians should still be obsessed with college degrees. With higher education now available to an increasingly larger segment of society, declaring that you are a college graduate would today elicit at best feigned interest, expressed in between yawns. The exception would be if you were to graduate from Oxbridge or an Ivy League. That might draw some attention, at least initially even in sophisticated circles.

If after a few minutes of conversation it turns out that your association with those august institutions was merely attending one of their *culup* ("quickie") courses that were open to all who could afford the exorbitant fees, then whatever impression you may have created initially would vanish. You need not reveal whether you are a genuine product or not, the content of your conversations would suffice. Less than a minute into Barack Obama's or Sarah Palin's speech and you could tell who came from an Ivy League and who is from the local community college.

Both Obama and Palin attract huge crowds with their captivating oratory. In deciding who to vote for, we should go beyond their academic pedigrees and flourishes of their speeches to seeing the clarity of their vision, weighing the substance of their ideas, and judging the effectiveness of their leadership.

At another level, despite the unabashed nationalism and pride in everything local as expressed in such jingoism as "Malaysia *boleh*!" (Malaysian can!) there is still this obsession with everything foreign, especially university parchment papers. Again here, that says more on the state of local universities than the regards Malaysians have of foreign ones.

I was not surprised that Kamalanathan could earn his Australian degree without ever setting foot on that continent, let alone on the campus. In these days of on-line courses and "distance learning," there is nothing unusual about that. If anything, those are significant improvements over the old correspondent courses and external degrees.

The more significant—and disturbing—revelation is this. Although he attended the local Olympia College (its academic director confirmed that) to get his Australian degree via "twinning," the college no longer has his academic records. I graduated over four decades ago, and I could still retrieve (if I am so inclined) from my alma mater my transcript, including my freshman English grades. Kamalanathan had his degree barely six years ago, and already his college has purged his records.

As mentioned, this controversy reveals more about local institutions than it does of foreign colleges.

Vetting Candidates

Higher education has not been spared the invasion and innovation of modern technology. At the criminal plane, with digital technology I could easily reproduce those impressive diplomas, complete with original signatures, intricate seals, and those fancy Latin phrases and dates. That makes it even more difficult to ascertain the veracity let alone quality behind those certificates.

At the legitimate level, modern technology has radically altered the manner of teaching and delivery of instructional materials. Today I can in the comfort of my living room listen to the same lectures given to those undergraduates at MIT. My continuing professional education is increasingly being delivered through "webinars," CDs, and other multimedia modules.

With the greater appreciation and subsequent growth of "non-traditional learning," the task of evaluating the quality of college credentials becomes even more complicated. The boundaries between blatant degree mills, virtual colleges, on-line courses, "external" degrees, and the traditional "board and mortar" campuses are becoming more difficult to ascertain.

In my profession where such decisions could have literally life and death consequences, we go beyond merely ascertaining the validity of those pieces of papers to directly contacting the issuing institutions and getting attestations on what those certificates signify. Failure to truthfully disclose could expose those institutions as well as their personnel to both civil and criminal liabilities.

The problem with Kamalanathan could have been resolved had a non-governmental organization concerned with the conduct of honest elections queried that Australian university on whether he was a legitimate student. The problem would not have arisen at all had Barisan leaders verified the matter before selecting him. Had those leaders institutionalized the practice, they would have been spared the embarrassment of picking a disbarred lawyer as their election candidate, as had happened recently.

This vetting of candidates is tough and tricky. Even when everything seems clear and legitimate, we could still have difficulty detecting fraudulent applicants.

I was on the selection committee to fill a senior position at our hospital recently. On perusing the resumes of the short-listed applicants, one stood out–impressive undergraduate degree from a leading university and a prestigious MBA. She also stood out in the interview; articulate and well informed. When my turn came, I congratulated her on her MBA and then innocently inquired whether she had taken any classes from a certain star professor at her school, and if so, could she share her experience. I must have hit something for she became flustered and began fanning her suddenly reddened face with her hand.

"I... I," she stuttered, "did not get my MBA from that Columbia!"

Her interview went rapidly downhill from there. At the end of the session, the committee went over her application carefully to see where we had slipped. There it was, her resume clearly stated, "1997–MBA (Columbia)," and she had duly submitted a copy of her diploma in which it was equally clear that her Columbia was not the one in New York City. The mistake was obviously ours, in making the leap in assumption after perusing only her resume.

The sad part was that her undergraduate degree and her experiences were impressive enough. That should have been sufficient for her to be the top choice. By needlessly embellishing her qualifications, she doomed her prospects. As can be further noted, this urge to inflate one's resume is not confined only to the academically unsophisticated.

Then there is the other end of the spectrum. A while back an accomplished young Malaysian returned home for an interview with a GLCs. He decided after the interview that he did not wish to risk his future to a company whose CEO could not tell the difference between the Stanford of Palo Alto and the local Stamford College.

I am less concerned with a two-bit politician trying to hoodwink simple villagers with his inflated resume. I am more perturbed that Malaysian leaders too could easily be taken in. Within UMNO alone, there are quite a few senior leaders including chief ministers sporting imposing titles like "Dr." They are not physicians, dentists, or veterinarians, because for those professionals there are statutes governing the use of that title so as not to confuse the public. Not so for those with other doctorates, legitimate or otherwise.

There are many foreign degree mills, with a few focusing on aspiring Malaysian politicians and corporate figures. The recipients are not even embarrassed; on the contrary they go out of their way to showcase their 'achievements' through paid self-congratulatory full-page advertisements in the local papers to celebrate their 'graduation.'

One UMNO leader publicly bragged about having a doctorate from Preston University. When he pronounced it, he made sure that it sounded like Princeton, the Ivy League university in New Jersey, the academic home of Einstein and other luminaries. Meanwhile Preston, whose mailing address is somewhere in the prairies, offered degrees based on your "life experiences." That 'university' has since left the Midwest after the state had a crackdown on diploma mills.

I would not have cared if this slimy character had managed to convince only the Mat Rempits and UMNO Putras of his pseudo academic prowess. Judging from the high praises he has been receiving from other top UMNO leaders, he had them duped too. That is the disturbing part.

Leaders To Bring Us Together

July 26, 2009

In having to appoint a Royal Commission of Inquiry to investigate the Malaysian Anti-Corruption Commission (MACC) following the death of one of its witnesses, Prime Minister Najib clearly demonstrated his lack of leadership and inability to be in command of a rapidly evolving crisis. Events forced Najib's hand; he was reacting, not leading.

Najib was not a leader, at least not the type that Malaysia desperately needs today. His meteoric rise in the party and government was less an expression of talent, more the gratitude his party had for his late father. For his part, Najib had not shown any indication that he had benefited from those splendid opportunities. On the contrary, like a spoiled child, those amenities merely indulged him.

It was unfortunate for Najib, but more so for the nation, that there were no 'training wheels' to the Prime Minister's office.

Najib's deputy Muhyiddin is in the same kampung league. Earlier, Muhyiddin dismissed calls for a royal commission, insisting that the police and the MACC were quite capable of undertaking the investigations. It reflected his low standing in the cabinet that many, including fellow UMNO Minister Rais Yatim, pointedly pushed for the setting up of the commission. Even the lowly UMNO Youth leader did not share Muhyiddin's faith in the police and MACC.

Consider a different scenario. If upon his return from his Middle East trip, Najib had summoned his Home Minister Hishammuddin and the Director of MACC for an immediate briefing. They of course would not be able to give a coherent explanation. Whereupon Najib would at a press conference announce his directing the MACC to put the involved officers on immediate administrative leave pending a full and independent investigation.

Had Najib done that, with his commanding baritone voice, he would have projected an image of a decisive leader who was on top of the situation. He would also put an immediate end to the current ugly spectacle of an unfortunate death degenerating into a polarizing political and increasingly racial issue.

As senior statesman Tengku Razaleigh noted, there have been too many deaths while under custody, and Teoh Beng Hock's demise marked a watershed in the attitude of the public towards the government, setting a new low. This essence was missed by many in the government.

The ordering of a coroner's inquest or Royal Commission should have been an executive decision. Najib did not need to involve his cabinet. The cabinet should be deliberating substantive issues, like how to make the economy competitive or reform the rotting education system.

Najib should have learned how his late father handled the national tragedy of the May 1969 race riot. Tun Razak stood in front of the cameras and in a solemn voice and serious demeanor announced the immediate imposition of martial law and a "shoot to kill" order for the police and military. He struck a reassuring and take-charge image, in stark contrast to the hapless weeping Tunku Abdul Rahman, who was the then Prime Minister.

The world may condemn Razak as a dictator or worse, but there was no disputing that he established law and order quickly. To put that in perspective, the modern flare up of sectarian violence in Northern Ireland began at about the same time as the Malaysian 1969 race riot. Today, while to most Malaysians that nightmare is but a dim distant memory, the folks in Northern Ireland are still busy settling old scores.

The evolving public furor over Teoh's death showed every sign of continuing its destructive downward spiral, fed by racist opportunists of all flavors and colorations, with Najib on the sideline reacting. A leader he was not.

What stunned me were not the responses of the bigoted and uneducated; their chauvinistic views were expected and perhaps excusable because of their ignorance. It would be too much to expect them to have a perspective beyond their clan or kampung. To them this crisis is nothing more than yet another ethnic Chinese Malaysian being victimized by Malay officialdom, or the belligerent Chinese not missing an opportunity to mock Malays.

What took me back instead were the responses of those 'educated' ministers and leaders. They just could not comprehend the public outrage over the MACC's interviewing a 'friendly' witness into the wee hours of the morning and who would later be found dead outside its premises. Perhaps those civil servants were trying to impress the public on how diligent and hardworking they were in attending to their duties! If that was how MACC's personnel treated their 'friendly and cooperative' witnesses, I shudder to think the reception a suspect would get.

Far from expressing condolences to the poor bereaved family, these ministers went on to impute evil motives on the victim and those who were outraged by the needless tragedy. How would these ministers feel if it was their son who had been victimized? Don't they have any empathy?

To their credit, Najib Razak and his Women's Affairs Minister Sharizat Jalil did convey their condolences to the deceased's family. The two were the exceptions. Najib was even thoughtful enough to send his personal representative to the funeral. The vulgar behaviors of the others, especially Muhyiddin, were eagerly picked up by the toadying commentators and columnists in the mainstream media, fueling the fire.

In seeking answers and justice to this cruel death, citizens should refrain from injecting additional unnecessary and divisive elements. The case was complicated enough; there was no need to inject or impute extraneous factors. As *The Star* columnist and Law Professor Azmi Sharom observed, people were angry over the needless death of a young Malaysian, not a young ethnic Chinese, and what they perceived as the abuse of power by MACC officers, not the abuse of power by Malay civil servants.

Malaysians should be mobilized to remedy this injustice. Malaysia is a democracy and public opinion matters. Thus far public outrage had caused the cabinet to set up the Royal Commission, but that should not be enough. Without continued public pressure, the commission's findings would suffer the same fate as befell the Police Commission and the one investigating the so-called Lingam Tape. Nothing happens. Continued public pressure would be needed to make the coroner's inquest and the Royal Commission be open and transparent, with their findings made readily available.

There is an art to mobilizing public opinion, and I am not attuned to its many subtleties. I do know that many share my disappointment that at one public rally over Teoh's death, most of the speakers were unable to convey their outrage in the Malaysian national language. Many were young and presumably born and raised in Malaysia, yet they were unable, unwilling or uncomfortable to speak in the national language. That was *not* the way to seek broad public support.

Likewise, I was similarly unimpressed with the rallying cry of HINDRAF, *Makkal sakthi* (People Power). That would be fine to gain public support in Kerala, India, but if it is fellow Malaysians you wish to influence, then you had better articulate your arguments in the national language. HINDRAF would have converted a few more to its cause had it substituted its slogan with *Kuasa Rakyat* (citizens' power). Elementary public relations!

Being a plural society, Malaysia faces many challenging and continuing centrifugal forces threatening to rip it apart. The nation needs leaders who must recognize this grim reality and then mobilize countervailing forces that would bring citizens together. Malaysia needs leaders who would view the nation's diversity not as a liability but an asset, and a valuable one at that.

Despite his much touted "1Malaysia" slogan, Najib Razak is not that kind of leader. Neither is his deputy Muhyiddin Yassin. Instead, the nation needs leaders the caliber of Tengku Razaleigh, Anwar Ibrahim, and Zaid Ibrahim. The challenge for Malaysia is to make sure that they prevail.

May There Be Many More Such Encounters!

March 29, 2009

I congratulate Ustaz Sheikh Mahmud for bringing Prime Minister Abdullah Badawi and Opposition Leader Anwar Ibrahim together recently for a luncheon honoring Prophet Muhammad's birthday. I also applaud Anwar and Abdullah for their very public display of civility towards each other on that occasion.

Along the same vein I am pleased to see on the last day of the UMNO General Assembly Tun Mahathir and Abdullah Badawi shaking hands. Despite the many harsh exchanges between them recently, at least they could still manage a brief show of courtesy. Supporters and commentators may read many things on that, but the fact they could bury their personal differences even if only momentarily is praiseworthy enough.

Such public gestures of cordiality and mutual respect are sadly lacking in Malaysian society today. As with everything else, that could only change with some very visible examples set by leaders. We can do without such obscene displays as when a supposedly "Honorable Member" called the Deputy Prime Minister a murderer in the hallowed hall of Parliament, or when the Minister of Education branded the leader of the Opposition "a traitor to Malays!" Splendid examples for local school children!

I wish academics as well as heads of NGOs, think tanks, and professional bodies would emulate Sheikh Mahmud. They too should bring together leaders of different persuasions to discuss issues that deeply affect Malaysians in settings other than the political arena.

Unnecessary Conspiracy Theories

It reflects the rarity of the event, as well as the volatility of the current political climate, that a social encounter between Anwar and Abdullah would raise eyebrows among local political observers. Otherwise perceptive and sensible commentators are reduced to concocting mysterious conspiracy theories purportedly to explain and interpret such a happening.

Relax and quit being suspicious or invoking conspiratorial tones lest citizens might discourage or frighten other leaders from taking similar initiatives. Even if Anwar and Abdullah had discussed nothing more than their host's *rendang* on that day, the fact that they had shared lunch together at the same table was enough. Anwar and Abdullah need not apologize for what they did. On the contrary they should thank their host publicly and profusely for that opportunity.

Anwar should not dismiss the meeting as mere "coincidence" as he did. Even if it were so, he should still make full use of the opportunity. Likewise, Abdullah should not pretend, as he too did, that Anwar "unexpectedly" dropped by. I know this is Malaysia where an invitation from a friend of a friend to visit another friend is valid enough!

Imagine if either Anwar or Abdullah were to have said something along this line: Someone from the Ustaz's office had approached me about the meeting and I readily agreed to it. To add some religious pizzazz to the response, make some references to the sunnah (practices) of the Holy Prophet to suit the occasion. The one that readily comes to mind would be the Prophet's offer to negotiate with the Meccan leaders that culminated with their signing the peace treaty at Hudaybiyyah. That spared a potentially bloody battle between the followers of the prophet and the then pagan Meccans.

If Anwar or Abdullah had responded thus to the many ensuing queries instead of trying to dismiss this important encounter, even if it was truly happenstance, imagine the valuable message of reconciliation and respect it would have sent to the citizens, especially their followers.

I am also pleased that Anwar had brought along his wife Azizzah. I wish that Abdullah too would have done the same. Spouses of leaders play a major role in moderating and supporting the views of their respective wives and husbands.

I am not in tune with the Malaysian social protocol but arriving after the Prime Minister or any special guest on any occasion is a definite "No! No!" However, Anwar had a ready explanation for his late arrival as he had to put up with some shenanigans at the courthouse.

Learning From Others

During the height of the American presidential election last year [2008], candidates Barack Obama and John McCain took time off from their hectic campaigns for a joint appearance at an annual charity event, the

Alfred E Smith Foundation Dinner, where they poked fun at each other, and shared the same dining table.

Likewise, former Presidents Bush, Sr., and Clinton, once fierce political competitors, were able to combine their considerable influence and prestige to head a charitable fund to help victims of the Asian Tsunami and Hurricane Katrina.

As Prime Minister in the 1950s and 60s, Tunku Abdul Rahman made it his practice to invite Members of Parliament and their spouses for a social evening of *joget* dancing at the Sri Perdana on the opening day of Parliament. The Tunku was a gracious host; he knew how to make his guests feel at home and have an enjoyable evening. Even parliamentarians from PAS felt at ease at such parties.

Such social interactions serve a useful purpose; they help smooth and cement relationships in other spheres. Such interactions are what enabled the late Tan Chee Koon, Malaysia's "Mr. Opposition," to be a trenchant critic of the government and yet earned the admiration of many, including government leaders.

It is not a surprise that the Selangor state government under Datuk Harun Idris, an UMNO ultra, gave Tan, a socialist and in the opposition, a land grant for him to build Sentosa Hospital. Such goodwill gestures across the political (as well as racial) divide are unimaginable today. Witness the current very ugly and public spat between Selangor Mentri Besar Khalid Ibrahim and his predecessor Khir Toyo. And they are both Malays! Imagine if they were of different races! As it is, you can bet that you would not find them at each other's "Open House" during Hari Raya.

Speaking of Hari Raya "Open House," it was commendable of Anwar to be at Abdullah's soon after he (Anwar) was released from prison. Alas, that was then. It seemed so long ago!

UMNO Youth used to organize an annual social golf tournament with its counterpart in Singapore's PAP Youth. To say that the political philosophies of UMNO and PAP are poles apart would be an understatement, yet their members were able to set those aside for an afternoon of friendly rivalry on the greens. If UMNO Youth could do this with PAP Youth, why not with PAS Pemuda? If those folks at PAS are not into golf, then why not try Quran reading sessions or *zikir barat* contest?

Instead we have that ugly scene of Hishammuddin calling Anwar Ibrahim a traitor. Even factoring in the highly partisan atmosphere of the recently concluded UMNO General Assembly, I still find that utterance offensive and unpardonable. And this character fancies himself leading UMNO and Malaysia some day!

I hope that new Prime Minister Najib Razak would reinstate the Tunku's practice of having a social gala at the "People's Palace" in Putrajaya on the opening day of Parliament so legislators and their spouses, as well as senior government officials, could get together for an evening of fun and relaxation. Surely those folks could put politics aside for the evening.

I would also like our future Prime Minister to make it his practice of meeting regularly with the leader of the opposition to discuss pending major legislations. That would help smooth out Parliament's operations.

It would be too much to expect Najib and Anwar to spend a quiet social evening together as President Reagan did with the Democratic Speaker of the House Tip O'Neill. It is not the place for Anwar to seek such regular meetings, but it would be the courteous and civilized thing for Najib as Prime Minster to initiate the gesture, just as President Reagan did with Speaker O'Neill.

There was something else remarkable and heartening about the Mawlud Nabi event at Ustaz Sheikh Mahmud Al-Mazjub's place, quite apart from the presence of both Anwar and Abdullah. The occasion was also graced by the presence of not only ulama from neighboring countries but also the head of the Buddhist Monastery in Bangkok.

I hope that leaders and Malaysians generally would learn something from this great alim, and that at the next national Mawlud Nabi event they should also invite the heads of other religious organizations in the country. Malaysians should go further and expect their leaders to visit each other's "Open House" during the festive seasons. Wouldn't that be wonderful! That would truly be a worthy legacy for this great *alim*.

Chief Secretary Sidek Should Not Behave Like A Chief Clerk

February 11, 2008

Judging from the gushing praises he is receiving, Chief Secretary Sidek Hassan is performing miracles with his Special Task Force to Facilitate Business (PEMUDAH, its Malay acronym) committee to streamline the civil service. A reality check is in order.

It reflects how out of touch Malaysian top civil servants are from the realities on the ground that it took Sidek and his Director-General of the Public Service Department, Ismail Adam, to make an unannounced visit to a District Office in Selangor for them to realize how difficult it is to pay one's "quit rent."

Then they were shocked to find that the District Officer was out of his office. Again, that reflects their naivety and ignorance of the current sorry state of the government machinery. These top civil servants put too much faith on the recent glowing report of IMD's World Competitive Yearbook that placed the Malaysian government ahead of Japan and Germany in terms of efficiency. The Malaysian public knows better.

It is pathetic that these top civil servants are reduced to being chief clerks checking on the *keranis* (junior clerks) to make sure that they are at their desks attending to their clients and customers.

Sidek's unannounced visit is now fast becoming a legend, of a meticulous and diligent top civil servant paying attention to the smallest of operational details. Even previously cynical commentators are now heaping praises on the man. This chorus of approval is repeated by the seasoned corporate figures co-opted into PEMUDAH.

If those corporate figures were impressed, then it does not say much of the crispness of their own management. Alternatively, they had such low expectations of the civil service that any improvement would impress them. My hunch is that their praises are nothing more than shrewd maneuverings to be on the good side of the government. In a country where the nexus between government and private sector is fuzzy, this is to be expected. It would not surprise me that their companies do substantial business with the government.

Interestingly, although Sidek had been interviewed umpteen times, no one asked what disciplinary actions (if any) he took against that errant District Officer and, more importantly, his immediate superior.

If the past is any guide, the poor underpaid *kerani* (lowly clerk) would bear the heaviest punishment, with the District Officer reassigned, and *his* immediate superior left untouched.

Misplaced Emphasis on Process Instead of Policy

PEMUDAH's emphasis has been exclusively on administrative processes. It reflects the deep rot that a simple procedure that would have been simple only a decade or two ago would today be tortuous and drawn out. Nonetheless that does not stop PEMUDAH from trumpeting its easy victories. These administrative details should have been streamlined at the mid management level; they are essentially staff work.

What Sidek should be doing is to teach those middle manages how to identify, analyze, and solve their problems. That would have been far more effective than surprise visits and issuing edicts from high above. Sidek could not possibly know the operational problems at the various land offices; the issues in rural Ulu Selangor are different from those of urban Petaling Jaya. With the latter's more educated clients, the civil service could introduce on-line payments, for example. That might not be possible in Ulu Selangor.

Back in the 1970s Tun Razak hired the American consultant Milton Esman to spruce up the civil service. Esman's personal accounts are highly illuminating. During his first meeting with top civil servants, he was confounded that they behaved like little school kids. Their attitude was: "You are the expert; you tell us what to do!"

At Treasury, he asked them their major issues. Their immediate response: "Overworked and understaffed!" They could also have added, "Underpaid!"

They complained of the volumes of vouchers they had to scrutinize. Esman suggested that they study the bills they had already processed and group them by their face value. To their surprise, a substantial portion of the vouchers that were under a certain amount were routinely paid without further auditing. Esman suggested if they were to henceforth make a policy that all such bills be routinely paid or better yet, authorize the various departments to pay them without referral to Treasury, their workload would be reduced considerably. They would then have extra time to scrutinize the details of the big-ticket bills. As for the smaller vouchers, do random checks (say one in ten) for quality control.

Through such exercises Esman taught those civil servants how to isolate and solve their problems. It was far more effective than lecturing and making surprise visits. Oh yes, and Esman did not spend his time giving press interviews!

On to a more substantive matter, by the time civil servants reach the top, certainly at the Secretary-General and Director-General levels, their concerns should not be staff, administrative, or operational details rather with policy analysis and policy making.

Consider the government's recent decision to restrict the sale of subsidized essential goods to non-Malaysians. Such policies should first be vetted by senior civil servants, addressing such issues as their practicality and cost of implementation. Does that mean that consumers must show their passports or identity cards when shopping? What about citizens buying for their non-citizen neighbors?

On another major issue, consider the graduate employment scheme. What are the social, economic, and other consequences for the government to be the employer of last resort? Egypt has such a policy; its civil service is the most bloated and inefficient while its universities remain unresponsive to the needs of the marketplace.

Back to Chief Secretary Sidek, he and his colleagues should be studying and recommending solutions to the cabinet on the impact of the current American credit crunch and impending recession, not checking the timecards of clerks in a district office in Ulu Selangor.

Ambrin Buang, Not Sidek Hassan, The True Hero

Sidek need not look far to find examples of excellence; he could find it within his own civil service, in the exemplary performance of Auditor-General Ambrin Buang.

Ambrin could have reduced himself to simply doing the traditional "bean counting" activities, of making sure that there are receipts for expenditures and other accounting minutiae. Make no mistake, those are essential details. The greater fallacy would be to assume that those are the only or even major duties of an auditor.

It reflects the diligence and professionalism of Ambrin that his Annual Report regularly grabs headlines. It also says much about our politicians and civil servants that they do not read those reports. Ambrin is not at all bashful in commenting on such boondoggles as the Sports Ministry's planned facility in London, as well as the RM50 screwdrivers.

Ambrin's report gives a far more accurate (and depressing) picture of the sorry state of the government machinery, far more realistic than that depicted by IMD Yearbook or PEMUDAH's too frequent glowing press releases. It also reveals much that Ambrin is *not* a member of PEMUDAH.

The reality for most public institutions is that they serve their own self-interests while attempting to put a public face to it.

Recent policy initiatives such as restricting the sale of subsidized items only to citizens and the graduate employment scheme serve nothing more than to expand an already bloated civil service. The currency among civil servants is the size of their respective departments as measured by the number of employees and budget allocations, not whether certain policies would ease poverty or improve the education system.

The wisdom and success of President Reagan and Prime Minister Margaret Thatcher was their recognition of this essential truism. The folly of the Abdullah Administration is its naivety in believing that what is good for the civil service is good for Malaysia and the citizens.

RCI On Lingam Tape: Boys Sent To Do Men's Job

February 11, 2008

Regardless of the outcome of the Royal Commission of Inquiry (RCI) on the "Lingam Videotape[3]," these public hearings have already given Malaysians a rare and instructive glimpse on the inner workings of their government at the highest levels, and of the caliber of the individuals entrusted in such positions.

---

[3] A surreptitious cellphone videotape of a lawyer caught bragging to the Chief Justice about the judges he (the lawyer) had in his bag!

This is also clearly demonstrated by the commissioners themselves. Their individual impressive credentials notwithstanding, they are merely boys sent to do men's jobs.

In forcing Prime Minister Abdullah to convene this Royal Commission, Anwar Ibrahim has done a great service to the nation. Malaysia owes a huge debt of gratitude to him, as well as to the son of that businessman Loh Mui Fah for having the foresight to tape that infamous conversation in the first place, and to the anonymous individual who gave that tape to Anwar.

The alternative media like *Malaysiakini* and *Malaysia Today* together with various bloggers and members of non-governmental entities helped ensure that the evolving scandal could not be ignored by the government. The mainstream media were, as usual, irrelevant. They not only missed this most important story but tried to dismiss it, at least initially.

Third World Proceedings

Not being at the trial, I missed the important dynamics, such as the demeanors and body language of the various participants.

A few years back I was a spectator at a medical malpractice trial in Malacca. The judge and lawyers looked impressive, the lawyers solemn in their black gowns, the judge wise if not owlish in his robe and wig. Unlike the Malaysian courtrooms of yore, this one was mercifully air-conditioned.

Alas only the appearance was First World. Once the trial proceeded, the Third World mentality and culture oozed out. There was for example, no court recorder, computers, or overhead projectors. As a result, the judge was reduced to scribbling furiously, barely paying attention to the witnesses and lawyers. No wonder Malaysian judges are notorious for their delinquent written judgments; they are busy being secretaries!

With no overhead projectors, valuable court time was wasted circulating important documents and exhibits. This RCI was no different.

In an inquiry of intense national interest, I would have expected the proceedings to be videotaped, and if not broadcasted live then at least posted on the website. Or at least the transcripts should be. Alas the Commission does not even have its own website.

Poor Staff Work

The Commission's poor staff work was evident. The commissioners and lawyers relied too much on official documents and mainstream media reports. In questioning former Chief Justice Eusoff Chin, no one bothered to present the damning evidence garnered through the investigative reporting of *Malaysiakini*.

If the Commission were a nefarious attempt to embarrass former Prime Minister Mahathir, now one of the Commission's key witnesses, then that too was a bumbling failure. The Commissioners were easily flummoxed by Tun's repeated "I-do-not-recall" responses. They were either incompetent or intimidated by Tun. The Tun easily dismissed them and their queries, and with a condescending smile to boot. They could not elicit anything substantive from the old man.

Those Commissioners forgot that no one was obligated to make their work easy.

The Tun reduced prosecutor Nordin Hassan to a bumbling first year law student in a moot court. Nordin would have gained more if he had asked general questions on the Tun's philosophy and mode of filling senior appointments instead of trying to force him to recall obscure details. If nothing else such queries would have revealed how we ended up with a sleepy head like Abdullah Badawi as Mahathir's successor as Prime Minister. It was naïve for the prosecutor to think that Mahathir could recall (or try hard to) specific letters written six or seven years ago.

The omissions were equally revealing. There was for example, no criminal investigation to the leaked official letters.

There were a few illuminating moments related to the proceedings. *The Star* dutifully published a photograph of seven members of the Malaysian Youth Secretariat carrying placards mocking Mahathir for his repeated memory lapses. This is the paper that did not see fit to print pictures of the recent massive BERSIH and HINDRAF rallies. What do you expect from editors who are only too eager to receive directives from the government?

Naïve Inquiry

It is an axiom among savvy lawyers never to ask witnesses questions they (the lawyers) do not know or anticipate the answers. This requires considerable legwork. If you anticipate "I do not recall" responses, you should avoid asking specific details and instead relate some favorable events the witness might have done or said at the material time. He would then be more likely if not eager to recall the details. Only after that would you sneak in questions on details of specific items. The witness would then appear sneaky if he or she were to claim loss of memory.

The Commission has considerable authority including the granting of immunity and prosecuting those who perjure themselves. It should have used that power to depose (get sworn statements) of minor witnesses like Lingam's brother and secretary, as well as the secretaries to Tun Mahathir and Eusoff Chin well ahead of the public hearings. In calling star witnesses like Eusoff China and Tun Mahathir prematurely, the Commission committed a major strategic blunder.

The Commission is now halfway through its public hearings. Like the earlier one on the police misconduct, this one too will prove to be an exercise in futility. Prime Minister Abdullah will, as usual, form yet another committee to "review" the findings, and within a short time, all would again be forgotten.

Nonetheless we have learned much on how senior governmental positions are filled and the caliber of those appointed. That should embolden us in cyber world, alternative media, and non-governmental organizations to continue holding those in authority accountable.

Sex And The Politician

January 6, 2008

Between the salacious reporting on and the holier-than-thou responses to the sexual escapades of former Health Minister Chua Soi Lek, three important points are overlooked. In a country where an intrusive government could as a law enforcement exercise barge into people's bedrooms (consider the many *khalwat* raids), these points bear pondering.

One, what if she (the Minister's alleged sex partner) had not been a "personal friend" (presumably Chua also has "non-personal friends") but a foreign intelligence agent, and he, somebody important, like the Minister of Defense? Rest assured then that she would be smooth and sophisticated; she would not let herself be blown to pieces or let the tape be released. It would be more valuable kept secret than be exposed, more useful as a blackmail tool than as an expose.

Two, what if my wife and I had stayed in that same room a few days immediately before, when those "technicians" were having their "practice" runs, or a few days later, when their voyeuristic lust is not yet satisfied? Those peeping toms could not blackmail us of course, but we would have still felt violated. The hotel would be liable, legally and morally, for the damages suffered by us just as surely as if the management had handed the duplicate keys to our room to known thugs.

Last is the lack of any sense of perspective. In this escapade two people had great fun, with one subsequently paying dearly with his career. No one was killed, or potentially killed, assuming they were not engaged in any exotic risky sex. Yet the police expended considerable resources on the case. Meanwhile the recent brutal sex slaying of a young Nurin Jazlin remained unsolved and forgotten.

An Old Reliable Tool

The use of pretty girls (and boys too!) to bring down the powerful is nothing new or particularly ingenious. Only the scene, theme, actors (and actresses) vary. When such acts are exposed, the end results are equally predictable. Not always, as much would depend on the prevailing norms and the personalities involved.

The American Central Intelligence Agency (CIA) had secret tapes of Sukarno cavorting with pretty blonds (yes, more than one at a time!), presumably on one of his many trips to Washington, DC. In the 1960s when he was lurching far to the left, the CIA discretely let loose those tapes in the cinema halls of Jakarta.

The hope was that those pious Indonesians would be so repulsed as to start a revolution to topple him. Imagine the horror of the embassy folks when the crowd instead cheered their local stud.

President Kennedy's fondness for pretty dames was well known and equally well tolerated if not catered to. Only when he strayed too far and shared his toys with the Mafia bosses were there dismay in the intelligence community.

To me the greatest threat to national security is not those sexual scandals that were exposed rather those that are still secret. They would then be a much more formidable weapon.

When Prime Minister Tunku Abdul Rahman signed that defense treaty with Britain following Malaysia's independence, was that his considered choice or one that was imposed upon him? As it turned out it was a fortuitous decision. It spared the nation from spending heavily on the military and instead used the funds on education.

It would have been easy for Britain to impose that defense treaty. During his student days there, the Tunku acquired a widely acknowledged taste for fine scotch. He also acquired the taste for some other finer British "things." Those could have been used to blackmail the man.

Whether Tunku's avowedly pro-Western stance was his personal conviction or otherwise, we will never know.

A college friend of mine was a fast-rising political star in a neighboring country. On a visit to France, he suddenly discovered the exquisite taste for French wine and other equally "fine" offerings that Paris had to offer. His country's leader became aware of the potential danger and brusquely put an end to the young man's political career.

The mark of a wise leader is how well he or she recognizes and thus avoids such a trap. In not demanding Chua's immediate resignation, Prime Minister Abdullah failed to grasp the threat to the nation of Chua's extracurricular adventures.

Lee Kuan Yew in his memoir wrote contemptuously of the many *joget* parties hosted by the Tunku where apparently hookers were readily available. I do not know whether Lee's indignation arose out of his moral conviction or the fear that he and his boys could be put in potentially compromising situations. He was wise to be wary.

Leaders like Sukarno and Kennedy were immune to sexual scandals because everyone knew and had long tolerated their weaknesses.

Incendiary Racial Component

This being Malaysia, the racial element is never far. Already there are ugly racial stereotype comments and videos posted in blogs and on Youtube. Those would have been pardonable if they were funny; but they were not; they were simply crude.

Speculations were that Chua was set up by his many rivals within his party jealous or fearful of his trajectory rise. I wish for the sake of Malaysia that that were true. If this seems a perversion, consider the alternative, that is, this is the scheming of others within the Barisan coalition, specifically UMNO, fearful of his forceful defense of Chinese causes.

If this were so, then I would say that those UMNO operatives were not very smart in releasing the tapes. I would have kept the video secret, and then would support him on his leadership drive. When he reached the top, then you would have full control of him, or stated crudely, you have him by the balls.

Returning to the Tunku, one of the inflammatory accusations leveled at him was that he was "too pro Chinese." The prevailing thinking then was that the rich Chinese were providing him the necessary cash for him to indulge his expensive drinking and other hobbies. They controlled him.

Strong Offense A Strong Defense

I commend Chua for coming out clean so quickly and for maintaining his poise in his press conference. He even displayed a fine sense of humor in inviting the reporters (presumably the females only) to view the tapes with him! A note of caution; be careful what you ask for!

Chua needs to do more. He should have hired the most skillful and vicious lawyer to sue the hotel for invasion of his privacy and breach of contract. When you rent a hotel room there is an implied contract that you are entitled to its private use. As those cameras were not portable, the managers should have known they were being installed and thus be held liable. I am assuming that Chua paid for the room. If the room and its "services" were free (meaning, paid for by someone else), then you get what you pay for.

Even if Chua were not to prevail in the lawsuit, at least he would have the satisfaction of forcing the management to spend money on its legal defense. It would have also encouraged others who were guests at the hotel, specifically those who had stayed in the same room, to join him in the lawsuit.

Chua could not possibly be further damaged by more revelations no matter how kinky. When you have some mud on you, that would be dirt; when you are totally covered, that would be a mud bath, and could be therapeutic. Then it would be those who touched you who would get soiled or smeared.

A vigorous offense is often the best defense. By suing, Chua could discourage future voyeuristic hotel operators from indulging their fantasies. That could only be good for the tourist industry. Who knows, it might even discourage the government, especially its religious authorities, from snooping around in private places.

No Glitter To Malaysia's 50th Golden Anniversary

December 30, 2007

By right, Malaysians should still be relishing the afterglow of their 50th Merdeka anniversary celebrations. Alas, the much-anticipated euphoria was short lived; the grim realities of Malaysian life soon intruded.

Even the mainstream media carry daily headlines of gory crimes. If those were not scary enough, residents now live in fear that their basic freedom is being threatened, not by some external enemy rather by their very own government. Malaysian leaders mistook their electoral mandate for a license to trample on citizens' basic rights, as in the right to free assembly and the freedom of conscience.

Those breaches, as expected, did not grab the headlines in the mainstream media; you would have to read the alternative media or international publications to get the real news. The mainstream media instead highlighted Prime Minister Abdullah's "small" wedding to his "downstairs lady."

The images of Malaysia projected onto the world stage towards the end of the year were not of a modern nation poised for Vision 2020, rather the typical backward Third World state with a stubbornly bumbling warden as its leader.

The scenes on Al Jazeera and CNN were of the police tear gassing and firing water cannons with abandon upon thousands of peaceful citizens who dared exercise their basic rights to a free assembly. If those images were not ugly enough, there was Minister of Information Zam in a fit of *latah* (echolalia) in front of the television cameras for the whole world to see and hear his sheer stupidity.

Zam was a poor imitation of Saddam Hussein's Information Minister "Comical Ali." At least Ali entertained us with his outlandish bravadoes; Zam nauseated us with his blabber.

Just as Malaysians thought it could not get worse, there was Deputy Internal Security Minister Johari Baharum declaring that only Muslims could use the word "Allah" (God). He threatened banning the Malay version of the Catholic Church publication that dared use that word.

The startling observation was that this moron of a minister could get away with such idiocies. By his silence, Abdullah revealed that he was equally moronic.

How did a nation that was so full of bubbly confidence as encapsulated in its *"Malaysia boleh!"* (Malaysia can!) spirit only a few years ago descend so fast and so low, and with so few protesting?

To be sure, Malaysia is still far ahead of Pakistan or Zimbabwe, at least thus far. It is unfortunate that far too many, especially the leaders, take comfort in that.

Annus Horribilis

Malaysians had premonitions for their long *annus horribilis*. It began ominously with the southern part of the peninsula being flooded and hundreds of thousands displaced. It was the worst flooding in decades.

Where was Prime Minister Abdullah in his nation's hour of need? Off to Australia for his scheduled sailing vacation and the opening of his brother's *nasi kandar* restaurant! His "bright" young advisors did not see fit to advise their man to cancel his vacation in the face of a national emergency. The old man was of course clueless and oblivious.

The floods soon receded, and the residents went back to their daily grind, helped by many generous fellow citizens and non-governmental bodies. When you see your fellow Malaysians in need, you pitch in. That should come way ahead of your holidays. You cannot teach these simple human precepts, not even to an Oxford graduate. You either have that sense of human decency or you do not. It was fortunate that many Malaysians have it while their leaders do not.

Allah (permit me to use that word here) was trying to impart some important lessons on Malaysian leaders for a few months later there was yet another massive paralyzing flood, this time in the heart of Kuala Lumpur.

As for that Australian grease spot whose opening was graced by the Prime Minister, it closed soon after.

Horrible In Between

Between the terrible beginning and the horrible ending to the year, there were plenty of hideous fillers.

The tenures of the Director of the Anti-Corruption Agency Zulkipli Mat Nor and Chief Justice Ahmad Feiruz were not renewed. Both left under a cloud. That should have been a feather in Abdullah's cap, except that Abdullah was intent on keeping them both! Only unrelenting public pressures forced him to back off. Abdullah may not have wanted the people to challenge him, but they did anyway.

Ahmad Feiruz was the "off stage" star attraction later in the year in the infamous "Lingam tape." You would not find that in the headlines of the mainstream media. Thanks to former Deputy Prime Minister Anwar Ibrahim, we had a sniff of the filth that was (and still is) the Malaysian judiciary.

Weakened by his endless displays of ineptitude, Abdullah was in no position to brave public opposition. A few weeks after the Johore floods, Raja Petra Kamarudin's *Malaysia-Today* carried a detailed expose of the Prime Minister acquiring a luxurious corporate jet, at public expense of course. Raja Petra had the details nailed, down to the jet's tail number.

Malaysia-Today's phenomenal success is the one rare bright spot. No wonder *World Business* named Raja Petra, together with Bank Negara's Governor Zeti Aziz and former Prime Minister Mahathir among Asia's Top 20 Progressives. Meanwhile *Tokoh Wartawan Negara* (National Journalism Award winner) Zam remains a *jagoh kampung* (village champion). He and those who honor him belong there.

Raja Petra made other headlines. The police had questioned him and his wife Marina separately over some activities purported to be harmful to the state. Presumably one of those could be his release of the sordid details of the messy divorce settlement of one "double Muhammad," a senior UMNO operative. Raja Petra went further; he challenged this double Muhammad to a public debate to expose this discredited politician, but the latter chickened out.

The police interrogations of RPK and his wife went nowhere; they were flummoxed. Marina refused to answer questions claiming that as a Muslim she is entitled to have her husband present beside her. The privilege of being a Muslim in Malaysia!

Lina Joy did not think so. Her celebrated case, a simple and routine administrative matter of changing the religious designation on her identity card, attracted worldwide attention when Malaysia's top court ruled that, the norms of civilized society notwithstanding, there is no freedom of conscience in the country. Malaysians cannot change their religion on a whim, according to the wisdom of Chief Justice Ahmad Feiruz.

Pursuing this theme, the religious authorities in Perak charged a young Malay mother for "encouraging immoral activities" while singing in her sleeveless blouse in a nightclub.

Pursuing the moronic theme again, some well-meaning supporters ("arse lickers," Raja Petra's inelegant term would be more appropriate) of Abdullah nominated his late wife Endon as *Anak Gemilang Malaysia* (Illustrious Daughter of Malaysia). Mercifully, they withdrew her name, but not before some very unkind jabs by bloggers. I do not blame the poor lady for being made the butt of jokes. Instead I would rap the knuckles of those idiots who set her up.

I was uncertain which was more idiotic, that or the hysterical reactions among the leaders to a student's sophomoric rap rendition of *Negara Ku* (the national anthem), or that character Mat Zakaria Derus and his mansion built amidst the slums of Klang.

The annual Auditor-General's Report too made headlines, again! There was the Port Klang Free Zone development project debacle that cost a hefty RM4.2 billion, and the equally lavish Sports Ministry's spending sprees. The list goes on.

I am certain that the theme will be repeated next year; only the players, projects, and price tags would vary. At least Malaysians can be comforted by the fact that those boondoggles still make the headlines. The day may come when they would not, and that would be a tragedy. With Abdullah in charge, that day might not be far off.

UMNO Is The Problem

Reformasi UMNO (I)– Why The Party Must Be Reformed

May 13, 2018 (*First of Two Parts*)

UMNO was severely mauled in the recent [May 2018] 14th General Election. The wounds it suffered could prove fatal. Nonetheless with some skillful interventions by its more enlightened leaders and an abundance of patience, the party could recover and be rehabilitated to emerge stronger, wiser, and more effective. That would serve not only its members but also other Malaysians and thus the nation.

There is also the other possibility. It could be permanently scarred and crippled, reduced to a laughingstock as its members forever demand their dues from others as a matter of privilege based on the party's claim of having brought independence to the country. The party would mock its slogan of "UMNO being Malay and Malay, UMNO," perverting it into the very antithesis of its noble original intent. Such a fate would be far worse that if the party were to just fold and disappear.

The future of UMNO is not divinely ordained. Its fate depends less on prayers, more on the collective actions and wisdom of its leaders as well as members. The signs thus far are not encouraging, despite its president Najib "taking responsibility" for the electoral debacle by resigning.

Its electoral defeat notwithstanding, the fact remains that UMNO remains the party with the largest number of seats in Parliament. Yet its members behave as if they are in a fast sinking ship, bailing out fast, not wanting to be the last sucked in under the waves.

There are many compelling reasons for reforming and thus saving UMNO. For Malays and Malaysia, the party is iconic. Its motto, *Bangsa, Agama, Negara!* (Race, Faith, Country) is no empty slogan. UMNO was the first force to wake Malays up and made us emerge from our slumber of parochialism and feudal insularity. Before UMNO, Malays thought themselves only as subjects of their local chieftains and sultans. Malays still harbor much of that residuum of localism and feudalism.

On a more sentimental level, UMNO is the rare if not only Malay entity that has proven itself that it could survive more than a few years beyond its showy opening ceremonies. Most Malay organizations have the lifespan of fireflies. Peruse the records at the Registrar of Companies and Societies. They are filled with volumes of titles of Malay organizations that now exist only in those stacks. Many have fanciful names and noble objectives. The only thing they lack is durability.

Not UMNO. Many Malays trace their UMNO membership through generations.

For Malaysians, there is another beyond sentimental reason to save the party and restore it to its original vigor. It is the party that spearheaded and then successfully negotiated for the peaceful independence of the country. That ought to count for something. Many others too had the same aspiration and tried, peacefully and otherwise. The central and key point remains. It was UMNO and its brother parties in the old Alliance that succeeded. In the final analysis, that is what counts, not the what-might-have-been or I too had tried.

A more practical reason to save UMNO is that Malaysia—indeed any democratic system worth its name—needs a strong viable opposition, one capable of taking over the government at any time. I do not see any other party outside the winning coalition that had survived the shellacking of GE-14 let alone be ready to govern. MCA and MIC are just about dead. GERAKAN is already there. PAS is too busy reciting the Koran and hadith. Those other parties in Sabah and Sarawak have not bothered to even think of spreading their influence in the peninsula, that is, when they are not consumed squabbling with each other.

Thus far current UMNO leaders have not proven themselves or shown any indication that they are up to the difficult task of reforming the party. That is unfortunate and sad. Consider the party's 72nd Anniversary held a few days following the debacle of GE-14. It looked less like a birthday celebration, more a funeral. There were no inspiring speeches from the leaders to rally and inspire the troops after the humiliation they had just endured. Instead they resorted to a collective reciting of Surah Yaseen, the traditional last rites and funeral ritual for Muslims. I am uncertain whether the symbolism escaped the participants.

Or it could well be that they were all aware of the straits they were in and that the occasion was not celebratory, rather the dispensing of last rites, if not the actual burial of the party.

It is not enough for party president Najib Razak to resign, though that was a necessary first step. *All* his enablers in the party should also follow suit. That would include the party's deputy and vice presidents, the heads of all three wings (Youth, Women, and Princess), as well as all members of its governing and policy-making Supreme Council. They *all* contributed to and are responsible for the party's shellacking. Najib was not smart or charismatic enough to get things done his way without the explicit approval if not encouragement of these others—his enablers.

While they all too should have resigned with Najib, they must stay in their posts until the new team takes over. Meaning, they have a responsibility to call for the party's General Assembly as soon as possible to ensure a smooth transition. It would be irresponsible for Najib or any other leaders to just walk away.

As I see things developing now, the same old, tired characters of Zahid, Hishamuddin, Mat Hassan, and Khairy are all angling for the top leadership. They have not yet even acknowledged their responsibilities for the debacle. They should have the grace to withdraw from consideration for the new leadership. They too should take the blame and then get out along with their president. They did not; grace and class are the very qualities so lacking among its leaders. That's UMNO's fatal weakness.

Reformasi UMNO (II) –Decoupling Party Positions From Governmental Appointments

May 20, 2018 (*Second of Two Parts*)
In the 1999 Tenth General Election, UMNO lost many seats and its Barisan Nasional coalition reduced to a simple majority. Najib Razak, then widely touted to succeed Mahathir, squeaked through with the slimmest majority, thanks to the late arrival of "postal votes" in his constituency.

Contrary to the belief of many, the mysterious and late arrival of ballot boxes is not a recent phenomenon. It started long ago during Mahathir's first tenure when he led Barisan. In the current [2018] euphoria over Mahathir's *defeating* Barisan, it is good to be reminded of that fact.

Back in 1999 just before the election, I wrote in my *The Malay Dilemma Revisited: Race Dynamics In Modern Malaysia* that only Mahathir had the skills, courage, and personality to undertake the much-needed radical changes in UMNO. The party needed major revitalization even then.

No one then (or now) in UMNO leadership came anywhere close to Mahathir in political acumen and organizational skills. Today there are plenty of pretenders–Mahathir wannabes–like that showy "Brigadier-General" Khairy Jamaluddin. A genuine general would have committed *hara-kiri* after letting his troops down. Apologies alone would not do it.

Reading again now what I wrote then about Mahathir, I ponder the irony that by being out of UMNO, as with his voluntary resignation in 2003, he forced the most profound changes in his old party, far more radical than he could have achieved while in power. To be sure those were regressive changes resulting in the party's defeat a decade and a half later.

I had suggested then that UMNO's top priority was to remove the "no-contest" directive for the party's top two slots. That regressive move was put in by–who else–Mahathir, to reduce "undue politicking," or so he claimed. Human nature being what it is, that rule merely moved those maneuverings underground and generated even more dangerous rifts.

As Mahathir was then anticipated to retire soon, that would have been a good time to do away with that stricture. Alas that was not to be. As a result, UMNO and Malaysia were blighted by the inept leaderships of Abdullah and Najib. Being weak, both found that provision a convenient if not necessary crutch.

I had also suggested then a revamp of UMNO's Supreme Council. While it is true that the party president could not control who gets *voted* into that body, he does have the considerable power to appoint up to 15 members to complement the 25 elected ones, over a third of the body. That is substantial and reflects the power of the party's president. Mahathir could have used that route to recruit new talent into the party's upper echelons, a technique Tun Razak had used with great effectiveness. Instead, Mahathir selected the flunkies.

As for his successor, I had suggested that Mahathir buck tradition and pick someone from other than his three sitting vice-presidents. All three were duds. He had already fired his capable Deputy President, Anwar Ibrahim. Mahathir should have scouted the field much wider in search for a potential successor. Had he not picked Abdullah and Najib, the party would have been spared the current humiliation. The past precious decade and a half would also not have been wasted, and Malaysia would not have been saddled with a trillion-*ringgit* debt.

Mahathir also failed to address the core problem of corruption (euphemistically referred to as "money politics") in his party. As UMNO was then the ruling party, corruption in UMNO meant corruption in government. It is corruption, specifically of 1MDB, that brought Najib and UMNO down in the 2018 election.

One initiative I had proposed back in 1999 was to decouple party positions from governmental appointments. That is, once you are appointed to a government position, whether as Prime Minister or the local dog catcher, then you would have to give up your party position. That meant the Prime Minister would no longer be party president and the Deputy Prime Minister, deputy president.

It is tough enough being a cabinet minister without also being UMNO treasurer. Such decoupling would also dilute and diffuse power, creating some semblance of a system of checks and balances. Both are sorely lacking in UMNO (as well as in the government). Najib was Party President as well as Prime Minister and Finance Minister. Bad things happen with the concentration of power, quite apart from the fact that you could not possibly commit 100 percent of your time and effort to any one position.

A perennial divisive issue in UMNO (as well as the other parties) is selecting attractive candidates for the general elections. The current process is opaque and encourages local "war-lordism." Worse, the process does not attract fresh capable faces.

Back in 1999 I also suggested that the local divisions nominate four or five viable candidates, listing them in order of preference, and then have the central committee select one together with an alternate from that list, and only from that list. Such a mechanism would accommodate both local input and a central quality-control mechanism. It would also discourage or dilute the influence of "money politics" as you would have to bribe both the local decision makers as well as the distant central ones. A more difficult proposition.

A major problem for UMNO is that it no longer attracts talented Malays, especially young professionals. Those who join the party do so to spearhead their otherwise lackluster careers. The not-so-terribly smart lawyers on becoming UMNO members get a crack at some high-profile cases and contracts. Accountants who could not attract private clients become chairman of a GLC. Likewise, academics who have published nothing original except their theses, upon joining UMNO are catapulted to the Dean's or Vice Chancellor's office. No surprise that genuine entrepreneurs, professionals, and scholars shun UMNO.

A major obstacle to young successful Malay professionals joining UMNO is that they do not wish to waste their precious time working their way up the party's entrenched hierarchy. They are busy with their careers. To overcome that I suggested having a central admission pathway so they could bypass the parochial and ever-jealous local divisional chiefs.

The responses of UMNO leaders thus far to their recent [2018] debacle have not been encouraging. Najib resigned immediately. That was the right decision, but he should have stayed on at least until the party had had its new leadership elected by the members in an open leadership convention.

For his part, Acting President Zahid, with the backing of his fellow Supreme Council members, was scheming to join the ruling coalition, however improbable or laughable a proposition that was. Vice-President Hishammuddin was silent, nodding to whatever Zahid (and Najib earlier) had said. Women's leader Shahrizat mumbled about a post-mortem. Youth leader Khairy emphasized stabilizing the membership (thus inadvertently revealing that many are contemplating bolting), and on being a good opposition party. He also talked about "collective responsibility." Had he really believed in that and acted on it, he too would have joined Najib in resigning. As for the Puteri division head, she remained demure, like an ornamental princess.

In short, I see nothing that would lead me to believe that UMNO leaders are ready, willing, or able to undertake the much-needed radical changes. Meaning, UMNO's implosion has just begun.

The 14th Malaysian General Elections

He's Back! A Monumental Task Awaits Mahathir

May 9, 2018

While most Malays half his age are obsessed with attending mosques and consumed with pondering their fate in the Hereafter, Mahathir was in his elements campaigning. It was not so much a campaign as a mission to save his nation. And he did, with the messianic zeal of a man driven.

The results showed. Malaysia got rid of her corrupt and incompetent leader Najib Razak, the US Department of Justice's "Malaysian Official 1" who had been plundering the nation and corrupting her values. Mahathir decapitated UMNO. Najib did not even have the dignity to address his UMNO members on election night. No class; the Bugis *lanun* (pirate) in him showing.

Mahathir personifies the true Islam. He acts on the central Koranic injunction *Amal ma'ruf, nahi mungkar* (Command good; forbid evil). In getting rid of Najib and his gang of plunderers, Mahathir forbids evil from gripping his country. In galvanizing Malaysians to vote their conscience and without fear, Mahathir commanded them to do good.

Mahathir is a better representative of Islam than those Koran-thumping, hadith-quoting bearded ulama in their overflowing robes, jungle Arab-wannabes.

At 92, Mahathir could not afford to revel in his victory. He has a monumental task ahead and precious little time to execute it. The last decade and a half have been more than just a colossal waste. The country has slipped further downhill and is now hopelessly corrupt, heavily indebted, and her institutions corroded. Most of all her values have been perverted. Bribes from the Arabs are now regarded as *borkat* (divine gifts) from the holy land of the prophet, if not Almighty himself.

During the campaign Mahathir pledged to punish those responsible for 1MDB, targeting Najib in particular. That should remain Mahathir's top priority. Unless Najib is punished, and punished hard, others following including those in Mahathir's own new team would be tempted to follow up that crooked path.

Mahathir should also focus on two other objectives: developing future leaders with the associated orderly, predictable succession plan and rebuilding ravaged institutions. The two go hand in hand. Let others run the country. He is fortunate in having many young and capable members elected with him. Learn from his earlier fiascos of picking duds like Abdullah, Najib, and others. Do not pick a third one.

Mahathir's campaign promise of a royal commission on 1MDB would be too slow and cumbersome. A better and swifter route would be to appoint a special prosecutor who could file charges as soon as there is enough evidence, instead of having to wait for the final Royal Commission Report which could be months or years later.

As an immediate step the special prosecutor should impound the passports of all those involved, including and especially MO1, as well as its former and present directors and CEOs. As Najib's cabinet was or should have been involved with 1MDB's decisions, Malaysia being a cabinet government and thus with collective responsibility, I would also impound their passports.

The special prosecutor should pick the best forensic accountants and most aggressive litigators. Such talents are rare in the Malaysian public sector, so give the special prosecutor leeway in hiring from abroad if need be. Besides, Malaysians are so polarized now that it would be difficult to get someone local who would be viewed as impartial.

Malaysia should co-operate with USDOJ and seek separate legal representations in the current American suit. There are plenty of American lawyers who have been following the case closely. Choose one of them to be Malaysia's counsel. That would be expensive but even more so if Malaysia were not to be legally represented.

The best candidate for that special prosecutor would be former Attorney-General Gani Patail as he already has considerable background knowledge. It was rumored that he had prepared the arrest papers for Najib a few years back, the reason he was fired.

The 1MDB mess should also prompt Mahathir to reassess the whole concept of GLCs. They are now nothing but conduits for political corruption. Sell them all! Focus on building institutions not companies. Leave that to enterprising individuals.

Two things are clear with the corrosion of Malaysian institutions. First, that started during Mahathir's time. To his credit he has owned up to his responsibility. Najib and Abdullah on the other hand, have taken the destruction to a whole new low level.

Mahathir should focus on two critical institutions—the police and Anti-Corruption Agency (ACA). Do not fire their current chiefs, instead let them stay on and select a new number two with the clear understanding that he would investigate his superior as well as all other senior officers. As Malaysians have been so polarized it is unlikely that you could get a local candidate who would be viewed as nonpartisan. Recruit from abroad if need be. Besides, a local second in command by culture would hesitate to investigate his superior.

The functions of the new de facto chiefs would be to investigate the current top officers for possible criminal conduct and prosecute them. If found guilty they would then lose their pensions. That would serve justice better than just firing them or letting them resign. The other equally critical function is to nurture talent within their departments.

If the police and ACA are efficient and trustworthy, the whole government machinery would be clean.

The police and ACA should troll the Internet for those videos where cold cash had been distributed openly during the campaign. Identify the perpetrators and use them on threat of prosecution to "flip" their *kakis* (superiors) who supplied them with all that cash. In addition, scrutinize the bank statutes to see whether banks should report those who made large cash withdrawals weeks before the election. That should lead to many fruitful trails.

As for nurturing talents, Mahathir had picked many duds before. In addition to spectacular ones like Abdullah and Najib, there are the Shahrizat Jalils, Tajuddin Ramlis, and hosts of others. Mahathir had groomed some stars, like Daim Dzainuddin, Rafidah Aziz, Vincent Tan, and former Petronas Chief Hassan Merican. Why not tap their skills and have them screen and evaluate potential new candidates for the new team?

Beyond the police and ACA, other key institutions Mahathir should focus on are schools and universities. Make them the pride of Malaysia, not skyscrapers, companies, or palaces. Make teachers the respected profession and first choice career among our brightest, as in the past.

Allah has been gracious and generous to Mahathir in giving him a chance to rectify his errors. I am gratified with his immediate post-victory statement of seeking a pardon for Anwar and bringing him into the administration. Much has flowed under the bridge between those two; there is little need and even much less value in going over that. Instead the pair should focus on developing the next generation of leaders and in guiding Malaysia's historic first female Prime Minister. I wish both Anwar and Mahathir much success. The nation owes much to both, and they in turn to the nation.

Pondering The Possible Outcome Of The 14ᵗʰ General Election

May 7, 2018

By Thursday morning May 10, 2018, the outcome of the 14th Malaysian General Elections would be clear. Or perhaps not. This being Malaysia, count on "power failure" or last-minute arrivals of "postal" and "absentee" ballots at many counting stations, or worse.

Dispensing with those and other infinite possibilities that could mar and interfere with the final tallying, the results of this election could be placed along a spectrum of expectations. At one end would be the supreme sweetness of a supra-majority win by the Mahathir-led coalition. The other would be the nightmarish scenario where neither Mahathir's coalition nor Najib's Barisan wins a clear majority, prompting Najib to have his UMNO party join PAS to form a Malay-only government over the objection of his Barisan's non-Malay partners. In effect Najib would destroy Barisan in order to retain power even with a shaky and narrow communal majority.

The outcome of this election would probably fall somewhere in between. The closer the outcome is to the first scenario, the better it would be for Malaysia. I would put a clear Barisan victory, though unlikely, closer to the other pole in terms of its effect on the nation. In fact, that would a total disaster for Malaysia. Najib and his band of crooks would take that as a license to continue their plundering of the country. Malaysia cannot afford that.

Back to the first possibility, the only other ingredient that would add to the sweetness of the victory would be for UMNO to lose a few more states, including in particular historically-significant Johor where the party was started, and PAS to be kicked out of Kelantan, the only state it had governed before the election. Then even if Najib were to be defeated in his own Pekan constituency, that would not add anything to the already sweet victory for the country.

By imagining the consequences should the election outcome be at one end or the other of expectations, we could then contemplate and be prepared for when the results fall somewhere in between, as they most likely would be.

With Mahathir's overwhelming victory there would be much jostling for power among members of his erstwhile fractious component parties. After all, the coalition is very recent, being formed just before the election. Mahathir had been through this many times before with his old Barisan, so he should be able to handle this minor crisis with ease, tact, and aplomb. Just reminding them where they were before he joined them would inject a much-needed sobriety and sanity among the most ambitious and rambunctious members.

Some minor crises with respect to key ministerial appointments and other plump positions are to be expected. The good news is that with the exodus of those sympathetic to the previous regime, there would be plenty of jobs for those not getting ministerial posts. Remember, there is always the Ambassadorship to Timbuktu.

I do not expect Mahathir to have difficulty keeping his over enthusiastic team members in line. He also has the luxury of an abundance of talent, which he did not have when he was with UMNO and Barisan. Someone made a tally on the number of PhDs from excellent universities in his coalition in contrast to those with degrees from Preston in UMNO; it was impressive!

Mahathir should focus on his central campaign promise, to hold accountable those responsible for the 1MDB mess, specifically Malaysian Official 1. Impounding his passport should be the first critical step!

Now to the other extreme of possible election outcomes where no party or coalition would win an outright majority. That would prompt Najib and Hadi (of PAS) to join forces. The two and their followers have often hinted at such an outcome during the campaign. The obscenity of that political consummation would assault the collective Malaysian sensibilities. The two would play hard on overt communal sentiments, one using the overtly racist slogan of *Ketuanan Melayu*, the other exploiting the simplistic "Islam is the Answer" caliphate call. Both are potent sentiments, and both would be very distracting as well as destructive.

Najib would have little qualms throwing the non-UMNO members of his coalition under the bus. That would give him immense perverse pleasure. Remember his infamous "What more do the Chinese want?" after his shellacking at the 2013 elections?

More ominous is that there would be more than a few in Mahathir's own new coalition who would not be able to resist the seduction of that powerful chauvinistic siren song. That would only embolden Najib's dark instincts and those sinister forces aligned with him.

That is the one critical reason to hope for the first outcome. With Mahathir's overwhelming victory, the inevitable crossing-over of a few would not jeopardize his coalition. More to the point, Najib would not even try and few would be tempted.

Just this simple mental exercise of contemplating the two extreme possible outcomes for GE14 should guide voters as to which party to vote for. The choice is clear. Give Mahathir and his team an overwhelming victory this Wednesday, May 9, 2018.

The Shifting Political Wind

May 5, 2018

In the animal world, once you are perceived as being weak or desperate, your predator would pounce on you fast and without mercy. This is also true if not more so in the animalistic world of politics.

Najib's political desperation was evident long before he dissolved Parliament. There was the fast passage of the Fake News Act, the blatant and obscene gerrymandering exercises, and last but most despicable of all, his making the police and armed services chiefs pledge allegiance to him instead of king and country, as they were sworn to do upon taking office.

Najib hoped that those silly antics would strengthen his position ahead of the election.

Najib's low was on nomination day when Mahathir could not fly to Langkawi to file his papers. His pilot said that the plane was not safe. Mahathir charged sabotage. Najib did not factor in the kindness of others, or that he could not control everyone and everything. Mahathir found another plane. That sabotage attempt was not only pathetic but also dangerous. We are talking about lives being endangered here, that of the pilot and his passengers.

Najib threatened to charge Mahathir under the new Fake News Act. Mahathir ignored him and kept repeating the serious charge. Najib's threat was but an empty one, his impotence exposed for all to see. Or may be that Mahathir's charge of sabotage was not fake news after all.

The top military commander also retracted his earlier misplaced allegiance to Najib after Mahathir sent him and his fellow commanders an open letter reminding them of their oath of office. A few days later the naval chief issued an unprecedented command to his sailors. They were free to vote for whichever candidate and party they choose. He assured them that their votes would remain secret. He was widely lauded for his brave action.

Brave is not too a strong a word here. After all this is Malaysia. The fact that he had to issue that command in the first place speaks volumes of the country's democratic processes. The police chief too followed suit and issued a similar statement.

Mahathir's open letter was more powerful than whatever Prime Minister Najib may have said earlier to his police and military chiefs. Or those chiefs had put their wet fingers in the air and felt that the wind was changing direction.

Najib's most comical act of desperation was having his Elections Commission (EC) issue a directive to tear down Mahathir's pictures on election billboards! It was a sorry sight to have those otherwise unemployable young Malays in their EC uniforms climbing the scaffoldings to tear down those giant posters. In the end, unable to complete their task fast enough, they resorted to just cutting out Mahathir's face. Then still not fast enough, they just pasted on blank sheets to cover his portrait. Pathetic!

The order was given out so hastily and without much thought that, conspicuous by its absence, I did not see those workers wearing any safety harness when they were climbing those billboards. Their supervisors were either irresponsible or too dumb not to think of their workers' safety. Or, those workers' lives were cheap and expendable in order to save Najib.

Realizing that the 1MDB scandal was a major issue, Najib sent the company's CEO to campaign for him. A PR man—and not a good one at that—masquerading as chief executive! The poor man bitterly complained that no one came out to hear him. Touching! He would have been better off and more persuasive had he simply released 1MDB's audited financials, standard for all companies. He could not; the company had none. That is the crux of 1MDB's problem. It does not take a CPA or MBA to figure that out, and fast. Any CEO who does not grasp that on his first day at work is not chief executive material.

Long before Najib announced the election, he had his Registrar of Societies, a mousy Malay lady, her impressive title notwithstanding, deny the registration of Mahathir's party. As such its candidates, Mahathir included, could not use the party's name or symbol. For added measure and not satisfied with just tearing down Mahathir's pictures, EC directed that Mahathir could not campaign beyond his constituency as he is not head of a registered national party. He blithely ignored that and stormed the country, taking his campaign right to Putrajaya and Pekan, Najib's hometown, and drawing huge crowds.

Mahathir's flouting EC's directives again exposed Najib's impotence. Most heartening of all, despite his 92 years of age and recent frequent attacks of bronchitis, Mahathir had no difficulty delivering his pungent messages. And they resonated with the electorate. The campaign invigorated him; a patriot on his mission to save his country.

What a contrast to Najib; he was inarticulate, stumbled over his words, and could hardly wipe off the saliva drooling from his lips. A thief caught with the loot.

This Wednesday, May 9, 2018, election day, voters will have a chance to be predators and rid Malaysia of her weak and desperate leaders. Go for the jugular and grab Najib by the neck and decapitate him as well as his party, UMNO.

It is time for Malaysia to have strong, competent, and confident leaders with integrity. Elect Mahathir and his coalition.

A New And Very Dangerous Low For Malaysian Politics

May 1, 2018

The tampering of the plane that would have taken former Prime Minister Mahathir to Langkawi last Friday, May 27, 2018, to file for his nomination papers for the upcoming election marked a new and dangerous low in Malaysian politics.

Tinkering with your opponents' car, sound system, or power supply is a standard ploy in third-rate Third World politics, the Malaysian variety included. Those tricks could be performed with ease and by a saboteur with no-to-minimal skills. The results of such mischief are rarely catastrophic, except for the occasional car explosions. Not so with the tampering of airplanes.

For Malaysians, that brought back haunting memories of the plane crash of June 6, 1976, dubbed the "Double Six Tragedy" that killed the just-victorious Chief Minister of Sabah, Fuad Stephens and some of his senior ministers. The report of that "accident" is still classified to this day.

What was stunning about Friday's incident was the uncharacteristic silence of Prime Minister Najib. He commented only much later. Najib accused Mahathir of engaging in the "politics of lying." The irony escapes Najib, of course!

I commend incumbent Transport Minister Liow for responding immediately. The others were in their typical civil service mode, still waiting for a report or *arahan* (orders from above). The Chief of Police and Chairman of Civil Aviation admitted in a bland statement that there was "a minor and routine technical fault." They would be smarter and gain a modicum of credibility had they released the full report, if indeed one was done. *Any* malfunction on a plane must be taken seriously. There is no such thing as minor and routine. That would come *only* after a thorough inspection.

What the pilot did was spot on, that is, refuse to fly the plane. A true professional. It is his life as well as those of his passengers that he would be risking.

It would take someone highly skilled to tamper with an aircraft to avoid detection by the pilot during the routine pre-flight checkout, as well as bypass a modern jet's sophisticated warning and back-up redundant systems. As such those saboteurs do not come cheap. They were either strongly motivated or highly compensated, or both. Meaning, there must be a strong, elaborate, and well-funded background support system.

This upcoming May 9, 2018 election already shows every sign of being competitive, a novel experience for Malaysia in recent years. This election also brings many eerie reminders of a similar hotly contested one back in 1969 that resulted in the horrific race riot, except for two significant but not widely acknowledged differences. That election saw the ruling coalition defeated for the first time in many states. Voters' polarization then was interracial, between Malays and Chinese. By contrast in the current contest, it is *intra* racial, among Malays. That can be even more volatile and explosive.

UMNO and other Malay chauvinists try to inject into the current intracommunal schism racist elements in order to galvanize their base. They hope to subvert it into a Malay-Chinese conflict. Hence the constant harping on Malay unity and using the predominantly Chinese DAP in the opposition coalition as a convenient fuel and scapegoat. There was even a malicious suggestion that DAP members would assassinate Mahathir once they win the election. Laughable and preposterous! Such malicious thoughts and rumors reflect more the desperation of Najib's supporters.

The other difference is that this election has been reduced to a contest between two personalities—Najib and Mahathir. Hatred, passion, and other strong emotions have been personalized and focused on them.

Najib is a formidable campaigner not because of his personal magnetism (he has none) or oratorical prowess (he lacks that too) rather he is the incumbent and Finance Minister. He holds the key to the Treasury. With that he has been disbursing cold cash to potential voters with the desperation of a hawker getting rid of his pile of unsold overripe durians. Like overripe durian, the stench is fast becoming overpowering.

Mahathir is a cool campaigner and has great aura about him, qualities so conspicuously deficient with Najib. Nobody could call Mahathir an amateur politician or statesman. Najib tried that and ended up making a fool of himself.

Mahathir's supporters are bound to him by commitment, emotions, and most of all a missionary zeal in the singularity of their purpose—to get rid of Najib. Najib's supporters on the other hand are *dedak*-driven (cash-driven) and conspicuous by their lack of personal enthusiasm for or commitment to their man. Once Najib runs out of *dedak*, as inevitably he would, his supporters would wither away or worse, turn against him, as many have.

Despite the airplane incident, I do not worry of any attempt at doing away with Mahathir (divine intervention excepted). Instead I fear for Najib. If ardent Mahathir's supporters feel that their man is being in any way threatened or even humiliated, the fury heaped by them upon Najib would be merciless. Imagine if harm were to befall upon Mahathir! Remember amok is a uniquely Malay word. No word in any other language could signify the furor, frenzy, or savagery of amok.

I could not care less of Najib's personal fate, but I worry about the impact of such an action on the nation. Once that dangerous line is crossed, there would be no turning back. Welcome to Pakistan!

Mahathir's supporters do not take lightly last Friday's plane incident. They and other Malaysians remember only too well the Double Six tragedy as well as what had happened to that Mongolian model, the banker Hussain Najabi, and prosecutor Kevin Morais. All under Najib's watch; all unbelievably gruesome. The pattern is hard to miss.

As for civil wars, Malays are not immune to that. Many had been camouflaged as insurrections against the sultans and their colonial backers. The most protracted and gruesome in the Malay world was the Padri War across the Strait of Malacca. That led the opponents of the Padris to seek help from the Dutch. The Dutch continued "helping" those natives for over a century.

The dynamics today remain the same, only the players have changed. If a civil war were to break out among Malays, and the minority Chinese be threatened, rest assured that China would not remain idly by but would "help" *ala* the Dutch in Sumatra. What with China's already significant investments in Malaysia, such interventions could with ease be justified on the world stage as being a humanitarian intervention.

UMNO recently sent its Secretary-General to China's Communist Party 18th National People's Congress. Rest assured that he was not received there as an exalted guest rather as an emissary from a vassal state, reliving the memory of the 15th Century Malacca Sultanate.

Those thoughts ought to temper the excesses of and sober up those Malays within and outside of UMNO with their delusional *Ketuanan Melayu* aspirations.

As a side observation, I am surprised that Mahathir, being a former Prime Minister, does not get the equivalent of Secret Service protection. In America, former presidents as well as all presidential candidates get that. Mahathir had it until recently. The withdrawal of such protection for him must have been a decision taken at the highest level.

Najib's continued silence on last Friday's plane incident reveals volumes. Today it is a minor aviation tire leak. Tomorrow?

The Thirteenth Malaysian General Elections (GE13)

Elections – A System For Checks And Balances

April 7, 2013 (*First of Four Parts*)

When he dissolved Parliament on April 3, 2013 to make way for the general elections, Prime Minister Najib advised Malaysians to "think and ponder appropriately" before casting their votes.

There are two mental exercises to help Malaysians "think and ponder appropriately" before casting their votes. One would be to imagine the best and worst possible consequences of one's vote, that is, perform a "downstream analysis" of one's decision. Two, reflect on the greater role of elections as an effective bulwark against abuse of power by those in authority.

I will discuss the latter first. Subsequent essays will be a downstream analysis of the only three possible outcomes to this election: Barisan Nasional returning to power; Pakatan Rakyat to prevail; and third, a "hung" parliament.

The most effective check on those in power is the knowledge that they could be replaced in an election. The more this is a reality and not just in theory, the more effective is this critical role. Elections serve as periodic useful and powerful reminders.

Even where elections are fair and free, but if the same leaders and party were to be re-elected over and over, they would sooner or later succumb to sclerosis and abuse of power regardless how competent and well-meaning they were initially. It is the rare leader who could escape this all-too-human tendency. We must have actual periodic changes in government through elections, and not just the promise of change.

With rigged and fraudulent elections, or where the process is merely illusory, as with having only one candidate per slot (Russian elections of yore and the "election" of UMNO President), the less effective they would be in keeping those in power accountable. Saddam Hussein bragged that those who did not like him could always vote him out, but Iraqi elections under him were a sham. Had he kept those elections honest, he would have discovered his people's true sentiment much earlier, and the price to both him and his country would have been considerably less.

The British decided through elections that their popular and effective wartime leader Churchill would not be the best person to lead them during peacetime. They wisely concluded that he would quickly turn the Cold War into a "hot" one, as reflected by his hawkish and haughty Iron Curtain speech.

Yes, the British were grateful to him for leading and inspiring them during the war, but that gratitude could be expressed in many other ways. Elections are for selecting the best *future* leaders, not for expressing gratitude for or rewarding past performance, no matter how exemplary.

Foremost and at the practical level, election is a way to pass judgment on the incumbent. It is not, as some have suggested, a contest between the incumbent and challenger. It is for the incumbent to prove that he deserves another term independent of the merit or capability of the challenger. The incumbent's performance is a matter of record, and thus could be readily scrutinized.

If the incumbent has proven to be less than capable, then he should be voted out even if the challenger is thought of as potentially not up to the task of taking over. The argument there would be that the incumbent has *proven* himself incapable while the challenger is only *regarded* (meaning, only potentially) as such. There is the possibility that the initial assessment was wrong, and that the challenger would prove otherwise. There are many ready examples of previously underrated candidates later shining in office; Harry Truman being one.

The first and only question voters must ask before casting their votes in this next election is whether the current Barisan government is deserving of another term. All other matters, as whether other parties are capable in taking over, are irrelevant and besides, conjectural.

Consider the three critical areas: the economy, education, and level of corruption. Barisan's economic leadership is passable. It is exemplary only when compared to that of Zimbabwe. Granted, by the figures Malaysia outperforms America and Western Europe (and even Singapore), but remember those countries are already cruising at high altitude. Malaysia is still ascending; she *needs* faster growth. Malaysia should be compared to China and Panama. Even Ghana and Laos surpassed Malaysia last year.

More pertinent especially to those under the sway of PERKASA and the *Ketuanan Melayu* spell is the aggregate economic performance of

Malays. After nearly six decades of UMNO rule, Malays still could not achieve their initial modest 30 percent goal in the private sector.

Then consider education. No one, not even the Minister of Education himself, is satisfied with our schools. Those who can afford it have long ago abandoned the national stream. Looking from the PERKASA and *Ketuanan Melayu* angle, only poor Malays are stuck with the rapidly declining national school system. Consider this. While a generation ago I could still find many Malays at the leading universities of the world, today Malays there are as rare as integrity among UMNO politicians.

The much-heralded growth of the private sector in education is not a sign of health rather the contrary. It reflects a deteriorating public system. Alberta and Singapore do not have robust private-sector education because their public systems are so much superior.

As for corruption, there is no point dwelling on it. Malaysia is past the tipping point; she is now where Nigeria was in the 1980s. The only way to stop corruption is to deprive UMNO of power. The recent Court of Appeal decision granting one Eskay Abdullah, an UMNO strongman and a member of the slimy "Datuk T's" trio, his RM20 million "commission" on the aborted crooked bridge in Johor reflects the rot in UMNO. We cannot blame non-Malays for seeing that as *the* characteristic of contemporary Malay politics and ethics.

Elections are like multiple choice tests. You pick the best answer or candidate from the list offered. The incumbent would always argue that his past performance had been superior or at any rate better than what his opponents could ever hope to achieve; the challenger offers the promise of a brighter future. Voters balance the risk of changing horse midstream versus being stuck with a lame one to face an incoming flood.

Malaysians already know how lame their current horse is. Worse, it has a voracious appetite that is severely taxing citizens, literally and figuratively. This next election is an opportunity for Malaysians to send this lame one to the glue factory and hitch a ride on a new vigorous steed.

There is only one effective way to teach those who have long been in power and grown arrogant into believing that they are destined to rule forever. Vote them out of office. Then even if their successor were to prove less than satisfactory, it would still have served a salutary lesson.

Mexico's PRI of today is a much superior political party and led by a much younger, more capable, and decidedly less corrupt leader than it was a decade ago when it was booted out after having been in power continuously for the preceding 71 years.

Those who believe that UMNO is rotten to the core, no amount of calls for transformation and reform from within or without would be as effective as throwing the party out of power.

Malaysia has another and equally important reason to see regular changes in government. Stated briefly, it is to teach the Sultans specifically and the permanent establishment generally the important lesson of being politically neutral. They cannot bank on or be overly cozy with the ruling party. That Malaysian Sultans and civil servants have yet to learn this crucial lesson of democracy was demonstrated by the ugly political mess in Perak, and to a lesser extent in Selangor and Trengganu following the last [12ᵗʰ GE, March 2008] election.

It is also for this reason that I am optimistic of a smooth transition at the federal level with the upcoming general elections should Barisan be booted out. We are fortunate to have Kedah's Sultan Halim as Agung, not because he had that role earlier, rather his recent experience with the smooth transition from UMNO to PAS in his home state following the 2008 election. His performance then shamed his brother rulers in Perak (especially), Selangor, and Trengganu.

Malaysian Sultans and members of the permanent establishment too need frequent reminding on the need to be politically neutral and to be professional about it.

A Barisan Win Is No Victory For Malaysia

April 14, 2013 (*Second of Four Parts*)
There can only be three possible outcomes to the next election: A comfortable victory for Barisan; for Pakatan Rakyat to prevail; or a hung parliament. A comfortable victory is one where the expected hopping of a dozen or so successful candidates would not materially affect the political balance. A hung parliament is where the buying or the shifting of

allegiance of a handful of elected members would significantly alter the political balance.

Contrary to the pronouncements of many, the worst possible outcome would not be a hung parliament but a Barisan victory. The best possible outcome would be for Pakatan to secure that majority. A hung parliament is not the worst or best possible outcome.

I begin with Barisan being returned to power, not with a supra majority for not even Najib Razak is predicting that, not in his wildest dream. In his speech dissolving Parliament, he implicitly conceded the possibility of defeat. His fanatic supporters fantasized a big victory, but that was because they had been high on their free *tapai* (fermented rice).

If Malaysians relish precious public funds being squandered through bloated contracts (think of the scandalous "commission" that slimy "Datuk T" secured for the non-existing crooked bridge) and outright pilferages (as with the "cow-gate" scandal and the purchase of the used Scorpene submarines that would not submerge), then expect more of the same with another Barisan victory. Only this time the scale would be even more outrageous both in scope and amount, difficult though that may be to imagine. Barisan, and UMNO specifically, would look upon their victory as approval if not vindication of their corrupt and wasteful ways. That is what Najib meant by not changing horse midway. He and his cronies wish to remain on its gilded saddle.

With a Barisan victory we would never get to the bottom of the "cow-gate" scandal or the outrageous civil settlement between Khazanah and ex-Malaysian Airlines' boss Tajuddin Ramli. Consider that had Barisan won Selangor in 2008, that Khir Toyo character would still be its Chief Minister and not the convicted criminal that he is today. There are many Khir Toyos at the federal level; only a Barisan defeat would expose these scumbags. Only with a Pakatan victory could they be held accountable and be prosecuted.

For those expecting political stability or continuity as their reason for voting Barisan, that delusion would quickly be shattered. There is little chance for Najib to better his predecessor's performance of 2008. If they started to scheme for Abdullah's downfall before the total votes were tallied, this time the power struggle to replace Najib would be even cruder, more vicious, and utterly destructive. Forget about the old Malay *budi bahasa* (niceties); it would be the *Mat Rempits* gone amok, complete with the roar and gore.

After the 2008 electoral fiasco, Muhyiddin unhesitatingly turned on his erstwhile patron, Abdullah Badawi. The temptation for Muhyiddin to topple Najib post-election 2013 would be irresistible. Being seven years older than Najib, this is the only opportunity for Muhyiddin to do it. By the time the next general election comes around he would over 71 years old, a spent force.

Muhyiddin's body language all along could barely conceal his contempt for Najib, both the man and his policies. Expect Muhyiddin to launch an even more emboldened and naked challenge. I disagree with veteran UMNO observer Abdullah Ahmad who noted that Najib would more likely to be challenged by younger leaders, not Muhyiddin. It would only *appear* that way, at least initially.

This vicious do-or-die battle between Najib and Muhyiddin would have all the trappings of classic class rebellion of feudal times, between *orang bangsawan* (aristocrats) and *orang hamba* (peasants). Expect the royal class to be involved; no marks for guessing which side they would favor.

At the personal level, it would be a brawl between a streetwise pugilist who has survived many such encounters, versus a soft-cocooned brat long used to having his way by hiring others to do the dirty work for him. The irony this time is that Najib would be at the receiving end of those calculating leaders who weigh things on what they would gain personally, an art Najib had perfected throughout his political career.

The junior members of Barisan, the Chinese and Indian parties as well as those from East Malaysia, would be reduced to being anxious spectators and helpless prey. Prey because their members would be vulnerable to tempting offers to switch sides. There would be no political stability, instead endless scheming and shifting alliances. The ensuing looting of the public treasury to finance such shenanigans would be on an unprecedented scale.

Najib's ballyhooed promise of transforming his administration is just that—hot air. He will again field his sclerotic ministers and they will all be back in his cabinet. Nothing would have changed.

Malaysians are already getting a preview of Barisan's shenanigans during this campaign with Najib furiously bribing voters with taxpayers' money. Make no mistake, after the election he will be expecting and collecting his dues. That would be the ugly scenario that would await a Barisan victory.

The RAHMAN prophecy has it that the "N" refers to Najib; he would be the sixth and last UMNO Prime Minister. If Barisan were to return to power this coming election, then that RAHMAN prophecy would have an even more ominous meaning. It would mean the end of Malaysia as we know it. As National Laureate Samad Said put it, this is the only chance to spare Malaysia such an awful fate.

A Pakatan Victory The Best Outcome

April 21, 2013 (*Third of Four Parts*)
The best outcome would be a decisive Pakatan victory. That would be the only way to effect much-needed changes, specifically to end the current culture of corruption, cronyism, and rent-seeking activities that are enmeshed and fast becoming the fabric of Malaysian—specifically Malay—society. Addressing the concerns of those under the sway of PERKASA and *Ketuanan Melayu* doctrine, Malays would never advance until we get rid of this destructive culture, of which UMNO is the prime enabler.

I am heartened that more than half of PKR's candidates are new, with a substantial number of young faces. That is the best hope of bringing about change—with new personnel. Najib considers recycled and rethreads as fresh. How can he ever hope to transform the country with the same tired, tainted, and tattered team? It is significant that he has resurrected Isa Samad, the slimy character suspended from UMNO a few years ago for "money politics." Najib is scraping the very bottom of the fetid UMNO barrel. Rest assured that tainted characters like Isa Samad would be in Najib's cabinet or be key players outside it.

Malaysia's myriad problems would not miraculously vanish with a Pakatan victory; they may well get worse, at least in the short term. After the long drought years, it would only be human to expect Pakatan leaders and their patrons to treat their victory as *durian runtoh* (fig. bountiful harvest) and get carried away with their excesses. There are more family squabbles during the good times than during the lean.

Expect Pakatan leaders to behave like the long-deprived family that had won a big lottery just before Christmas, Hari Raya, or Chinese New Year, engaging in greedy squabbles on who would get the more expensive presents, the bigger *duit raya*, or more generous *ang pows*. Likewise, expect predictable fights over who would be Deputy Prime Minister, specifically whether a Malay or non-Malay, and fights over critical portfolios like Finance, Education, and Home Affairs.

I am confident that under Anwar Ibrahim's leadership, Pakatan would overcome these expected teething problems. Many still harbor doubts about him. I have tremendous faith in the human capacity to change. Anwar today is a much better person and an immensely wiser leader then he was 15 years ago. He has been through a dramatic reversal of fate, been literally battered, and survived nearly six years in jail until his conviction was overturned. Lesser mortals would have been crushed but Anwar emerged stronger and with his reputation enhanced.

Anwar is not dumb. His years in solitary confinement have taught him a thing or two about fate and human nature. He is now a well-tempered steel, not easily corroded, and able to withstand the tempest, exactly the kind of leader Malaysia needs.

The Chief of Police who battered Anwar was finally convicted and jailed. It is significant that Mahathir and others in UMNO have yet to express regret much less condemn the despicable performance of this Chief of Police. That reflects the ethos of Najib, Mahathir, and UMNO. That will never change; hence the need to get rid of them.

The religiously inclined, more pious, and less worldly-driven PAS leaders could be a positive influence. They could impress upon their Pakatan colleagues to regard their victory not as a cause for celebration as with a Hari Raya, but the beginning of a long difficult stretch, as with the start of Ramadan. Their victory should thus call for restraint, patience, and generosity, a time for shared sacrifices, not a fight over the spoils of victory. There would be plenty of time to celebrate later once they have succeeded in rehabilitating the country.

There would also be the inevitable temptation to reward old stalwarts for their loyalty and past efforts. Yes, thank and honor them but the nation now needs a new beginning. Malaysia needs new leaders. It would be a tough sell, but it would have to be done, and done gently, firmly, and with class as well as magnanimity. The torch has passed on to a new generation. Time for the elders to step aside, tough though that may be for some of them.

The more human and likely response from them would be, "Finally it is our turn!" Those seniors would then look upon the younger leaders not as the next generation of torch bearers but usurpers. "We have struggled for decades and now these upstarts are grabbing the rewards!"

Were the older leaders to react that way, it would be a tragedy for them as well as their new coalition and Malaysia.

"The old order changeth, yielding place to new, / And God fulfills himself in many ways" (48,49) wrote Tennyson in "The Passing of Arthur," "Lest one good custom should corrupt the world." (50) That newness after the election refers not just to a new party but also a new generation.

Those seniors should instead heed this Tennysonian wisdom: "When every morning brought a noble chance / And every chance brought out a noble knight." (38,39) The 2013 election will be a new morning for Malaysia, and with that the chance for a new breed of noble knights. Seize upon that!

There would be other potential and unmasked dangers. If perchance PAS were to win big relative to the other members of Pakatan, then expect its leaders to overreach. They would want to implement *hudud* and declare Malaysia as an Islamic state, a move that would fatally split the coalition and be a tragedy for the country.

With its sizeable victory, PAS could be the de facto ruling party. Its members could threaten or be bribed by UMNO to "return to the fold." Historically PAS was an UMNO splinter group. UMNO would not hesitate to throw its non-Malay partners MCA and MIC under the bus, if that be the condition imposed by PAS. UMNO would do anything to hold on to power.

If that were to happen, non-Malays would have every reason to be worried. I do not expect another race riot. Malaysians are now too smart and too far developed socio-economically to fall for such chauvinism. Instead expect a massive brain drain and capital flight out of the country. This time those highly educated non-Malays would be joined by Malays, at least those who have qualifications recognized outside of Malaysia. Those Malays have seen Saudi Arabia and Afghanistan; they have no wish for Malaysia to be like those countries.

An UMNO-PAS coalition would survive; the demography supports that. Malaysia would not, at least not in her current form.

Lastly, a Pakatan victory will have a salutary effect on UMNO. Presently it is burdened with corrupt, incompetent, and sclerotic leadership. Despite Najib's much-ballyhooed and increasingly futile "transformation" and "change or be changed" exhortations, the party is incapable of reform or self-renewal. Deprived of the loot from having lost political power, a defeated UMNO would implode in no time. That would be the bad news for the party.

The good news is that only the honest, competent, and committed would be left. *They* would rebuild UMNO slowly and painfully, inspired by its past glories. The example of Mexico's PRI cited earlier is instructive.

There are fear mongers out there intimating that Malaysia would risk another horrific "May 13 incident" with a Barisan loss. The irresponsibility factor aside, such fears are misplaced. If Malays are easily swayed by the frothy mouths like Ibrahim Katak, then we have a far greater problem. Non-Malays are smart enough not to be bothered by characters like him. The Ibrahim Kataks could easily be bought out and effectively silenced by a few cheap directorships.

What I fear more is not a Malay versus non-Malay riot, rather a vicious and protracted intra-Malay conflict. Intra-communal conflicts have always been underestimated. Syrians now suffer much worse than when their country was at war with Israel. Further back, Mao's communists killed more Chinese than did the invading Japanese. Malays now are more deeply polarized along social, political, and religious lines. The fact that Malay leaders across the spectrum are blissfully unaware of these simmering fault lines makes that even more dangerous.

The recent Lahad Datuk incursion in Sabah was widely viewed as an "invasion." Stripped of the nationalistic jingoism and militaristic bravado, it was nothing more than an intra-ethnic fight. What startled and frightened me most about the incident was that the most virulent and violent sentiments were expressed not by non-Malays but Malays. Not a single person, least of all a Malay, had suggested any peaceful solution. It took a foreigner in the person of the UN Secretary-General Ban Ki Moon to urge an end to the violence and to encourage dialogue for a peaceful resolution.

I view the current race taunting and fear mongering as nothing more than Barisan's crude and ineffective tactic into scaring Malaysians from voting for change.

A Hung Parliament Is Not Necessarily Bad

April 28, 2013 (*Last of Four Parts*)
Many would fear a hung parliament. They think that would lead to chaos, uncertainty, and instability. Those are possible but not inevitable. I see many potentially redeeming aspects that could benefit citizens, the permanent establishment, and yes, even those politicians.

For citizens, seeing these freshly victorious politicians brazenly jockeying for positions would be both instructive and revealing. It would be quite a sight to watch them behave worse than hookers. At least hookers are consumed with satisfying their present customers first and would solicit new ones only after they have done that. More importantly, they do both discreetly. Those politicians on the other hand would be openly and lustily auctioning themselves to the highest bidder without even a promise of satisfactory performance to their current customers—citizens who had only recently voted for them. Those politicians would whore themselves shamelessly. What matters would only be the price their new customers be willing to pay. Damn the consequences, for them or the country.

The jockeying would be intense, shameless, and endlessly shifting, threatening both Barisan and Pakatan. It would not be below MCA for example, to align itself with DAP and throw their weight behind Pakatan, demanding an outrageous price in return. Or MCA could demand a stiff price for remaining in Barisan. Not to be outdone, as alluded earlier, PAS could bolt out of Pakatan and align itself with UMNO in an ugly chauvinistic attempt at reviving *Ketuanan Melayu*. UMNO would sell its soul to get PAS support, and PAS in turn would readily sign a pact with the devil given the right price. There would be only one certainty; these politicians would at last be exposed for all their corruptness and hideousness, with citizens and Malaysia paying the terrible price.

Perhaps Malaysians would need such a sordid spectacle to jolt them into realizing that elections have consequences, and that the politicians and leaders of today are a far different breed and caliber from the earlier generation that brought merdeka.

On the other hand, Malaysian politicians may well surprise the citizens. Without being unnecessarily Pollyannaish, a few might discover that politics is after all a noble profession, and at its best and essence, a fine exercise in the art of compromise to get things done for the good of all. You gain some and lose some, just as with the other parties involved.

At the very least a hung parliament would prompt Malaysians to be more prudent when voting the next time and not be so casual with this important exercise of democracy. If that would also encourage otherwise thoughtful Malaysians to offer themselves as candidates, then the whole exercise would not have been futile.

A hung parliament would also have a salutary effect on the permanent establishment. The last time there was a similar debacle, in Perak following the 2008 elections, the permanent establishment including the Sultan, did not acquit themselves well. Who could forget the spectacle of the Speaker being hauled out of the Assembly while desperately clinging on to his chair, or the Raja Muda, the Sultan's representative, being forced to cool his heels in an adjacent room while waiting out the mayhem? It was not pretty. The stench stained all and stayed to this day.

You could be certain that this time, with the real possibility of Barisan being toppled, members of the permanent establishment would be more circumspect for their own selfish reasons. As such I would not expect such blatant and crude displays of partisanship as was seen in Perak. To add flavor to that, the King today, Sultan Halim, was the Sultan of Kedah when PAS took over from UMNO. The prospect of working with a non-UMNO chief executive would not be a novelty for him.

Once that reality is established at the federal level, all the other sultans at the state level would follow suit. They would out of concern for their own survival no longer be so blatantly partisan. That can only be good for them and Malaysia.

A hung parliament is nothing to fear; it is just another though less clear-cut expression of a Barisan defeat. Or stated differently, a hung parliament is a not-so-pretty Pakatan victory.

BERSIH 3.0 Broke Many Glasses

Part I: Including A Few Glass Ceilings

May 6, 2012 (*First of Two Parts*)

In the aftermath of the largest public demonstrations against the Barisan government, the officials' obsession now turns to the exercise of apportioning blame and the associated inflicting of vengeance. Both are raw human reactions, but hardly enlightening, sophisticated, or even fruitful. Besides, there is plenty of blame to go around. I prefer to look at the bright side and on the lessons that could and should be learned.

BERSIH 3.0[4] clearly demonstrates that Malaysians no longer fear the state. In that regard Malaysians are a quantum leap ahead of the Egyptians under Mubarak, the Iraqis under Saddam, or the Chinese under Mao (or even today). When citizens are no longer afraid of the state, many wonderful things would follow. BERSIH is also the first successful multiracial mass movement in Malaysia. In a nation obsessed with and where every facet is defined by race, that is an achievement worthy of note. Another significant milestone, again not widely acknowledged, is that the movement is led by a woman who is neither Malay nor a Muslim. Ambiga Sreenevasan broke not one but three Malaysian glass ceilings!

On a sour note, BERSIH 3.0 revealed that Barisan leaders (and a few from the opposition) have yet to learn and accept the fundamental premise that dissent is an integral part of the democratic process and expressing it through peaceful assembly a basic human right. At a more mundane level though no less important, the authorities' performance in BERSIH 3.0 also exposed their woeful incompetence and deplorable negligence in basic crowd control.

In any mass rally you expect a minority to get carried away or be willfully indulging in criminal acts. It is the duty of the authorities to prevent and apprehend them, but not to use that as justification to treat

---

[4] Lit. Clean, an NGO committed to clean government.

as criminals the vast majority who are otherwise peaceful, or for the police in turn to behave like criminals in responding.

To keep things in perspective, and with no intent to insult those injured, whose properties were damaged, and those otherwise inconvenienced, the mayhem last Saturday was no worse than one following an American college championship game. More to the point, considering the much larger crowd and more pivotal issues at stake, no lives were lost.

Discerning The Winners and Losers

As with a college championship game, there were definite winners (and champions) from last Saturday's contest. As for the losers, there too were many. If you were to appear late on the scene or just a distant observer like me, it would not be terribly difficult to figure out who were the new champions and who were the sore losers just by watching their reactions.

It was a tribute to BERSIH's leaders that they did not gloat—the hallmark of genuine champions. They remained cool and confidently went on to target their next trophy, the removal of the Chairman and Vice-Chairman of the Elections Commission for the pair's blatant political partisanship by being, among others, UMNO members.

Although BERSIH was a coalition of NGOs, it nonetheless welcomed participation from all, including members of the political parties outside the ruling coalition. There were generous representations from them as they too shared BERSIH's objective of clean and fair elections. It was a tribute to BERSIH's enlightened and sophisticated leadership that it welcomed their participation and did not try to control or otherwise censor their speeches and actions. BERSIH leaders respected individual freedom, again reflecting their maturity and sophistication.

As for the political players on either side of the issue, it was also easy to discern the winners and losers among them. KEADILAN's leader Anwar Ibrahim described the event as a "celebration of unity, an awakening for liberation. [It] … shall go down in the nation's history as Merdeka Rakyat when 300,000 spoke in one voice to demand a free and fair election. . . . .[Those who] came down in full force were encouraged by a sense of justice to demand liberation from usurpers. Their message cannot be mistaken—a free country cannot be enslaved anymore."

He continued, "BERSIH 3.0 represents the hopes and dreams of all Malaysians that the political legitimacy of any government in the future can only be attained through a genuine democratic process." That is the confident voice of a winner.

Contrast that to the reactions of Prime Minister Najib, his Deputy Muhyiddin, and Home Minister Hishammuddin. Muhyiddin was first to the draw, threatening to make BERSIH pay for the damages, presumably including those caused by those ubiquitous razor fences, tear gas explosions, and blasting water cannons. For his part, Hishammuddin contemptuously dismissed the smashing of journalists' cameras as "standard operating procedure," only to be contradicted later by his Chief of Police. The police smashed more than just cameras.

Najib's hospital visit to the injured journalist Radzi Razak was a gracious personal touch. The heavily covered media event however, backfired. It revealed too much. Radzi's facial expression during Najib's nearly quarter-of-an-hour monologue where he (Najib) apparently apologized to the injured reporter showed that he (Radzi) was anything but comforted by Najib's words or presence. Later, Najib blasted the demonstrators for not respecting a court order banning entry into Dataran Merdeka, conveniently forgetting his Administration's contempt for citizens' right to a peaceful assembly. The irony; Dataran Merdeka—Freedom Square!

In short, the political trio of Najib, Muhyiddin, and Hishammuddin behaved like typical losers, blaming others and seeking vengeance. They were the three blind mice running around as if BERSIH had cut off their tails. The trio may not be blind, but they are myopic, unable to see beyond their whiskers.

Futility of the "Blame Game"

Trying to apportion blame at this stage of the game, even when attempted by well-meaning and neutral observers, would be a futile exercise. When done by political hacks, as they most surely would be, the exercise would serve only to aggravate old wounds.

When you have dry rubbish strewn all over, cans of gasoline purposely left open, and match boxes recklessly tossed around, the question of who lit the first matchstick becomes mute if not irrelevant. There will always be someone who saw somebody else who struck the match earlier. Then the analyses and debates would degenerate into or be consumed with interpreting what certain gestures and phrases may or may not mean in the heat of the occasion. Such puerile exercises are already well underway. Worst, they are being taken seriously by the authorities!

A more useful endeavor would be to learn ways of, metaphorically speaking, getting rid of the dry tinder, the thick brush of mutual suspicions, the open cans of inflammatory slimes, and the ready availability of matches. Such an exercise would require of Najib, Muhyiddin, and Hishammuddin to be other than the three blind mice that they are. Mice, blind and otherwise, thrive on rubbish.

Najib, *et al.*, need to look far beyond their whiskers and ponder whether the laying of razor fences at Dataran Merdeka and turning the center of modern peaceful Kuala Lumpur into an Israeli-occupied West Bank, Korea's Demilitarized Zone, or Stalin's Gulag is not the equivalent spewing more fuel. This point was forcefully made by a poster on one razor fence, "Welcome to Tel Aviv!"

There are hundreds if not thousands of such pictures as well as personal accounts of BERSEH 3.0. One touched me immensely.

"Up 'til Friday afternoon I was still unsure about going," one participant wrote. "… [T]hen I saw the photos of the police rolling out the barbed wire and I saw red. Since when did our police, or whoever is their boss, roll out barbed wires against their own people? Are Malaysians thugs? Terrorists? Thieves?"

The observer who wrote that is no raging anti-establishment anarchist. On the contrary, Marina Mahathir is a thoughtful commentator, very much mainstream. She saw only the *pictures* of police laying down those razor fences, and she was incensed. Imagine if she had been strolling down the street and been rudely confronted by that hideous sight? What if she were a foreign tourist?

Ponder the mindset of those who proposed the idea in the first place, or the personnel who laid down those razor fences. Did they think that Malaysians are such unruly hooligans that could only be controlled by those menacing barriers? Or were the authorities sadistically imagining and salivating, anticipating some innocent citizens being ripped apart by those sharp blades? We judge others through our own image. To their leaders, Malaysians must be a nation of thieves, thugs, and terrorists because they are.

Najib and others with glee referred to the damages done by the demonstrators while conveniently overlooking those incurred by the police, as with the unnecessary and provocative road closures long before the event. I wonder how many ambulances and doctors were delayed on their way to the hospital to attend to some emergencies *before* the rally because of those massive road closures. Violence was perpetrated upon the city long before the first demonstrators arrived.

Do not expect much introspection from these Malaysian leaders; sore losers are incapable of that. They could not for example, fathom that the laying of razor fences, widespread closing of streets, and heavy police presence *contributed* to the violence. Such an insight escapes them.

Part II: Lessons To Be Learned

May 14, 2013 (*Second of Two Parts*)
Many have asked, in barely concealed rhetorical tone, whether the day would ever come when a non-Malay could be Malaysia's prime minister. My view is that when such an individual emerges, the question would become irrelevant. Today no one wonders whether America would ever have a Black President. It is well to remember that it took nearly two centuries before America elected its first Catholic President (Kennedy), and had to wait another half a century before electing a Black (albeit only half) one. America is still waiting for her first female President.

Today, a few bigots and unrepentant chauvinists excepted, no one would deny that Ambiga Sreenevasan, BERSIH's leader, had captured the imagination of all Malaysians, young and old, Malays and non-Malays. This despite the many earlier ugly attempts, and not just from the lunatic fringes of PERKASA, to make her ethnicity, sex, and faith an issue, with epithets like "traitor" and "the anti-Christ for Muslims" recklessly hurled at her. Thankfully, that fizzled out fast.

"The irony of the BERSIH 3.0 rally," Mariam Mokhtar noted in Malaysiakini, "was that it was Ambiga Sreenevasan and not premier Najib Razak who managed to unite the *rakyat* and give true meaning to his favorite slogan, '1 Malaysia'."

There are two relevant observations, specifically with respect to Malay politics. First, to get support especially among the youth, Malay leaders must articulate issues that affect the masses. Fair and free elections being one, honesty and competence in leaders would be another. Malay leaders can no longer wrap and thus hide their corruption and incompetence around the cloak of "*Agama, Bangsa, dan Negara*" (Faith, Race, Nation–UMNO's slogan). Malays were disabused of that a long time ago; BERSIH 3.0 was a reminder only to those thick-skulled and memory-challenged, as well as those intellectually challenged.

The second is a corollary to the first. Any leader regardless of faith, race, or sex can be assured of support from the Malay masses if he or she were to address these critical issues. It has dawned upon Malays (and other Malaysians) that if Malaysia would have had free and fair elections, these corrupt and incompetent scoundrels would not be where they are today, and Malaysia a far better country. If Malaysia had been an Islamic state, as these characters have been endlessly championing for, more than a few of these leaders would have been publicly whipped for corruption, and a few stoned to death for adultery!

BERSIH is a tribute to Malays as we have finally escaped the trap of tribalism, which still ensnares even some of the most sophisticated societies. Malays now judge and follow leaders based on their abilities, not sex, shared racial kinship, or even commonality of faith. This achievement is worth emphasizing and frequent reminding. Consider that America is still struggling with the prospect of a Mormon becoming president, this coming so soon after it agonized and finally accepted a Black man as one.

Ambiga eschews political ambitions; I applaud her for that. If she were to succeed with the goal of having free and fair elections for Malaysia, she and her movement would have done a great national service, beyond any that could be achieved by the current crop of politicians. As it is, in breaking through the sex, race, and faith glass ceilings, she had already achieved much and inspired many. She effectively and elegantly demonstrated that Malaysians could serve the nation in many other ways besides politics.

Momentous Movement

That Saturday's event was deeply traumatic, though thankfully not in the same physical sense or league of lives lost and properties damaged as with Tiananmen or Tahrir Square. Nonetheless it was as momentous as both. BERSIH 3.0 cut deeply into the Malaysian psyche, and not just of those whose cameras were smashed, eyes burnt, and heads cracked. I hope it seared the conscience of those ethical police personnel who had been ordered to treat their fellow citizens as thugs and hooligans.

UMNO Deputy Minister Saifuddin Abdullah read it right when he said that the violent and chaotic scenes at BERSIH pointed to an angry and divided nation. He wisely suggested that Barisan leaders must take special care in addressing this fact. His was a distinct exception among UMNO leaders.

Having suffered through that Saturday's trauma, the nation desperately needed a healing and soothing balm. Alas there was none. Instead of comforting angry citizens and sympathizing with their sufferings, Prime Minister Najib and other Barisan leaders found perverse pleasure in aggravating the pain of many and deepening the divisions amongst Malaysians. Najib saw himself as Prime Minister of only those opposed to BERSIH. Those in PERKASA and UMNO found comfort in his post-BERSIH shrill partisan utterances. Those other thousands of law-abiding demonstrators who were exercising their basic rights to a peaceful assembly were not. Such is the caliber and nature of Najib's leadership. Perhaps Malaysians could be comforted by the fact that he and Hishammuddin did not brandish their *kerises* in denouncing BERSIH. Yes, I am lowering the leadership bar considerably here.

In my earlier recounting of winners, I missed one significant figure, National Literary Laureate Samad Said, or Pak Samad as he is reverently referred to. This soft-spoken writer bravely moved barefooted after he lost his shoes amidst the tear gas canisters and water cannon attacks of the earlier BERSIH 2.0 rally. This time he obligingly posed with his fans in blue uniforms, leading many to mistakenly report that he had been arrested! As I said, there were some conscientious police personnel.

The 76-year-old Pak Samad shamed many Malaysian retirees whose lives revolve around golf, tending their orchids, and *ratap* (meditation) at the suraus. Pak Samad has given the nation much with his literary talent; he now inspires Malaysians with his leadership and tenacity. He best personifies the essence of Islam, "Command good and forbid evil." He saw evil in the conduct of the elections and sought to forbid it; he saw the good in BERSIH and supported it.

BERSIH 3.0, like earlier rallies, exposed the gross ineptness of the authorities in managing dissent and handling crowds. The mindset of the authorities was locked in the premise that any view at variance with the official stand must *ipso facto* be treasonous and must therefore be suppressed–both the idea and its subscribers.

These leaders pay only lip service to the notion that democracy is essentially a contest of ideas, and that freedom of peaceful assembly and association is enshrined in the Universal Declaration of Human Rights. For added assurance they invoked hallowed traditions to justify their suppression. Demonstrations and mass rallies are just not part of Malay culture, they claimed with detached air of haughtiness.

They conveniently forgot that it was mass demonstrations and rallies that derailed the Malayan Union even after it was ratified by the Sultans. Those senior police officers should review their departmental archives to see how their British predecessors adroitly handled those rallies that aborted the Malayan Union. Those colonial officers had every reason to be contemptuous of the uppity brown natives with their notions of independence. Yet the colonial authorities did not react as local native officers and leaders did to their own people last Saturday. Had the colonials been as indiscriminate and vicious in their treatment of all those natives demonstrating for merdeka, there would not be an UMNO.

Malaysian police should be guided by the Public Order and Preservation Ordinance (POPO) that specifies, among others, using minimal force, issuing ample warnings, identifying the ring leaders, providing ready avenues so the crowd could disperse easily without harming themselves and others, and most importantly, rendering assistance to the injured instead of kicking those already down. Laying down razor fences effectively shut dispersal routes. Someone suggested that the unexplained interruption of the public transit system towards the end of the rally was a meticulously planned malicious scheme to strand and thus trap the demonstrators so they could be easy prey for those rogue cops. Until a better explanation is offered, I share those views.

Yes, POPO was a British idea and a good one. I see no reason why the natives could not learn from it. Malaysia sends her officers abroad on "study" tours and while there they visit such places as Disneyland. Mesmerized by the glitz, they missed seeing how well the Disney staff handles crowds or keep their facilities neat and beautiful. This incompetence in crowd control is not limited only to public officials. Observe the Malaysian Airline counter at Los Angeles Airport. They let the crowd spill over onto the neighbors' areas. You would think that they would learn from the other airlines, like opening the counter earlier, having the supervisor open additional counters, or putting a separate line for those most likely not to encounter problems, like single travelers and those with no checked baggage, for example.

It is this, the unwillingness to learn from and emulate those who are successful, that is the major Malaysian cultural deficit, not our fondness for rallies and demonstrations.

Malaysians Abroad Should Not Vote

November 6, 2011

Malaysians abroad are misguided and plain wrong in agitating for exercising their right to vote in Malaysian elections.

I can the see the validity for students, diplomats, and others on temporary assignment abroad demanding such rights, but then they already have that. For others, especially those who have acquired permanent residency status elsewhere, their clamor for retaining their right to vote in Malaysian elections is misplaced.

Foremost is that since they do not live in Malaysia, they would not have to bear the burden of the consequences of their voting decision. These Malaysians are seeking representation without taxation. That is presumptuous. As they had sought permanent residency status abroad, their focus should be to prove to their new host country that they are deserving of such a status. Meaning, they should focus their attention, indeed loyalty, to their adopted land.

Then there is the considerable added costs to having Malaysians abroad vote in Malaysian elections. I would rather have the government spend that money and resources in Malaysia.

Elections Have Consequences

For an action to be meaningful, its consequence must affect the participants, otherwise the exercise is merely academic or worse, a game. It may be a fun game for those abroad to vote in Malaysian elections, but for the locals who live with the consequences, it would not be so. In short,

Malaysians abroad participating in Malaysian elections are engaged in a fraudulent act, quite apart from muddying the waters for the "natives" who would have to live with the results.

It is presumptuous for those residing abroad to seek political representation and at the same time dispensing with paying their share of the costs, meaning, Malaysian taxes. Americans abroad have a right to vote not only because they are citizens but also because they are taxed on their worldwide income. An American may earn her entire income in Malaysia and in *ringgit*, nonetheless she still pays her share of income tax to Uncle Sam as if she had earned that income stateside. As such I can see her demanding her right to vote and that the local American embassy should provide her the necessary facilities so she could exercise that right.

Malaysians abroad do not pay any Malaysian income tax, unless they have Malaysian sources of income, and those Malaysians already retain their right to vote. If the rallying cry of those original New England "Tea Party" colonists back in the 17th Century was "No taxation without representation," today we have Malaysians abroad who pay no Malaysian tax yet perversely demand that their right for representation without taxation. Absurd if not arrogant!

The Election Commission's retort to them should be, paraphrasing the famous words of John Hampden uttered at the height of the English Civil War, what a Malaysian abroad has no right to demand, their home government has a right to refuse.

Malaysians abroad on permanent residency visas should not seek or be given the right to vote in Malaysian elections because they have essentially decided that there is no hope for them in Malaysia. If they were to harbor any sliver of hope for change, then they would have stayed behind and agitated for change from there, where their efforts would have the potential of having the greatest impact.

Besides, having made the emotionally wrenching decision to emigrate, their focus now should be to adjust to that decision and make the best of it. They should endeavor to plant roots in their new adopted community, to be an active and contributing member, and not be bothered with matters (especially political ones) they left behind.

If they should be clamoring for any voting rights, it should be for the right to vote in the affairs of their new community, if for no other practical reason than that those decisions would directly impact them.

If after adjusting well in their new adopted community, these émigré Malaysians still retain a reservoir of goodwill and gratitude for their homeland and wish to contribute, then there are other more productive avenues to do so than to agitate for the right to vote in Malaysian elections.

Eradicating the "Temporary Abode" Mentality

There is something irritating when I see Malaysians holding green cards or otherwise having permanent resident status being more concerned with Malaysian affairs then they are with those of their adopted homeland. If as a non-native in a new land I feel that way, imagine what the real natives would feel. In America I see frequent backlashes against Mexican Americans who are more concerned with affairs south of the border than they are with matters American.

A green card (or any permanent resident status) is a privilege; literally millions in the world would give anything to secure one. Having secured one and then to treat it so cavalierly is being disrespectful to the grantor state. Worse, that is the height of ingratitude. In some jurisdictions, any political involvement with affairs back in the "old country" would be grounds for rescinding that permanent resident status.

Permanent resident status is more than a long-term permit to work; it is a statement of your intent to be a permanent resident of that country, as the terminology of the document implies. In many countries permanent residents are granted nearly as full a privilege as citizens. It behooves the holders of such visas to exercise their privileges in such a way as to demonstrate to the host country that they value and are deserving of such a status.

If I were a native Singaporean, for example, I would not be too happy to see the republic's permanent resident visa holders more interested in Malaysian rather than the island's elections. There is now palpable backlash among the republic's citizens to these new permanent residents who treat the affluent island merely as a place to earn a good income and nothing more.

Malaysians too would not be enthralled either if foreigners granted Malaysian permanent residency status were to preoccupy themselves with matters in their former native land while ignoring local affairs.

A common complaint among Malays is that too many non-Malays treat their Malaysian citizenship merely as a stepping-stone for them or their children to emigrate to the West. Malays see the lack of enthusiasm by non-Malays to learning the national language as a manifestation of this "temporary abode" mentality. When these Malaysians emigrate and then agitate to have the right to vote in Malaysian elections, they are reverting to their old stereotypical "temporary abode" behavior, albeit not in Malaysia this time but in their new home country.

To be clear, I am directing my comments not to those Malaysians on temporary assignment abroad as students, diplomats, and other civil servants as well as company employees. For students especially, I would encourage and give them every facility to vote. Doing so would be the best way to get them engaged in the affairs of their homeland. God knows, if they were back in Malaysia their political activities would be severely circumscribed. At least abroad they would be free to partake in the political affairs of Malaysia.

If the Malaysian government were to pander to those abroad (parties in power tend to do that!) then I suggest that those voters be made to pay for the full costs of making the necessary accommodations. In my estimation, a fee of US$100.00 per voter would be appropriate, at least in America. That fee would be waived for those with proof of payment of their Malaysian income tax in the preceding year.

Impose that fee and then see how many abroad would remain "passionate" about Malaysian affairs to demand the right to vote in its elections. Now if those expatriate Malaysians were as passionate in seeking amendments to the Income Tax Act to making their global income subject to Malaysian taxes as they are in clamoring for their rights to vote in Malaysian elections, then I would salute them, but I would still not support it simply because of the costs.

The Malaysian Election Commission faces a host of monumental problems not least of which would be to clean up the electoral roll and streamline the postal voting process for those already in Malaysia, as with the police and military personnel. The clamor of Malaysians abroad seeking the right to vote is so far down on the priority list that I can hardly see it. Further, I see little merit in representation without taxation.

Malaysians Passed The Test, Brilliantly!

July 10, 2011

A remarkable thing happened this past weekend. To many, the event on Saturday July 9, 2011 [BERSIH 2.0 Rally] was nothing more than a massive public demonstration that capped a long brewing confrontation between those advocating "fair and free elections" and those who deemed that Malaysian elections are already so.

As with any fight, the drama was played out long before the event, and by the time the actual battle took place, the participants had long forgotten the original issue. Instead, the preoccupation was on who blinked first, who outsmarted whom, and most of all, who lost and who won. These then became the new overriding divisive issues, eclipsing the original ones.

The losers would return to their corner with their new resolve: "Next time!" And the battle continues. They never learn! There were plenty of losers this weekend but few winners. The winners may be few, but their achievements scaled new heights.

To me, this weekend was one of those moments (much too frequent, I hasten to add!) that test the nation. This time Malaysians acquitted themselves well. The same cannot be said of the Najib Administration.

If this was an academic exercise, I would grade the performance of Malaysians as represented in BERSIH with an "A," while the Najib Administration flunked. So dismal was its performance that the Najib Administration should have no recourse to a remedial course or supplemental test; expulsion is its only option.

Terrible Trajectory

I would have thought that after the debacle of 1997 with the gross and inept handling of the *reformasi* demonstrations, and again a decade later with HINDRAF (The Indian community's NGO), the UMNO government would have by now learned a thing or two on how to deal intelligently with dissent and public demonstrations, two inherent features of a democracy. My expectation was not unreasonable considering that we were dealing with essentially the same characters in the Administration. Most of the ministers who were in power during the *reformasi* and HINDRAF (now dubbed BERSIH 1) were still there in Najib's cabinet during this incident.

It was obvious that they, individually and collectively, had a flat learning curve. They were incapable of learning. Incomprehensible considering that the consequences to them were so severe. The 1997 *reformasi* mess resulted in Barisan being thrashed in the 1999 elections, with Najib nearly being kicked out of his safe seat in Pekan, the same seat that his father had held for many years.

The price or cost escalated with BERSIH 1.0. The general elections of 2008 saw Barisan being humiliated with an unprecedented loss of its two-thirds parliamentary majority, along with five states, including two of the most developed—Penang and Selangor.

I would let readers plot the trajectory as to the consequences of this weekend's mess should the next general elections be held soon, as was widely predicted.

The iconic image of the *reformasi* debacle was of former Deputy Prime Minister Anwar's battered face; that of BERSIH 1.0 was of Information Minister Zainuddin Maidin frothing at the mouth, babbling incoherently in front of the international news media trying to justify his government's brutal suppression of its people. It was a classic demonstration of that uniquely Malay mental malady, *latah* (echolalia or verbal diarrhea). It was also a display of amok, another peculiarly Malay affliction, albeit in this case only of the oral variety.

The indelible image of BERSIH 2.0 was in contrast more refreshing, that of its leader Ambiga Sreenivasan, former Bar Council President, serenely leaving the Istana after an audience with the King. The symbolism could not be overstated, for the Najib Administration had earlier declared her organization illegal! Only the retarded would miss the message, and they are precisely the types we are dealing with here.

Winners and Losers

My award for courage and excellence in BERSIH 2.0 goes to those brave Malay masses who defied their government, their imams, and the party that had long proclaimed and presumed to speak on their behalf. In taking an active part in a movement led predominantly by non-Malays, those Malays showed that they are no longer trapped by tribalism; they had escaped the clutches of chauvinism. There was no going back.

This significant milestone is not acknowledged, much less appreciated. Those leaders who choose to ignore this do so at their own peril. For aspiring Malay leaders, it is no longer enough for them to display their nationalistic zeal or ethnic instincts. They would have to articulate the issues that matter most to the Malay masses: fairness, honesty, and justice, in elections and on other issues. I would also add competence. Those too are also the concerns of all Malaysians.

There was a time when these leaders could garner Malay support simply by justifying that the victims of their corruption, injustices, and unfairness were non-Malays. Those days are now long gone; get used to it! Malays now realize that while in the past those victims may be mostly non-Malays, today they are increasingly Malays.

The comforting corollary to my observation is that those capable non-Malay leaders would be assured of Malay support if they were to address the central issues facing all Malaysians.

BERSIH 2.0 had strong non-Malay support especially abroad. Unanswered is whether a similar movement with equally noble objectives but with predominantly Malay leadership would garner the same enthusiastic support from non-Malays. If *reformasi* was any indication, the answer would be a reassuring yes.

I was heartened by the responses of Malay NGO leaders like Marina Mahathir. When Najib, and others who took their cue from him, began demonizing Ambiga by maliciously injecting ugly racial and religious accusations, Marina unambiguously and passionately defended Ambiga. Marina was all smiles and gentleness, as is the traditional *halus* (fine) Malay way, but there was no disguising her contempt for such odious tactics and their purveyors.

The biggest loser was the Najib Administration, specifically Najib and his fellow UMNO ministers. Their inanity was typified by Home Minister Hishammuddin complimenting the police for keeping the peace and stability. Yes, but with the streets blockaded, stores closed, and citizens bludgeoned—the 'peace' and 'stability' of a prison "lockdown." That was KL all week leading to last Saturday's rally.

The conspicuous silence of other Barisan leaders was noted; that reflected solidarity not out of courage but cowardice. In contrast, even UMNO Youth defied Najib in declaring that it too would stage a counter demonstration.

Despite its defiance, UMNO Youth was also the loser, together with that ultra-Malay organization led by has-been politicians and past-their-peak professors, PERKASA. Good thing that the government had banned their leaders from KL; at least they had a ready excuse for their dismal performance.

The list of losers is long; there is little merit in commenting on more except for just this, and I do so with profound sadness. A few weeks before the event, all the mosques in Kuala Lumpur, including the National Mosque, were warning their Friday prayer congregants of the evilness of those who led BERSIH 2.0 and the sin that would befall those who would participate in the rally.

At a time when the community is divided, as with this central issue of fair and free elections, I would expect Malaysian ulama and religious leaders to be healers, to bring the citizens together, to be the balm to their collective wounds. Instead, those religious leaders were only too willing instruments of the state, what with their canned state-issued sermons demonizing those who saw merit in the objectives of BERSIH 2.0.

It was obvious that to the thousands of Malays who took part in BERSIH 2.0 protests, including that one particular old man in his *jubbah* who had to be helped to walk, those characters cloaked in their flowing robes standing at their *mimbar* every Friday noon are less pious ulama to be revered but more propagandists for the state to be defied. They may be Imams, but to the thousands who took part in BERSIH 2.0 last Saturday, they were but *carma* imams, to borrow National Laureate Samad Said's term. *Carma*, the Malay contraction for *cari makan*, seeking a living. Idiomatically, those who prostituted their honored craft or profession for money and position.

Those G-I Imams (Government-issued) have flunked their test; there is no remedial course for them either. That is one of the great casualties of last Saturday's event. For those *carma* imams, there is no corner they could return to hide.

Islam is a great faith. It had stood against the hordes of invading Mongols, the godless totalitarian regime of Stalin, and the rampant secularism of the West. Islam will have no problem prevailing over these bureaucrats masquerading as defenders of our faith.

Voters Drawing The Line

September 6, 2009

In the heyday of UMNO, the joke was that the party could field a dog as an election candidate, and it would still win! The party leaders must still harbor that delusion for in the recent Permatang Pasir state by-election they fielded a disbarred lawyer. This time voters wisely drew the line at the dog.

The surprise was not that Rohaizat Othman successfully hoodwinked UMNO leaders to secure the party's nomination as its candidate, rather how easily those senior leaders were taken in by this shyster. Now that their candidate has been thrashed, those UMNO leaders belatedly bemoan the fact that their chosen man had been less than truthful to them. That is the quality of UMNO top leaders – the inability (or lack thereof) to spot talent.

Even after the sordid details of the man's sleazy professional past and checkered personal life had surfaced, UMNO leaders still vigorously defended their choice. They had the nerve to suggest that those critics were trying to smear the UMNO candidate. Those UMNO leaders obviously did not realize that their man was already soiled.

Reflection on Muhyyuddin

Consider UMNO Deputy President Muhyiddin Yassin's comments. He went to great lengths defending the integrity of his party's standard bearer. He likened the Bar Council's sanctions as nothing more than a traffic violation! I recognize that traffic in Malaysia is terrible, but really! I wonder what it would take to be branded a crook and thus be disqualified by Muhyiddin's reckoning. I am making a huge assumption here, that is, the man has some standards.

A commentator in the mainstream media reported that Muhyiddin was livid on hearing the details of Rohaizat. Only his severe poker face belied his anger, so the reporter claimed. If Muhyiddin was truly angry, he sure did not reveal it in his actions; he was 'gung-ho' about his candidate right to the end. That commentary revealed more about the writer trying to suck up to Muhyiddin so early on. Try a different tack next time.

It is a recent tradition with UMNO that its deputy leader be the campaign chairman for by-elections. This Permatang Pasir election was the first to be under Muhyiddin. Hence his comments and actions bear scrutiny.

Muhyiddin's decision to continue with Rohaizat's candidacy despite all the blemishes says volumes on the judgment as well as ethical standards of Muhyiddin. Not to scare readers, this character is also Deputy Prime Minister, and going by recent Malaysian history, he could very well be Prime Minister one day.

If a two-bit disbarred country lawyer could dupe Muhyiddin with ease, imagine him as Prime Minister negotiating with his counterpart across the causeway on selling precious fresh water, or his participating in crucial international treaty conferences! That is a scary thought!

The brief Permatang Pasir election campaign revealed more than we ever wished to know about this crooked lawyer and his equally slimy personal life. While Rohaizat was disbarred by the Bar Council, he could still practice in the Sharia court. This is the same court that recently sentenced a young mother to be whipped for drinking beer. That tells us something of the 'Islamic' (at least the Malaysian variety) code of ethics.

This Permatang Pasir campaign revealed more about UMNO, specifically its culture and top leaders. What has been revealed thus far should scare all Malaysians who are concerned with Malaysia's future.

Muhyiddin's ethical blind spot was disturbing enough. More reprehensible was his performance during the campaign. He fell into the predictable pattern of past ambitious UMNO leaders-in-waiting. There he was, freely and irresponsibly playing up the race card, eerily reminding me of Najib's and Hishammuddin's brandishing of their *keris*. Aspiring UMNO leaders like Muhyiddin have this primitive urge to display their chauvinistic manhood during tough campaigns. That is their culture.

Unfortunately, as the party still garnered over a third of the votes (presumably Malay votes), UMNO leaders will continue with their bigotry. Now they blame non-Malay (specifically Chinese) voters for abandoning Barisan.

UMNO of The Future

To be sure there were a few—very few, in fact only two—UMNO leaders who spoke out against Rohaizat, and they did so early. Mahathir wondered out loud whether a liar could be a people's representative. Tengku Razaleigh was much more forceful, "… UMNO is projecting the image that it lives by a different moral code from the rest of Malaysia."

"Either that, or this is the best we can do," he continued. Indeed!

Alas, both Mahathir and the Tengku represent UMNO's past. To gauge UMNO's future, look at the leaders of its Youth and Puteri wings. They not only endorsed Rohaizat but aggressively campaigned for him. I would like to ask UMNO Youth leader Khairy Jamaluddin specifically whether he feels that a disbarred lawyer and a man who lied about his wife is a worthy representative of UMNO.

The situation with UMNO Puteri is even more interesting. I wonder how those pretty, young girls in their distinctive pink *baju kurong* feel about campaigning for a man who took a second wife secretly, and then lied about it publicly. The Puteris' stand-by-your-man stance may be praiseworthy in other circumstances but not when your man is a cheat and a crook. Instead of campaigning for him, Puteri members should be contacting the second wife to see whether her man had been a good provider.

The Permatang Pasir by-election could have been a splendid opportunity for UMNO to shine if only their leaders had been smarter and pursued a radically different tack. Imagine if upon knowing the sordid details of Rohaizat, UMNO leaders publicly admitted their mistake and demanded their candidate withdraw on pain of being expelled.

That would give PAS a walk-over, but that would not have changed the end results. Besides, UMNO had done this a few months earlier in the Penanti by-election. On the other hand, think of the message the party and its senior leaders would have sent to their members and Malaysians generally, and the impact that would have on all. UMNO would have won a great moral victory. As it was, UMNO lost the election as well as the moral high ground. The party had set a new low on what is acceptable.

Judging from the post-election comments by UMNO leaders, from Najib Razak and Muhyiddin on down, UMNO has yet to learn this pertinent lesson from this latest debacle. The party still harbors the delusion that even its flawed candidates could still win.

The next time around expect UMNO to reach even lower to a new bottom in their search for talent. It would be difficult to find someone more unworthy than a disbarred lawyer. Trust me, UMNO will find one.

Losers On All Sides

May 24, 2009

It reflects how low public respect for Malaysian judiciary is when a unanimous reversal by the appellate court of a High Court's decision should be greeted with such widespread scorn.

We await the Appeal Court's written judgment so we could weigh its wisdom, legal and otherwise, and compare it to that of High Court Judge Aziz Rahim who made the initial ruling in Nizar vs. Zamry over their claims to be Perak's rightful Chief Minister following GE12 (12th General Elections). Justice Aziz gave his judgement within a week. Let us hope the Appeal Court judges, being more senior and higher in the judicial pecking order, would do better and come out with theirs faster. After all they must set the proper example.

At least the Appeal Court had the common sense to have a quorum of three to hear the appeal. It would have been better on a case of such import involving fundamental constitutional issues to be heard with the full quorum. At least those judges showed better judgment if not common sense than Appeal Court Judge Ramli who in his wisdom decided to hear by himself the appeal on the previous associated stay of execution.

Regardless, this case is headed to its final level of appeal. Let us hope that the Federal Court would hear this case with its full quorum and not just the minimal. While that is not a legal requirement, it is from the perspective of public credulity. At a time when the image of Malaysian judiciary is anything but pristine, this would be an opportunity to restore some credibility.

Thus far these are what we have. In favoring the plaintiff, Justice Aziz Rahim effectively declared that the Sultan of Perak, Raja Azlan Shah, erred in appointing Barisan's Zamry as the state's Chief Minister to replace Pakatan's Nizar. Justice Aziz cited principally the precedent of the 1966 case of Stephen Ningkan vs Abang Openg.

What is unique here is that Raja Azlan Shah is no ordinary Sultan, having served as the nation's highest judge from 1982 to 1985. In this decision, Justice Aziz is in fact telling the former Chief Justice and now Perak's Sultan, that the country's statutes and legal precedents do not support the Sultan's action. To state it simply and directly, the Sultan was wrong in his decision in this critical matter of state.

This precedent of Ningkan-versus-Openg of Sarawak state was set during Raja Azlan Shah's tenure as a judge, and long before he ascended to the Perak's throne. Meaning, he should be fully aware of the precedent and its attendant legal reasoning when he deliberated on Najib Razak's (as head of Perak's Barisan) request to have Zamry replace Nizar.

The only possible explanation for Raja Azlan's ignoring that precedent that he had set as Chief Justice, must be that he felt that it did not apply to him as a Malay Sultan. After all, how could a Sultan be compared to a mere mortal, the Governor of a state? In Malay culture, the Sultan is God's representative on earth; his mandate comes directly from heaven. It is not for mere mortals to trifle with. Sultans have *daulat*, a special divine dispensation denied those common-blooded Governors! Unfortunately for those Sultans, that is not what is provided for in the Malaysian constitution.

This delusion of having a special mandate from high above is an affliction affecting not only Malay Sultans but also all hereditary leaders everywhere, save the most enlightened.

In reversing the lower court decision, the Appeal Court effectively sided with the Sultan. The Sultan alone could decide whether the Chief Minister still commanded the confidence of the Assembly. The Sultan must have presumed that he had special divine powers to read the minds of the legislators and how they would vote *before* there was any voting!

In his appellate hearing, Justice Aziz Rahim made some uncomplimentary remarks about the role of the State Legal Advisor (SLA). The role of the permanent establishment as represented by the police and State Secretary, in addition to the SLA, merit an even greater scrutiny as they reflected the general degradations of Malaysian public institutions. I await the Appeal Court's written judgment to see whether those wise judges would also comment on this equally pertinent issue raised by Justice Aziz.

Had leaders of the permanent establishment been more professional and less partisan in discharging their duties and obligations, they could have acted as buffers and be the restraining force that would have prevented this crisis from escalating. Instead they became part of the problem, and a major one at that, instead of being part of the solution.

As to the SLA's claim of neutrality, Justice Aziz "will take it with a pinch of salt." The SLA admitted to being "instructed" from the respondent's solicitors in wording his affidavit, a term that took Justice Aziz by surprise. One would have thought that being a legal advisor and thus professionally trained, the SLA would act on his own judgment. Alas those are the caliber of Malaysian top officials.

Political, Not Legal Problem

All disputes ultimately will be decided by the courts. Whether that should or would is another matter. A perfectly rational and easily comprehensible reason could be advanced on whether certain disputes are best resolved outside the court system. This ongoing dispute in Perak is one such case. It is essentially a political dispute, and as such it would have been best resolved in the political arena. No less a veteran politician than Tengku Razaleigh has said this, and I agree with him.

Law Professor Shad Saleem Fariqi said it well and correctly. "… [T]his political crisis in Perak is like a hydra-headed monster that cannot be eliminated so easily by ding-dong judicial decisions."

Since the case has landed in court, it still could have played a crucial role in resolving it had the various participants and institutions been more professional and less partisan. Imagine had the court expedited the case and Justice Aziz rendered his decision prior to May 7th, before that disastrous legislative session where the Raja Muda delivered his speech. The nation would then have been spared the ugly spectacle of the mayhem in the legislature that saw the Speaker being physically ejected while clinging onto his chair. Now that singular repulsive episode will forever be engraved as part of the Malaysian democratic tradition.

Had the principal players demonstrated a modicum of restraint and (dare I say it?) wisdom and delayed the session till after the court' decision, that too would have spared Malaysia that shameful blemish.

Najib's appealing the case only added to the volatility and uncertainty; it was a major distraction and at a time when the nation could least afford it. Even if Barisan were to ultimately prevail, the price—political and otherwise—would be severe. More significantly, it would set yet another precedent on the enhanced powers for Malay Sultans. After the humiliation then-Prime Minister Abdullah Badawi suffered at the hands of the Sultan of Trengganu not too long ago, a reversal of Justice Aziz's decision would legitimize and cement the Sultans' enhanced powers.

On the other hand, if Barisan were to lose, this judgment would further strengthen the earlier Sarawak precedent. At the most elemental level, it would establish once and for all that the powers of the Sultan within a state are no different than that enjoyed by a Governor.

While I would welcome such a development, those who cling to the idea of *Ketuanan Melayu* or that Malay sultans have a "special" if undefined role in the nation, must pause and ponder the vast implications of such a development. I doubt very much that Najib Razak in his hasty pursuit of immediate short-term gains had reflected on this critical point.

This case thus far has only created losers on all sides. It already exposed the sorry ineffectiveness of local institutions. It revealed the inadequacies of the monarchy in ensuring a smooth transfer of power. It rekindled the sorry memory of the constitutional mess Malaysia went through in the 1980s. Most of all, the pitiful losers were the people of Perak. Their leaders, from the elected ones in the Assembly, to the hereditary ones in the palace, and the professionals in the permanent establishment, had all failed them.

To be reminded that these leaders were paid for by the citizens' hard-earned cash would merely add the proverbial salt to the still-raw wound, one that had yet to stop bleeding much less begin to heal.

This case awaits its final adjudication at the highest level. When it started, the first judge, Judicial Commissioner Mohammad Ariff Yusof, recused himself as he was formerly associated with PAS, Nizar's party. Now on its final stage, the sitting Chief Justice is Zaki Azmi, up until a few years ago a legal advisor to UMNO, a party in this dispute. Would Justice Zaki heed the example of Judicial Commissioner Ariff? It is on such simple and elemental matters that the credibility of the judicial system hangs.

This clear conflict of interest while readily apparent to the Judicial Commissioner, will elude Chief Justice Zaki Azmi.

The Lesson From Perak

May 10, 2009

The current political paralysis in Perak, the consequence of a few newly elected state legislators switching sides and thus altering the political balance, reflects the major failures of local key institutions. It is a total breakdown at the palace, legislature, and permanent establishment. It also exposes the glaring inadequacies of the judicial system which has yet to adjudicate this critical and urgent matter of state.

It is not the failure of the people, as some pundits have implied by quoting the adage that we deserve the government we get. It is voters' prerogative whether to grant the incumbent party a stunning victory, humble it with an unstable slim majority, or throw it into the ranks of the opposition. Canada and Italy have a long history of minority governments, and they have managed well.

A mark of a mature democracy, or any system, is the smooth and predictable transfer of power from one entity to another. Perak was a spectacular failure; it also served as a preview for Malaysia's future.

Perak was one of three state governments that changed hands following the 2008 general elections. In the other two, Kedah and Penang, the transition was smooth. In Selangor there were the ugly scenes of the destruction of state documents and properties, as well as the dissolution of the legislators' wives' club. That reflected more of infantile behaviors. Why was Perak the exception? That merits careful consideration.

It is assumed that if we have qualified and experienced people, then no matter how battered or inadequate the institutions, those key individuals would rise to the challenge. In Perak, we had a Sultan who by any measure was the most qualified and experienced, having served as the nation's top judge for many years. Yet his decision in this critical matter, which demanded the most judicious of judgment, proved to be unwise and precipitous. And that is putting it mildly.

That was not hindsight. Even at the time when he made that pivotal decision (which was the singular event that triggered developments which culminated in the spectacle of May 7), the voice of the people was loud and clear. Only that the Sultan had refused to hear or chose to ignore it.

No amount of subsequent royal pontifications would ever rectify or justify this error. Only a reversal of that earlier erroneous decision would resolve the issue.

It was too bad that Sultan Azlan Shah deputized his Raja Muda to the May 7th opening of the legislature. While that may have spared the Sultan the spectacle and embarrassment of being physically entrapped by the bedlam, he missed a splendid opportunity to witness firsthand what his modern-day version of *hulubalangs* (knights) were up to! Instead it was his Raja Muda who was left to cool his heels for a good six hours! Let us hope that at least it was an edifying experience for him.

It was nonetheless pathetic to see the Raja Muda reduced in his speech to pleading for respect! Few, not even the normally pliant mainstream media, bothered to carry his speech in full. So much for the respect that he desperately sought!

Amazingly in his speech, the Raja Muda did not deem it important or necessary to comment on the ugly spectacle he had just witnessed and been a part of. He remained aloof and strangely uncurious. He must have been in temporary suspended animation, oblivious of his immediate surroundings during his six-hour wait. He was from another planet, earlier programmed to deliver his royal speech and then leave! Nothing more; for that you would have to reprogram him again!

The principal political protagonists in this Perak crisis were Barisan Nasional's Zamry Kadir, a Temple University PhD, and Pakatan's Nizar Jamaluddin, a professional engineer fluent in multiple languages. Then there was the Speaker of the House, Sivakumar, a lawyer by profession. Their impressive diplomas and credentials meant nothing; they only looked impressive when framed and hanged on their office walls.

As for the permanent establishment, instead of being the stabilizing force and buffering factor, the State Secretary, State Legal Advisor, and the Chief of Police were hopelessly ensnared in the mess through their frank and ugly partisan performances. In no time they degenerated to being part of the problem (and a significant one at that) instead of being part of the solution.

As for the judiciary, it failed to appreciate the urgency and gravity of the crisis. The resulting lawsuit did not merit an expedited hearing but was let to meander through the usual slow judicial pathway. By contrast, the 2000 American elections that saw the Florida ballot counts being litigated, the case ended up at the Supreme Court for a definitive decision in a matter of days, not months.

Lessons Learned

Thanks to modern technology, those who were not there in Ipoh could still follow the unfolding events in real time, trumping the tight censorship of the government. Not that it was ever effective, just like the rest of the government.

There was not much that could be learned from the sorry spectacle. Even to declare that it reflected the sorry state of local institutions would be inadequate. There are already too many affirmations of that sad reality.

The next reflex reaction would be to declare, "Everyone is to be blamed!" While that is an understandable response, it does not solve anything, for the corollary to that statement would be that no one is to be blamed. That would be a cop out; they were not all equally culpable.

Everyone in the chain of events could have stopped if not reversed the destructive sequence right up to the day before the infamous debacle at the legislature. In the Malaysian system, the buck stops at the highest level—the palace.

Consider the chain of events again. First there were those renegade legislators switching party affiliations. No law against that; it was their choice. Perhaps that would galvanize the leaders of the party they had deserted to do a better job of screening and scrutinizing future candidates. Maybe primary elections among party members (as in America) instead of a decision from headquarters would produce better and more reliable candidates. That certainly would be one useful lesson.

This being Malaysia, things became more interesting fast. It turned out that those turncoats had earlier been investigated for corruption. Miraculously after their switchover, those investigations were not pursued! And no journalist saw fit to follow the lead.

Even if those turncoats were pure, their switching over should never have triggered such a mess. They could wait till the next sitting of the legislature to introduce whatever vote of no confidence they may have in mind of the leadership, and thus bring down the sitting government in the traditional and only legitimate way.

Even if leaders of the losing Barisan coalition were to petition the Sultan to dismiss the sitting Chief Minister (which they did), the Sultan ought to first hear out the incumbent before deciding. Common sense dictates that. One does not have to be a judge or have read the weighty tomes of legal luminaries to appreciate that elementary dictum. Hear both sides before rendering a decision! Any father knows that!

Sultan Azlan Shah could not pretend to be able to read or predict the thinking of his legislators after only a few moments of "chat" under the most severe royal protocol at the palace. That would be the height of royal arrogance. In any other circumstance, decisions made under such surroundings could be considered as coerced. Besides, it is their collective judgment expressed openly in a properly convened legislative forum that matters. Not only could you not predict individual behaviors, you could never foretell the group dynamics and the impact on the final decision.

If political leaders make a mistake, they should be held accountable. Just ask Abdullah Badawi. The buck with the present imbroglio stops at the palace, with Sultan Azlan Shah. However, in the present Malaysian system there is no effective checks and balances with respect to the monarchs, both at the state as well as federal levels. They are also immune to prosecution in the conduct of their official duties. There is no mechanism to fire or censure them. The Special Tribunal is only for prosecuting their *personal* misconduct. Well, at least that is a beginning, a measure of some royal accountability.

Regardless whether Malaysia has or does not have an effective system of checks and balances with respect to the Sultans, Malaysian society has changed. The old feudal order is gone, for good, never to return. Get used to that! In today's world, the people are sovereign. Ask the descendants of Shah Pahlavi and King Farouk, or closer to home, the Sultan of Sulu.

I tried to convey this in my poem, *Makna Merdeka 50* (Meaning of Merdeka 50), to commemorate Malaysia's 50th year of independence.

Rakyat negri bukan nya kuli
Untok di kerah ka sana sini
Zaman purba tak kan kembali
Mungkin menteri di buang negri!

Renungkan nasib si Idi Amin
Yang Shah Pahlavi pun tak terjamin

Pemimpin negri mesti menginggati
Rakyat—bukan Raja—yang di daulati!

[Blessed with freedom and reason are God's children
To lords and kings we are not beholden.
The old feudal order has long been toppled
Let's be clear, the sovereign is the people!

Ponder the fate of one Idi Ami.
That of Shah Pahlavi was equally grim!
Those realities our leaders must heed
"Power to the people!" is the new creed.]

That is the pertinent lesson from Perak.

"916" Is Not A Failure

September 28, 2008
September 16, 2008, or "916" as locals put it, was the date when Opposition Leader Anwar Ibrahim gave an ultimatum to then Prime Minister Abdullah to resign as Anwar thought he had enough votes to topple the government. That day came and went; Abdullah remained Prime Minister.

Nonetheless the possibility of Anwar Ibrahim taking over the government is now much more real. When (not if) he does, he would face the monumental twin problems of undoing the damage wrecked upon Malaysian institutions by UMNO, as well as containing the damages caused by the inevitable implosion of UMNO.

A failure in either endeavor would doom Anwar, his Pakatan coalition, and Malaysia. The good news is that both challenges could be handled simultaneously through the same strategy, and with the subsequent success benefiting all.

The blight on Malaysian institutions and governmental machinery, as well as the urgent need to rectify that, is well appreciated by all. Less recognized is the need to manage UMNO's certain breakup.

For those who venture that UMNO's fate is the least of Anwar's (or Malaysia's) concern, consider this. The tumultuous and unpredictable demise of the Soviet system may have ended the Cold War, but the world paid a severe price, one that could have been mitigated had the breakup been more orderly.

The world is still paying the price. There is the recurring nightmare that the Soviet's old nuclear warheads might fall into unscrupulous hands. Those still unconvinced of the price being paid, just ask the Georgians and Ukrainians.

UMNO dominated Malaysia for well over half a century; its implosion too would have many and unpredictable fallouts. If not skillfully managed, the consequences on Malaysia would be on a scale comparable to that inflicted on Eastern Europe by the collapse of the Soviet Empire.

Unity of Purpose

Even if Anwar were to secure more than the 31 promised crossovers in Parliament, his government would still be a coalition of political parties with diverse and often opposing ideals. Those parties have had only a brief experience of working together, not to mention the equally contrasting and conflicting personalities of their respective leaders.

Anwar could learn much from his predecessors. In the 1950s the distrust among the various races was even much greater. Yet Tunku Abdul Rahman was able to forge an "Alliance" (the name of his coalition) of UMNO with the Chinese (MCA) and Indian (MIC) parties into a formidable and effective force.

Tunku was able to overcome the considerable differences among his three-party coalition, Alliance, by focusing on the few agreed-upon objectives, among them the sharing of political power and seeking the end of colonial rule. Each party had to make considerable concessions to secure those common goals.

It helped that those early leaders genuinely liked each other, having shared their formative years together as students. They knew each other's families and attended each other's social parties. They harbored considerable personal goodwill towards each other that eased their subsequent inevitable policy differences.

Anwar successfully used his awesome political skills to make his coalition partners concentrate on their commonalities and less on their differences. Before the elections he made them focus on a singular objective: denying Barisan its supra-majority. He succeeded, and then some. In governing, Anwar should similarly emphasize the twin objectives stated in my opening statement, and only on those two. That is, rectify the damages that had been inflicted by UMNO, and manage the party's inevitable implosion.

Anwar is gifted with many of the personal charms and warmth of the Tunku. It is no mean feat for Anwar to bring Hadi Awang and Lim Kit Siang to the table! Anwar should continue using that special talent not only on his Pakatan coalition leaders but also across the aisle in Parliament. He should consider his earlier tenure as an UMNO leader an asset, and leverage that to foster greater cooperation with its leaders.

He must adopt the personal philosophy of President Reagan: party politics stops at 5 PM, and once you cross the border. The Republican Reagan used to invite the Democrat Speaker O'Neill over to the White House in the evening to share a glass of Irish whiskey. Reagan would also include many Democrats in his overseas trips.

Differences in policies and philosophies will always be there, but those ongoing social relationships would help lubricate those differences and prevent them from degenerating or reducing their proponents to the shrill denunciations of each other.

If UMNO Youth leaders could play regular golf tournaments with their PAP counterparts in Singapore, then surely Hadi Awang could listen to sermons by Abdullah Badawi, and vice versa.

Ramadan is a splendid opportunity for such social interactions by inviting non-Muslim fellow leaders in and out of Pakatan to a community *iftar*. Other opportunities include the wonderful Malaysian tradition of "Open House" during festive seasons. Those would provide excellent occasions for Malaysian leaders to socialize with each other, and more importantly, to be *seen* doing so. Such public gestures of goodwill would percolate down.

Government of National Reconciliation

Anwar could also take a leaf from another illustrious predecessor, Tun Razak. Following the May 1969 riot, Tun Razak formed a government of national reconciliation by inviting all parties to participate in his much-expanded Barisan Nasional.

Anwar need not necessarily expand his coalition, but he could tap outstanding members from UMNO and other Barisan parties for his cabinet. American presidents often have in their cabinet individuals from the other party, for example, Republican William Cohen serving under Democrat Bill Clinton.

Anwar would encounter considerable resistance from his side, especially those who consider ministerial appointments as the spoils of war, to be distributed only among the victors. To help overcome this, Anwar must select only the most capable from the other side. That would also demonstrate his commitment to meritocracy.

There would be resistance too from across the aisle. Used to the culture of corruption, they would consider such good faith gestures as attempts at corrupting or "buying" their members. To overcome that, Anwar should appeal to their sense of patriotism, and portray to them that this would be a national service. Also reassure them that they could still maintain their party affiliation.

One leading candidate to offer a cabinet position would be Zaid Ibrahim. His commitment to reforming the judiciary matches that of Anwar and Pakatan. Another would be Tengku Razaleigh, unless of course he wins UMNO's Presidency this December. His intimate knowledge of the economy and wide business experience would reassure the nation and the world. There are a few other promising candidates deep in the belly of UMNO Youth who have not yet succumbed to the corruption culture of their party.

Anwar should cast his talent net wide and deep. There are many capable Malaysians in academia, the professions, and private sector. A note of caution; they may have the knowledge and executive skills, but they often lack the necessary political polish. Nonetheless a brief tutelage by the master should equip them well in that deficit.

Inevitably there will be those over-exuberant members of Pakatan who would like to punch the final nail onto Barisan's (UMNO specifically) coffin. Resist that temptation. Pakatan's folks should value the importance of a viable and vibrant opposition. Relishing or helping in the collapse of Barisan or UMNO would not be good for anyone.

Unlike many, I do not consider the uneventful passing of "916" a failure. On the contrary, Anwar is wise in being cautious and not stubbornly adhere to some artificial self-imposed deadlines.

After over 50 years of domineering rule, UMNO's imprint is strong everywhere, in the civil service, academies, military, and even the private sector. Overcoming these considerable institutional inertias would be formidable. Go easy; let those operatives first get used to the *idea* of change.

Anwar's assurance of no "witch hunting" is appropriate and timely. Perhaps he could have a "Truth and Amnesty Commission" comparable to Mandela's Truth and Reconciliation Inquiry to ferret out corruption and abuse of power, granting amnesty to those who voluntarily come forward. Apart from saving the nation's precious resources in trying to investigate and prosecute, we could also learn something about the underlying mindset and culture. The educational value of such an exercise would be much more beneficial than any high-profile punitive prosecution.

Malaysia does not need a tumultuous or worse, an unexpected switch. That would be disorientating and could prove destabilizing. Instead, let the existing establishment be the first to get fed up with the present power struggle and ensuing uncertainty. Then they would be begging for someone, anyone, to take charge!

There is no need (as well as unwise) to involve the palace; that could come back to haunt you. Instead, wait for the palace to beg Pakatan to take over! If nothing else, there is more class that way. Similarly, dissolving Parliament and calling for fresh elections would not go well with the electorate. Citizens would not welcome yet another season of politicking and campaigning; they want the mess cleaned up! I am certain the palace is aware of voters' sentiment.

I would prefer that UMNO and Barisan collapse from within rather than through Pakatan's instigation. Pressure, yes, but not instigation. The difference between the two? Salesmanship, meaning, public perception.

Be patient. UMNO's infighting will intensify; UMNO and Barisan will implode. When that happens, be ready to pick up the pieces. Malaysians would be grateful to Pakatan for doing so. If Pakatan were to initiate the downfall and in the process trigger political instability, it would not endear itself to citizens. Public perception is supreme.

This is a time to tread carefully. UMNO's leadership convention will come soon enough this December. Relax and enjoy the expected fireworks. Like an overripe durian, UMNO will fall. Be careful that you are not underneath it when that happens. Stay to the side; UMNO would be yours for the picking when it falls under its own weight.

Last Chance To Save Malaysia

August 17, 2008

Before the last [March 2008] General Elections, I urged Kepala Batas voters to perform a great national service by rejecting their Parliamentary candidate Abdullah Badawi, thus automatically booting him out of the Prime Minister's office. That would have triggered a seismic shift in UMNO's leadership. With its ban on contesting top posts effectively circumvented, the party would get to preview other potential candidates.

If Kepala Batas voters were to shy away from exercising that historic opportunity, I suggested that Malaysians at large could still teach Abdullah a lesson by substantially reducing his coalition's victory. That would also trigger a challenge to his leadership, and thus the same effect as with the first scenario.

Malaysians did teach Abdullah a hard lesson at that election, but not hard enough. He and his coalition were barely returned to power, humbled.

Being a slow learner, Abdullah did not get the message. Now voters in Permatang Pauh, practically next door, will get a chance to deal Abdullah a third and final knock-out blow, one whose lesson he would surely get.

This upcoming by-election will be more than just electing the area's representative to Parliament. Permatang Pauh voters will get the unique opportunity to decide on behalf of entire Malaysia on who will lead the nation. It is as much an opportunity to vote for Anwar Ibrahim as it is against Abdullah Badawi, and to vote for Malaysia's future—on whether she would progress to join the developed world or continue with her current trajectory towards the likes of Zimbabwe.

Anwar Versus Abdullah

In Abdullah, Malaysia had a dull and pathetically detached leader who exploited the differences amongst Malaysians to remain in power. By contrast, Anwar is charismatic and well regarded especially internationally. He nurtures the commonalities of Malaysians and challenges them to rise above their differences.

Abdullah's "I am Prime Minister for all Malaysians" utterance rang hollow when he allowed, nay encouraged the racist taunting by UMNO Youth leaders. Illustrative of his opportunistic and exploitative character, right after the March elections when his party's position was threatened in many states, Abdullah initiated a series of secret meetings with the opposition PAS. In so doing he showed contempt for his existing Barisan coalition partners.

Abdullah was also insensitive, or more accurately contemptuous of the feelings of those non-Malays who voted for Barisan, UMNO and non-UMNO alike. The rewards he dangled must have been quite substantial to tempt the otherwise self-righteous PAS leaders to participate in those talks. It was fortunate for Malaysia that wiser heads prevailed in PAS; the discussions between UMNO and PAS were aborted.

Anwar does not have a formal leadership role. Yet as adviser to the new Pakatan coalition he successfully created a viable coalition, one effective enough to deny Barisan its two-thirds majority in Parliament and to dislodge it in five states, including such major ones as Perak, Penang, and Selangor.

It was a testament to Anwar's leadership skills that he could forge an alliance comprising DAP and PAS, two parties representing the polar extremes of political views in Malaysia. Anwar was successful because he focused and built on their commonalities, their yearning for a clean, efficient and transparent government, one not blighted by cronyism and corruption.

It is also the wish of all Malaysians, whether they embrace "Malaysia for Malaysians" or the "Islamic State of Malaysia" political ideals. It should also be the theme and aspiration of any Malaysian government.

I was also impressed with Anwar's ability to attract many young talents. While UMNO had to contend with such worn-out retreads like Ezam Noor, Anwar managed to attract many young educated individuals like Rafizi Ramli, Nik Nazmi, and Sim Tze Tzin.

It also reflected the perverted priorities of Abdullah and his lack of diligence as leader, that on such important matters as our energy policy he remained blissfully detached except for making empty silly remarks. With rocketing oil prices threatening the global (and Malaysian) economies, Abdullah and his deputy Najib are content busying themselves with whether Saiful (Anwar's alleged sodomy victim) would swear on the Koran as the truthfulness of his claim.

It was the height of obscenity to see this young man wearing his songkok and *baju Melayu*, symbols of everything pure and pristine in Malay culture, entering the sanctity of the holy mosque in the heart of Malaysia to utter, "... *telah memasukkan zakarnya ke dalam lubang dubur saya.*" [He inserted his penis into my anus.]

All so clinical, and so well-timed politically! It would have been obscene even without the ugly smirk on Saiful's face after he blurted his utterance. Thankfully, he spared us further lurid details, as he imagined them. One's fantasy could get quite vivid, especially when given some attention and encouragement. As for the frequency, Saiful had yet to decide on that. He was waiting to see Anwar's diary first!

With his right hand on the Holy Koran, witnessed by the Imam and nationally televised, those crudities issued forth from his sullied mouth, mocking the cleansing ablution that he took only minutes earlier before entering the mosque. That was merely a ritual, and a meaningless one at that. Surely Saiful, and others beside him including and especially the pious Imam, realized that by just uttering those crudities he had effectively nullified his ablution. Yet there he was, piously declaring *Allah hu Akhbar* (God is Great!), and then proceeded to his prayers. The perversity and obscenity!

I could not imagine a more despicable sight of the desecration of the Koran. I would not stoop to this college dropout's gutter level to even translate the entire obscenities coming forth from his soiled mouth.

Someone had put a microphone on the young man so the world could hear his filthy utterances. How thoughtful! The event was also broadcasted at prime time! I pitied those parents who would have to explain to their young the meaning of what transpired or had been uttered.

Such are the priorities of this dysfunctional duo of Abdullah and Najib. And they want Permatang Pauh voters to endorse their leadership!

Contrast that with Anwar's statesmanship. The day he would form the government, he declared, he would lower gasoline prices and release those prisoners of conscience held under the ISA. Regardless whether one agreed with his policies, there was no denying that Anwar had set his priorities and the national agenda right.

Respecting The Koran

I am appalled that many Malaysian Muslims are calling for Anwar to debase himself to the same sewer level as Saiful by swearing on the Koran and in a mosque. If the truth could be had so simplistically, we would not need the court system and extensive police force.

Those Muslims' commitment to things Islamic did not extend to their suggesting that the Sharia Court should take jurisdiction over this case. After all both alleged participants were Muslims, and Anwar had already lodged a complaint to the religious department. Somehow in this particular instance and circumstance, those Muslims suddenly had more faith with the secular criminal justice system than with the Sharia courts.

I would rather Anwar swear on the Koran to commit that, on becoming Prime Minister, he would uphold the constitution and lead a government that would be efficient, not corrupt, and have the interests of the people uppermost, as encapsulated in his *Ketuanan Rakyat* (Citizens' First) declaration. I would also challenge Abdullah and Najib to do likewise. That would be the proper and dignified use of the Koran, the symbolic enactment of the phrase, "Let Allah be my witness!"

It would also have been more meaningful and dignified had Saiful taken the oath over the Koran committing himself to be a diligent student when given the rare opportunity for a precious slot in a local university. Had he followed through with that and studied hard, he would have achieved something for himself and be of service to his nation.

Saiful should have realized that he was given an opportunity denied to too many other young Malaysians. Instead, he blew that chance for a moment of infamy.

A few years back, former Deputy Prime Minister Tun Ghaffar declared that UMNO could be had for a few billion *ringgit*, at most. He was referring to the endemic corruption in the party. As is apparent, that price had gone down considerably since. Today, a local college drop-out with only a promise of a cheap scholarship to a lousy local public institution could derail the whole UMNO government and paralyze the country.

I would have never imagined that the future of a Malaysian Prime Minister and his Deputy would hang on whether a young man's posterior had been violated. That is what Abdullah's and Najib's leadership had been reduced to, and how it would end, on Saiful's end.

If a struggling failed freshman like Saiful could create such a havoc, I would not dare imagine what a smart, savvy, rich foreigner could do to UMNO and Malaysia. There is one sure way to spare Malaysia such a fate: get rid of UMNO and the incompetent and dysfunctional team of Abdullah and Najib.

By voting for Anwar in the upcoming elections, Permatang Pauh voters would get to do just that, and thus protect Malaysia.

Index

About The Author

Malaysian-born and Canadian-trained, Bakri Musa is a surgeon in private practice in Silicon Valley, California. Although he left Malaysia in

1963, he has kept close track of her social and political developments.

He has given presentations on Malaysian affairs at Stanford University's Shorenstein Asia-Pacific Research Center, The Woodrow Wilson International Center for Scholars, The University of Buffalo, and Rochester Institute of Technology.

Apart from scientific articles in scholarly journals, his commentaries have appeared in mainstream Malaysian papers *The New Straits Times* and *The Sun Daily*. He was a long-time columnist for the on-line portal Malaysiakini (Malaysia Now) and a regular contributor to The Malaysian Insider.

Beyond Malaysia his commentaries have appeared in *The New York Times*, *International Herald Tribune*, and *The Far Eastern Economic Review*. His editorial on Malaysian affirmative action program was aired on National Public Radio's "Marketplace."

The author has written eleven books on Malaysian socio-political affairs and maintains a blog (www.bakrimusa.blogspot.com) that serves as a repository of his essays and commentaries. He also has a following on Facebook and other social media.